P9-DDV-408

VEGAN
IN VOLUME

VEGAN QUANTITY RECIPES FOR EVERY OCCASION

A NOTE TO THE READER

The contents of this book are not intended to provide personal medical advice. Medical advice should be obtained from a qualified health professional.

© Copyright 2000, The Vegetarian Resource Group
PO Box 1463, Baltimore, MD 21203.

Cover artwork by Lance Simons
Illustrations by Rowen Leigh

Library of Congress Cataloging-in-Publication Data
Vegan in Volume – Vegan Quantity Recipes for Every Occasion/Nancy Berkoff
Library of Congress Catalog Card Number: 99-73881

ISBN 0-931411-21-1

Printed in the United States of America
10 9 8 7 6 5 4 3 2 1

All rights reserved. No portion of this book may be reproduced by any means whatsoever except for brief quotations in reviews, without written permission from The Vegetarian Resource Group.

Dedication

This book is dedicated to Sherry, my heart, a friend to animals, an inspiration to all around her, a loving warm person, and the reason for all of us to try and make the world a better place.

VEGAN
IN VOLUME

VEGAN QUANTITY RECIPES FOR EVERY OCCASION

By Chef Nancy Berkoff, R.D.

The Vegetarian Resource Group
Baltimore, Maryland

Table of Contents

Introduction

We were of two minds when we started to develop the recipes for this book. Should it be no-holds-barred vegan using advanced techniques for veggie preparation, should it attempt the middle ground, or should it have a beginners' stance? When we thought about our choices during many late night discussions and spoke with some of our fellow food service cronies, we decided to take a beginning-to-middle view. Why? Because very few of us have the time to prepare complex recipes and many of us may not currently have the budget to add new ingredients. Also, the purveyors food service personnel deal with may not have all the veggie ingredients desired, and there may be neither time nor money to train staff.

Although we are confident a wider variety of veggie ingredients will become available in quantity packs and that more staff will become versed in vegetarian food preparation, you will find that the majority of recipes found in this book do not require ingredients you are not already using. The purpose of this book is to make your quantity veggie preparation easier.

Vegan events have become more and more popular. We have received an increasing number of "how-to" calls from caterers, schools and universities, health care facilities, restaurants, and community groups who want or need to provide vegan meals ranging form black-tie affairs to camping trips. We think the information in this book will fit the needs of most menus.

Cooking vegan is no different than preparing any cuisine. Using the highest quality ingredients, trying to buy produce in season, using simple preparation techniques, and paying attention to presentation are the hallmarks of all cuisines, including vegan. Keeping the interest up is also important. Pay attention to seasonings, variety (bell peppers come in more colors than green!), textures, and even temperatures.

Several hotel and restaurant chains have incorporated vegan cuisine into their menus, as have many schools and universities. We dined elegantly on braised portabello mushrooms, quinoa pilaf, olive and rosemary artisan bread, herbed, seasonal baby vegetables, and an almond-orange sorbet topped with golden raspberry sauce at a four-star resort in the Florida Keys. We had a blast at a college-dining hall in Nebraska with a vegan falafel bar, and we spent a quiet, homey dining moment at a nursing home in Colorado, sharing lentil-tomato stew and freshly baked corn-carrot bread.

If you have a passion for food you will enjoy creating menus from the recipes in this book. Work with the seasons and regional ingredients, create variations on these recipes, and make them your own. Above all, enjoy cooking and creating vegan foods, knowing you are pleasing and nurturing people and the planet.

– Nancy Berkoff, R.D., Ed.D., CCE –

Acknowledgements

Thanks to Reed Mangels, Ph.D., R.D. for doing the nutritional analysis for each recipe and offering valuable suggestions. I also greatly appreciate the editing Debra Wasserman did on the manuscript, as well as her laying out the material in its final form. Thanks to Lance Simon for designing the cover and Rowen Leigh for doing the artwork that appears throughout this cookbook. Thank you also to the following VRG volunteers who proofread parts of the manuscript: Amy Bottrell, Deborah Davidson, Jeff DeAlmo, Vikram Goel, Steve Maloney, Sheri Runtsch, Sheri Runtson, Amy Stausebach, and Margaret Wolf. And finally, thanks to all my students who helped test the recipes that appear throughout this cookbook and to Carolyn Peyvich and Rachel Himmelheber, former VRG interns who contributed information appearing in this book.

Chapter One

A FAST COURSE IN VEGAN NUTRITION

Vegetarian eating has existed through the ages and is becoming more and more popular. Your customers may have chosen vegetarian lifestyles for many reasons which can be philosophical, health-related, political, and/or religious, to name a few. Vegetarian diets can be classified by the types of foods not eaten. Vegans do not eat meat, fish, poultry, or animal by-products (such as dairy, eggs, and honey). Vegetarians do not eat meat, fish, and poultry.

People may have their own variations of vegetarian diets; for example, some may largely refrain from animal products but have an occasional egg or glass of milk. Many vegans exclude honey and refined cane sugar from their diets, as they consider honey an animal product and cane sugar may be processed with filters of animal origin. When a customer says they are vegetarian, it's up to you to ascertain what they mean.

The recipes and information in this book are vegan. This means we have excluded ingredients derived from animal products. Many health authorities back the idea that vegan diets meet the recommendations made to reduce the risk of major chronic diseases, such as heart disease and cancer. The key to a nutritionally sound vegan diet is the same as any type of diet. Be sure to choose a variety of healthy foods, such as whole grain products, leafy greens, nuts, seeds, legumes, etc.

PROTEIN

Garbanzo beans, black beans, peanuts, walnuts, tofu, and tempeh are some foods high in protein. Here are examples of vegan menu items that are high in protein:

- bean soup and crackers
- lentil soup with potato salad
- stir-fry tofu and almonds with rice
- veggie burger on a bun
- three-bean chili with pasta or barley
- peanut butter and bread
- pasta with pesto (which has pine nuts)

Calcium, iron, vitamin D, zinc, and vitamin B-12 are other nutrients of which we all need to be aware. Here are some helpful hints.

CALCIUM
The following vegan foods are high in calcium:
- calcium-fortified foods (soy or rice milks, orange juice, etc.)
- calcium-sulfate processed tofu (sometimes calcium is used and sometimes other items, such as nigari (a sea vegetable) are used; look on the label for listings)
- blackstrap molasses
- commercial soy yogurt
- sesame seeds and almonds
- some dark leafy greens (collards, kale, mustard greens, etc.)

IRON
Good iron sources include enriched and fortified cereal, breads and grains, lentils, black-eyed peas, kidney beans, seeds, dark leafy greens, dried fruit, and cashews. Enhance your iron absorption by including vitamin C foods with your iron-containing foods, as vitamin C helps your body absorb iron. For example:
- add orange sections to a fresh spinach salad
- serve a tomato and pepper sauce with steamed kale
- have a glass of grapefruit juice with iron-enriched cereal

VITAMIN D
Ultra-violet rays from the sun help your body make vitamin D. Include a short amount of sun exposure every day, as possible, while walking or running. Be sure to protect yourself with sunscreen for prolonged sun exposure. Sunscreen is important for disease prevention; however, during the time sunscreen is worn vitamin D production is inhibited. Some fortified products such as soy or rice milk and cereals also contain vitamin D.

ZINC
Zinc is found in whole-grain breads and cereals, legumes, tofu, nuts, etc.

VITAMIN B-12

Vitamin B-12 is found in some fortified cereals, soy products, and vegetarian patties. It is also found in nutritional yeast (when purchasing nutritional yeast read the label to ensure that it does not contain whey, which is derived from dairy). Red Star Company's Vegetarian Support Formula is a yeast product containing a reliable source of B-12.

Nutritional needs change throughout life, vegan, vegetarian, or omnivore alike. Infants, children, and adolescents need enough nutrients and calories for growth (and to support both learning and playing). This can be a challenge as tastes and preferences change. Add dried fruits, nuts, and seeds to baked goods and snacks for extra energy and nutrients. Athletes need concentrated energy sources; think about granola, bean or legume soups, and "jazzed" up muffins (made with extra fruit, nuts, and soy milk). Older adults may neglect their vitamin D and B-12 requirements, so include foods rich in these nutrients.

We love to sneak extra nutrition onto the menu. In addition to the items listed above, we have been known to:
- prepare mashed potato mix with heated soy milk (instead of water)
- use cooked, puréed vegetables as a thickening agent in soups (this adds color, flavor, and creaminess)
- prepare dessert sauces from orange juice concentrate and soy milk (this resembles a thin custard and can be served with cake, frozen desserts, baked apples, and even as a dunking dip for cookies)
- pile sliced fruit on top of soy ice creams and sorbet
- freeze bananas whole and offer them for dessert rolled in peanut butter and coconut
- cook vegetables in vegetable stock or juice (this adds flavor and nutrients)
- garnish any sweet foods with chopped nuts, seeds, granola, wheat germ, and crushed cold cereal
- heap potatoes, rice, and grains with chopped veggies (such as carrots, peppers, fresh chilies, onions, celery, radishes, tomatoes, fennel, green beans, etc.) and beans (fresh steamed soybeans, black beans, lentils, navy beans, baby limas, etc.)
- mix in a little nutritional yeast with cooked grains or mashed potatoes

EXAMPLE OF A DAILY VEGAN FOOD GUIDE FOR YOU TO KEEP HANDY

This is a modified version of a meal plan originally created by Ruth Blackburn, M.S., R.D., for The Vegetarian Resource Group. Like any food plan, this should only serve as a general guide for adults. The plan can be modified according to your own personal needs. Individuals with special health needs should consult a registered dietitian or a medical doctor knowledgeable about vegetarian nutrition.

A. PROTEIN FOODS: 1-2 SERVINGS PER DAY
(Each of the following equals one serving.)

1-1/2 cups cooked dried beans or peas
8 ounces tofu*
4 ounces tempeh
2 cups calcium fortified soy milk*
1/2 cup almonds*, cashews, walnuts, pecans, or peanuts
4 Tablespoons peanut butter

B. WHOLE GRAINS: at least 6-8 SERVINGS PER DAY
(Each of the following equals one serving.)

1 slice whole wheat, rye, or other whole grain bread
1/2 whole grain bagel or English muffin
1 buckwheat or whole wheat pancake or waffle
1 two-inch piece cornbread
1 whole grain muffin or biscuit or whole grain tortilla
2 Tablespoons wheat germ
1 ounce wheat or oat bran
1/4 cup sunflower, sesame*, or pumpkin seeds
3/4 cup wheat, bran, or corn flakes
1/2 cup cooked oatmeal or farina
1/2 cup cooked brown rice, barley, bulgur, or corn
1/2 cup cooked whole wheat noodles, macaroni, or spaghetti

C. <u>VEGETABLES</u>: at least 4-6 SERVINGS PER DAY

1. Two servings per day of any of the following: 1/2 cup cooked or 1 cup raw broccoli*, Brussels sprouts, collards*, kale*, chard, spinach, romaine lettuce, cabbage, carrots, sweet potatoes, winter squash, or tomatoes.

2. Two servings per day (one serving equals half cup cooked or one cup raw) of any other vegetable.

D. <u>FRUITS</u>: 4-6 SERVINGS PER DAY

1. Two servings per day of any of the following: 3/4 cup berries, 1/4 cantaloupe, 1 orange, 1/2 grapefruit, 1 lemon or lime, 1/2 papaya, 4-inch x 8-inch watermelon slice; or 1/2 cup orange, grapefruit, calcium-fortified orange*; or vitamin C enriched juice.

2. Two to four servings per day of other fruits: 1 small piece fresh fruit, 3/4 cup grapes, 1/2 cup cooked fruit or canned fruit without sugar, or 2 Tablespoons raisins, dates, or dried fruit.

E. <u>FATS</u>: 0-4 SERVINGS PER DAY
(Each of the following equals one serving.)

1 teaspoon vegan soft margarine or oil
2 teaspoons vegan mayonnaise or salad dressing
1 Tablespoon soy cream cheese or gravy

F. <u>STARRED* FOOD ITEMS</u>: 2, 3, OR MORE SERVINGS PER DAY

1. Men should include 2 choices daily.

2. Women should include 3 choices daily.

G. ADDITIONAL COMMENTS:

1. Pregnant and lactating women, persons under 18 years of age, and persons with bone or muscle trauma or other special needs may require additional servings.

2. Vegans (people who do not consume any animal products such as dairy and eggs) need to include a vitamin B12 source regularly. Sources include some vitamin B12 fortified breakfast cereals and soy milks (check labels) and Red Star Vegetarian Support Formula (T-6635+) nutritional yeast (1-2 teaspoons supplies the adult RDA).

SEVERAL SAMPLE VEGAN MEAL PLANS BASED ON THE ABOVE GUIDELINES

A. Breakfast:
Oatmeal or kasha with raisins, chopped dates, sliced banana, and enriched soy
    milk
Whole grain toast with peanut butter
Orange juice

Lunch:
Spinach-potato-black-eyed pea stew
Steamed corn with tomato sauce
Sliced apple with chopped dried apricots

Dinner:
Steamed tofu with Asian vegetables
Brown rice with peas and almonds
Baked cinnamon pear

B. Breakfast:
Toasted bagel with margarine
Fruit smoothie (made with orange juice, nutritional yeast, frozen berries, and rice or soy milk)

Lunch:
Falafel (ground chickpeas) in pita with shredded romaine lettuce, carrots, and tomato wedges
Broccoli florets
Fresh grapes

Dinner:
Tomato vegetable soup
Pasta-lentil salad
Corn muffin
Sliced melon

C. Breakfast:
Cold Cereal with enriched soy milk and fresh or frozen berries
Orange-raisin muffin with margarine and preserves
Cranberry juice

Lunch:
Veggie burger on whole wheat bun with the works (sliced tomato and cucumber, shredded lettuce and carrot, sliced onion, alfalfa or broccoli sprouts, ketchup, mustard, and relish)
Peanut butter cookie
Chocolate soy or rice milk

Dinner:
Tomato stuffed with seasoned brown rice and mushrooms
Kale or spinach braised in vegetable stock
Dinner roll with margarine
Butterscotch pudding (made with soy milk) topped with banana slices

When you are preparing vegan meals, resolve to avoid plain or unseasoned foods. By adding that "something extra," you can increase the interest and the nutrition in many menu items. Challenge your flavor knowledge – see how many seasonings you can match up with ingredients. Throw a bay leaf into that pot of lentils; add rosemary, minced carrots, and onions to barley; use those extra chopped tomatoes in the salad dressing; top potatoes with salsa; or heat some soy milk with some cinnamon, raisins, and orange zest and serve over hot cereal. Muffins and pancakes call out for fruit purées or dried fruit; mashed potatoes like to be dressed up with garlic, rosemary, basil, or horseradish; and veggies appreciate being steamed with fresh herbs and vegetable stock rather than plain water.

Vegan diets can be healthy and interesting or boring and unhealthy just like any type of diet. Select foods that have pleasing flavors and textures and be sure to vary the colors, temperatures, and cooking styles. The result will be a menu that will keep them well-nourished and coming back for more!

HERE ARE SOME MORE SAMPLE VEGAN MENU SUGGESTIONS

Children's lunch box:
- Carrot sticks, raw green beans or pea pods with tomato salsa
- Pita pocket with shredded romaine, sprouts, shredded carrots, and tofu cheese slices
- Peanut butter raisin cookie
- Chocolate rice milk (enriched)

Adolescent grab and go breakfast:
- Cold cereal (enriched) mixed with chopped dried fruit and nuts
- Orange sections
- Fruit smoothie (soft tofu or soy yogurt blended with banana, fresh berries, and wheat germ)

Adult dinner party:
- Vegan Vichyssoise (see recipe on page 152)
- Carrot and spinach pate en croute (in pastry)
- Herbed orzo with fresh basil
- Tossed baby greens with walnuts and lime vinaigrette
- Apple-calvados sorbet (calvados is an apple liqueur)
- Tomato-thyme whole grain bread

Senior meal:
- Tomato vegetable soup with rosemary breadsticks
- Lentil and potato ragout
- Glazed baby carrots
- Four bean salad
- Baked apple with lemon sauce

(Also see individual chapters for theme-based menus.)

Chapter Two

THE MECHANICS OF THE OPERATION

A QUICK FOOD SAFETY REVIEW

In every food service operation and at every event where food is served, the rules of food safety have to be strictly followed. You want to get into the newspapers because of your excellent cuisine, not for how many customers wound up in the emergency room after eating one of your meals!

No matter the size of your operation, here are some food safety absolutes; for more detail, we have included a list of resources on page 23. Also see Appendix E on page 255. Practice food safety techniques all the time and be sure to train all your food-handlers, servers, drivers, volunteers, or anyone who will be preparing or serving your food.

Wash your hands: provide separate handwashing facilities which have hot and cold running water, soap, and single-use towels or an air dryer (for example, that means no washing your hands in the same sink in which the lettuce gets washed). In order to get rid of bacteria on the skin, you have to soap and lather for at least 20 seconds and then thoroughly rinse. It has been estimated that a food service employee working an eight-hour shift should hand-wash at least fifteen times! And, by the way, it has been estimated that at least 3 million cases of food-borne illness per year are caused by poor (or no) hand-washing practices. And we all know that rings, watches, bracelets, fingernail polish, and artificial fingernails have no place in the kitchen, right?

Avoid cross-contamination: bacteria can be spread from person to person, person to food, from food to food, and then make the circuit again and again. An example of cross contamination would be cutting tomatoes (which are going in the soup), then cutting lettuce (which is going in a salad) with the same cutting board and knife without sanitizing the knife and board between uses. If there was any dirt or bacteria on the tomatoes, we can hope that the cooking temperatures will kill the contamination. However, the lettuce doesn't stand a chance; it's going to be served in an uncooked salad. Any dirt or bacteria on the lettuce will be served right to the customer. This can be avoided by sanitizing equipment and utensils before and after use, either with heat (165 degrees or above) or with chemicals (good old chlorine bleach is inexpensive, effective, and vegan) for 20 seconds. We find the most convenient way to sanitize is to provide "bleach buckets." We purchase children's beach pails, fill them with water and bleach (a Tablespoon of bleach per gallon of water), and provide one for each workstation. A clean towel, soaked in bleach solution can be used to sanitize when using the pot sink isn't convenient. Other examples of cross contamination include an employee taking a smoke break or using the phone and going back to food prep without washing hands; placing unwashed produce or food containers on a food surface and then prepping food on the unsanitized surface; or shaking hands and serving food without sanitizing hands.

This would be a good place to speak about using gloves. Gloves can only serve as a barrier to bacteria if the person wearing them washes their hands before putting them on and uses fresh gloves between tasks (to avoid cross contamination). Employees with skin tears (like blisters or cuts) should wear gloves until the tear is healed. Frequently washed hands are the equivalent of gloved hands. Check what the local health codes require.

FIFO: This stands for "first in, first out." It is a rotation method that should be used for food and non-food items. Using FIFO ensures that ingredients are used at their freshest and their safest (this is a wise economic and quality method).

Keep hot foods hot and cold foods cold: Perishable foods (including all cooked foods, soy products such as tofu or milk, reconstituted egg replacer, etc.) support illness-causing bacteria if not kept above 140 degrees Fahrenheit (in a chafing dish, warmer, on the steam table, etc.) or below 40 degrees Fahrenheit (in the refrigerator, freezer, or on ice). If kept out for 4 hours between 40 to 140 degrees Fahrenheit, perishable food is almost guaranteed to get someone sick. Leftovers (for example, carrot soup or pasta primavera) must be reheated to 165 degrees Fahrenheit when served a second time. There are no more than two chances even with the most carefully handled food: prepare it and serve it, serve it as a leftover, and then, that's it! So, calculate your production needs accurately, so you don't waste time, money, and labor (and possibly risk getting someone sick).

When in doubt...throw it out!: Protein-rich foods, such as bean soup or soy products, should not be kept for more than 48 hours refrigerated (check local health codes). So if you over do it on the tempeh loaf, either freeze it right away (where it can be kept for several weeks) or plan some menus around it. Don't wait until something waves at you before discarding it! Remember, the taste test doesn't prove anything. If you don't recall when you made that batch of split pea soup, but it tastes okay, forget about it! Take your losses; better to lose a couple of dollars than customers.

Wrap, label, and date: If you do this consistently, you will probably be able to avoid the previous step. Some facilities have preprinted labels to which only dates need to be added and some use a color-dot system.

Serve correctly: train your staff to keep their thumbs out of the soup and the iced tea; to use separate utensils to serve separate items; to keep the soup hot in the chafing dish; and the salad iced down. No sense in taking all the correct food prep precautions just to be sabotaged by the service staff.

Sanitize, sanitize, sanitize: we want to see those bleach buckets (or whatever system you devise) in the kitchen and the dining room and we want to see them used!

Use reputable food sources: You can risk getting a "good deal" on a watch or on real estate. When it comes to the ingredients you are purchasing, be sure you have seen the warehouse, gotten references, and done whatever checking is necessary to ensure that your supplier is giving you the freshest, quality ingredients available.

Some people with whom we have worked have been trained to think of animal products (meat, dairy, eggs, etc.) as causing food-borne illness and non-animal products as more benign. This is not so! Bacteria need air, moisture, an energy source (food), a neutral environment (not acid or alkaline), temperature (remember 40-140 degrees Fahrenheit), and time (4 hours) in order to grow, multiply, and contaminate your food. Cooked rice and potatoes, lentil loaf, and soy milk can supply all these things to any bacteria, which finds its way onto them. Bacteria does not play by different rules for different foods, so keep a clean and sanitized work and service area, use FIFO, watch your temperatures, and all the other rules of food safety and your customers will enjoy their meals with you (and live to come back for more).

SOURCES FOR FOOD SAFETY INFORMATION

BOOKS

Applied Foodservice Sanitation, ISBN 0-471-54218-0, 1992, John Wiley & Sons, Inc.

National Restaurant Associations ServSafe Series (has different levels of courses, from videos and workbooks to college-level texts), NRA (Chicago, Illinois); (312) 715-1010

Foodservice in Institutions (Harger, Shugart, and Payne), ISBN 0-02-425940-3, 1990, MacMillan Publishing

ORGANIZATIONS

Centers for Disease Control and Prevention, Public Inquiries Specialist
 1600 Clifton Road, NE, Atlanta, Georgia 30333
Underwriters Laboratory (for equipment safety)
 333 Pfingsten Road, Northbrook, IL 60062
Educational Foundation for the National Restaurant Association
 250 S. Wacker Drive, Suite 1400, Chicago, IL 60606

WEBSITES

United States Department of Agriculture Homepage: http://www.usda.gov/
The American Dietetic Association: http://www.eatright.org/
The Vegetarian Resource Group: www.vrg.org
Institute of Food Technologist: http://www.ift.org/

USEFUL EQUIPMENT

Culinary apprentices are told that a good cook can prepare any dish with just a knife, a cutting board, and some assorted pots, pans, and bowls. This is true, but there are some pieces of equipment that can improve efficiency and generally make life easier. Vegan foods require the same amount of chopping, slicing, and combining as any type of menu. Depending on the size of your kitchen, you may already have many of these items. Again, they are not required, just handy:

- **Blender or food processor:** useful for puréeing soups and sauces, combining custards, and finishing salad dressings. You could use a manual food mill (or your mixer may come with a mill or ricer attachment), but the blender or food processor allows you to choose from many different textures.

- **Mixer:** mixing quantity foods by hand can develop muscles (and frustration). Choose the size of mixer best suited to your production sizes. Standard attachments should include a dough hook, a paddle, and a whisk. Other attachments may include a grinder (for vegetables) or a ricer.

- **Slicer:** if you will be slicing a lot of veggies (eggplant, potatoes, tomatoes, onions, zucchini, etc.), you may want to think about investing in a slicer. Check local laws to see who can operate this useful, but potentially dangerous piece of equipment (for example, some states do not allow employees under the age of 18 to operate slicers).

- **Rice cooker:** can also be used to steam other grains. Depending on the amount of rice you will be preparing every day, this could come in handy. One feeding program we know set up a rice cooker in the college dining hall. This saved space on the serving line and assured students they would always have soft, hot rice.

- **Food chopper (also called a "buffalo" chopper):** for large operations, this piece of equipment can chop or dice ten pounds of onions in about 45 seconds. These choppers are a big investment, but they seem to last forever and cut down on prep time. A caterer we know can chop the ingredients for 50 gallons of salsa in about 15 minutes (and the guy who formerly had to chop all the jalapeños by hand is darn grateful).

- **Knives and cutting boards:** sharp sturdy knives are absolutely essential. Chef's knives that fit the employee and are easy to sanitize and sharpen make kitchen work a little easier. Handles are available in various materials and blades in various lengths. Teach your employees how to use a stone or invest in an electric sharpener. There are also professional knife-sharpening services. Have enough cutting boards for the number of employees you have. Be sure they are not warped or have multiple nicks and scratches and show everyone how to sanitize!

COOKING VEGETARIAN FOR A CROWD
WITH THE GREATEST OF EASE

So you say you'd love to offer vegetarian selections from your kitchen, or maybe even go mostly "veggie," but you just don't have the time, the knowledge, or the equipment. You'll have to think up another excuse, because this section can set you on the path to cooking "veggie" easily.

After ascertaining what the crowd wants, you can have a little fun educating them. First, win over the people who will be preparing and representing your menus. Run mini-taste panels with your staff and employees, being sure to listen to their input. Then, have samplings, taste-testing, and cooking demos with your customers. Be sure to provide verbal and written information and recipes.

Now for your kitchen you need the same equipment you use every day: cutting boards and sharp knives, steam kettles, ovens, stove-tops, etc. If you have a blender or a food processor, great; it's not mandatory. Look in you pantry and your refrigerator – you'll probably find a great number of ingredients that fit the vegetarian bill. Staples, such as flour, grains, cereals, dried beans and legumes, and rice are vegetarian, as are spices, canned fruit, juices, and pasta. Canned vegetables and canned beans can be vegetarian, just read the label. Your cold storage probably has lots of vegetarian selections already – fresh produce, fresh and frozen fruit and vegetable juices, fresh and frozen potatoes, certain breads (again, read the label), etc.

Processed foods are where you must become a label reader. Pasta and noodles can contain eggs; bakery products may contain dairy and eggs; and instant soup bases and canned soups can contain meat extracts, etc. The same goes for convenience items, such as frozen, prepared entrées, salad dressings, etc. Nondairy creamers can have components of milk in them.

The good news is for every animal-containing product there is usually a vegan product that fits the bill. If you rely on some frozen convenience items to fill your menu, just sit down with your food purveyor and see what he/she has to offer. There are lots of vegan frozen entrées and side dishes that are equivalent in cost and quality. Ask to have a "cutting," that is, a sampling which contrast several products. Include your staff in on this activity.

We have sampled great veggie frozen entrées including pasta stuffed with savory fillings of spicy vegetables and tofu, stuffed peppers, and many other ethnic specialties.

SALAD DRESSINGS

Prepared salad dressings don't have to be dairy-based. They can be purchased or made with vegetables or vinegar as the base (and they're healthier this way, too). Make a great salad dressing by starting with vegetable cocktail juice (like

V-8) and blending in bell pepper, onion, and celery (this is also a good start for a hot sauce for pasta). Another salad dressing/marinade can be made with orange juice, vinegar, pineapple, and some other leftover fruit, such as strawberries, peaches, or grapes. Many of your side dishes are probably largely vegetarian now. Just check your cooking oil; if it's butter or lard (good grief!), it's time to make a change anyway. You can order nondairy margarine at no additional cost. Check your fryer oil blend to be sure it doesn't have any animal fat added.

SOUP STOCKS

If you make your own stock for soup, try a vegetarian stock by sautéing onions and garlic in a small amount of oil. Add chopped carrots, celery, mushrooms (a great way to use up those extra mushrooms or stems that are drying out in the fridge), a little vermouth, peppercorns, bay leaf, and parsley stems. Let this simmer with lots of water until you get the strength of stock you want. You can add greens, green beans, or beets if you want a darker color. Strain the stock and refrigerate until ready to use. For a fast vegetable-based stock, we start with tomato juice, add puréed vegetables (such as carrots, celery, and onions), a dash of pepper, and a dash of onion powder. Let it simmer for about half an hour. Both of these make a good base for sauces; just let them reduce or thicken them with flour, tapioca, or cornstarch. If you need a shortcut, purchase vegetarian soup bases (watch for the salt content).

Have you noticed that vegetarian cooking uses the same techniques and ingredients as you're using now, with less fat? Because you tend to cook with more flavor and color when you do vegetarian dishes right, the fat's not missed.

PROTEIN

What about the protein, you say? Soy products, such as tofu and tempeh, emulate the texture of meat and provide a complete protein (See Soy 101 later in this chapter). Here are some other ideas for vegetarian entrées: vegetable moussaka or lasagna (use roasted vegetables instead of meat), bell pepper and mushroom strata, bean and almond salad, cabbage and white bean stew served over garlic mashed potatoes, stuffed tomatoes or peppers (try an oatmeal-walnut stuffing), and vegetarian tamales.

Finding soup boring without meat or cream, you say? How about a roasted garlic and white bean soup, a cold three berry and wine soup, or a multi-colored curried lentil soup (did you know that lentils come in green, white, brown, and orange)? You can use your imagination (and a lot less fat) with vegetarian soups.

CALCIUM

My customers want calcium, you say. All right: if you prefer to stay away from soy products (which can be fortified with calcium), then incorporate greens (as in cooked or raw collards, kale, or Swiss chard), broccoli, cabbage, turnips, molasses (Indian pudding or gingerbread, anyone?), cooked beans, or corn tortillas into your menu. Already there, you say – surprise! You've been serving a calcium-rich menu and didn't need all those animal products.

DESSERTS

Desserts and baked goods can be made or purchased without eggs or dairy. Plant-based gels can be purchased and used just like the gelatin you usually use. Baked apples, poached pears, fruit compote (stew dried fruit with fresh apples, peaches, apricots or pears, and spices), sorbets, and seasonal fruit salads and sauces are colorful desserts that have always been and will always be vegan.

There now, that was easy, wasn't it? You can have a vegan menu in just about no time, using the kitchen and the ingredients you already have. You'll find that you're getting more creative with ingredients and your customers will be happy with their new menu.

THOUGHTS ON STOCKING THE PANTRY

It's easier to prepare foods if you have adequate supplies on hand. Here are the vegan items we like to have in our refrigerators and storeroom:

- **Refrigerator:** tofu (firm or silken), tempeh, seitan, chocolate and vanilla soy and/or rice milk, loads of fresh produce, fresh herbs (including ginger, garlic, basil, rosemary, oregano, etc.), soy sauce or tamari, okara, tortillas, pita bread, and assorted juices.

- **Freezer:** extra tofu and tempeh, soy ice cream, frozen soy beans and other veggies, apple and orange juice concentrate (in place of refined sugar), extra vegetable stock.

- **Storeroom:** canned tomatoes, soybeans, tomato purée, egg replacer, assorted flours, several kinds of rice, dried herbs and spices, canned and dried beans and lentils, pasta, couscous, quinoa, kasha, baking powder, baking soda, cornstarch, vinegar, mustard, assorted oils, flavoring extracts, and zests.

HOW TO USE QUANTITY RECIPES

My father had a saying he used quite a lot of the time, "if all else fails, follow the directions." Sounds simple, but, especially when it comes to recipes, it's often tempting or seems easier not to follow the directions. A newspaper food editor once told us about an irate reader who had called to complain that a salsa recipe that had been published the previous week was totally inaccurate. "I followed your recipe to a 't,'" huffed the reader, "although I didn't have any fresh tomatoes, so I used canned, and I had to substitute some ketchup for the tomato paste. I forgot to buy fresh cilantro, so I used dried parsley. Why didn't your recipe come out right??!!"

Why, indeed. Some culinarians will tell you that recipes are merely guidelines. This is true if you are an experienced chef who need not worry about variations in cost, quantity, or quality of the product. Most quantity kitchens benefit from a staff that is well trained in using recipes. Ever been to a restaurant and you know (without looking in the kitchen) that it's the chef's night off? That wouldn't happen if recipes were followed.

The recipes in this book list the ingredients, measures or amounts, and methods. Pay attention not only to the ingredient listed, but the form that the ingredient should be in (fresh garlic, minced onions, prepared mustard, etc.). Be sure to weigh solid or dry items (flour, rice, vegetables, spices, tofu, etc.) and to measure liquid items (juice concentrate, soy milk, oil, etc.) in order to use the correct amount of each item. Read through the methods before starting the recipe, so you can assemble all the necessary equipment, preheat ovens or steamers, allow for cooking or cooling time, etc. If possible, do a dry run (staff are good people to use as samplers) with a recipe before using it in an important situation (Thanksgiving morning is not the time to find out that the tofu-pumpkin pie needs a longer baking time in your ovens). Keep a written record of comments, so you can adjust the recipes to suit your facility.

Speaking of adjusting recipes, let's walk through how to convert a recipe (if you need more or less than the amount on the recipe). It takes a few minutes to do the calculations, but you'll benefit in the long run – you'll wind up with the right amount of food (saving time, labor, and costs).

TO CONVERT TOTAL YIELDS:

1. Divide the yield you want (the new yield) by the yield you have on the recipe (the old yield).
2. The number you get is called the "conversion factor." Simply multiply every ingredient by the conversion factor to get the new amount of each ingredient. For example, if the old recipe has 10 portions, but you need 15, just divide 15 by 10 (old into new) to get the conversion factor, which is 1.5. So, if the old recipe called for 3 pounds of tomatoes, the new amount would be 4 pounds 8 ounces (3 pounds tomatoes x 1.5 = 72 ounces or 4 pounds 8 ounces).

Now, what if only portion numbers are listed. You just have to do two preliminary steps. First, you find the yield (so you can get the conversion factor) by multiplying original portions x portion size (25 four-ounce portions becomes 100 ounces or a 6 pound 4 ounce yield). Do the same for the new amount you desire (for example, 30 five-ounce portions becomes 150 ounces or 9 pounds 6 ounces for the new yield). Then proceed as above.

A note of caution about using conversions with baking recipes: the converted amounts don't always work. Remember that baking recipes are akin to chemical formulas and rely on fairly exact interactions between ingredients. If you convert a baking formula, do a test run before putting it on the menu. This is a handy tool to use when you need to make new amounts! Science always wins out over eye-balling!

JUST A NOTE...

You will notice that there is no salt listed in the ingredient column of the recipes in this book, although salty ingredients (soy sauce, tamari, canned veggies, etc.) are used. Salt should be used at your discretion. If you need to use lower- or reduced-salt items (such as soy sauce), be sure to adjust other no-salt seasonings (such as lemon juice, garlic, onions, fresh herbs, etc.) to ensure an interesting flavor. We will make an exception to our salt rule for baking recipes, which require salt as part of the chemical reaction of leavening.

Throughout this book you will see "vegan" and "veggie" used interchangeably and occasionally "veggies" will be used to speak about, well, vegetables. We have to keep you on your toes somehow!

If you see "flour" listed as an ingredient in a non-baking recipe, you may use white or whole wheat, as you wish. If you want to use different flours, such as rice or lentil, you will have to play with the amounts.

If at all possible, try not to substitute dry ingredients in baking recipes (such as baking powder, baking soda, flour, etc.). Baking recipes depend on balance and ratio (and math!). So, if you are an experienced baker, have a try at it. If not, stick to the directions.

When substituting ingredients, be sure to do only one change at a time. If you substitute three ingredients and the final product is not successful, you won't know what worked and what didn't. Remember some basic cooking principles: dried herbs are twice as strong as fresh (so if substituting fresh for dried, use twice as much and vice versa). If substituting frozen fruit or veggies for fresh, remember that textures and liquid amounts will differ; so do a test run before putting it on the serving line. If adding frozen produce for fresh, be sure to thaw before adding (or you'll throw off the liquid amounts).

Honey and refined sugar are generally excluded from vegan recipes. We try to use fruit, fruit juices, and fruit juice concentrates in addition to capitalizing on the inherent sweetness in many foods (carrots, raisins, yams, etc.). Natural syrups like maple syrup or rice syrup are also suitable ingredients. When you see "dry sweetener" listed in a recipe, it means it is up to you (and the availability in your area) to experiment with some of the natural products on the market. Many of these products are made from minimally processed cane or beet sugar.

Oven temperatures are given for conduction (no forced air, no internal fans, type of oven Grandma used) equipment. If you are using convection equipment (the oven has a fan or forced air that allows hot air to circulate), the general rule of thumb is to subtract 25 degrees from conduction temperatures. This is because convection equipment gives a more intense, even heat. So, subtract 25 degrees from our directions if you have a convection oven.

If you are preparing vegan, vegetarian, and carnivore dishes, work efficiently to reduce labor and product waste. For example, don't make three separate versions of a Greek salad (containing feta cheese and anchovies). Prepare the total amount of green salad needed (including the olives, peppers, and spices) and set aside the amount needed for the vegan population, then add the feta cheese and set aside for the vegetarians, and finally, add the anchovies for the carnivores. Less time, good product!

Chapter Three

VEGAN INGREDIENTS

DESCRIPTIONS AND USES

You have a choice of the types of ingredients you will stock your kitchen with when offering vegan menu options. Your choices will depend on time, space, equipment, customer preference, staff skill and knowledge, and the need for choice. If you are a caterer who occasionally prepares a vegan menu, you may not feel the need to incorporate new ingredients, such as tempeh or okara (although new ingredients allow you to offer more options to customers). On the other hand, if you are a college food service director offering vegan selections to boarding students 7 days per week, then you will probably want to incorporate vegan ingredients into your menus. And, by the way, when we say "vegan" ingredients (such as tofu, seitan, soy milk, and some veggie burgers) we have found that just about everyone, regardless of their dietary preferences, enjoys them. Several school food service directors we have spoken with have noted that the "veggie" entrée is selected by more students than the non-veggie. So be prepared, you may be serving a lot more of your vegan meals than you anticipate.

As we have said before, it is not absolutely necessary to use special ingredients to cook vegan. Remember to exclude the appropriate foods and ingredients (see Figure 3.1 for a listing). Many of your menu items are probably vegan or easily made that way. Fruit salad, applesauce, breads (made without honey, eggs or dairy, as in rye bread and many types of bagels), raw and cooked vegetables (just lose the butter or the meat stock), eggless pasta, cooked cereals, baked, steamed, roasted, and hash brown potatoes, rice, veggie salads (like 3 bean and marinated mushrooms), vegetable and bean soups (without meat stock), and steamed or baked grains come to mind.

Some items you may be serving can make the transition easily. Take off the cheese and the sausage and load up a veggie pizza with marinara (tomato-vegetable sauce), chopped onions, peppers, garlic, mushrooms, and tomatoes. Mashed potatoes can be made with vegan margarine and vegetable stock. Add vegetable and mushroom stock to your list of stocks to be prepared every day (see recipes on pages 93 and 94); freeze stocks to have on hand when they're needed. Throw some sliced portabellos, tomatoes, and onions on the grill to be key ingredients in a grilled vegetable sandwich. Take out the meat and add a different type of bean to create a two-, three-, and four-bean veggie chili. Take out the meat and leave the beans, jalapeños, chopped vegetables, and salsa for vegetarian tacos or burritos.

If you would like to add some additional ingredients, here are some ideas (also see the Soy 101 section at the end of this chapter):

Tofu: available in different degrees of firmness and textures, tofu is coagulated soy milk (the coagulant can be nigari, an ocean product, or calcium sulfate) and is a perishable product. Unless it is aseptically packaged (the packaging that resembles those juice boxes), be sure to refrigerate tofu. Some people rinse their tofu before cooking. If your tofu is packed in water, change the water in leftover tofu every 3 days. Tofu can be frozen, but its texture changes (it becomes spongy and chewy). Frozen tofu is good for dishes such as chili, where additional texture is wanted. To many people, tofu has a neutral flavor and texture, so you must give it inspiration. Tofu can be marinated or seasoned prior to cooking or flavored during cooking. Tofu is very agreeable and will take on the flavor that it is given. On the other hand, if tofu is not seasoned, it will be bland and unappealing to many of your customers. Firm and Extra Firm Tofu holds up well to chopping and slicing, and will keep its shape when grilled, put in soups or stews, baked, or stir-fried. Soft Tofu is good for blending and when a creamy ingredient is needed, as in salad dressings, dips, beverages, and sauces. Silken Tofu is custard-like and has a faint, nutty flavor. It goes well in puddings, "cream" pies, casseroles, soups, and sauces. There are lower-fat versions of tofu and calcium-enriched tofu. You may also find smoked, "meat" flavored tofu as well as sweetened, pudding-like tofu. We like to marinate tofu in dried basil, oregano, and black pepper with a drop of vinegar for a Mediterranean flavor; in red pepper flakes, lime juice, and chopped fresh jalapeños for a Southwestern flavor; and in soy sauce, chopped fresh garlic, and green onions for an Asian flavor. To satisfy our sweet tooth, we add a couple of drops of almond extract to some maple syrup and let tofu marinate in that for several hours. We then slice it and serve it on top of sliced fresh oranges.

Seitan: sometimes called the "meat of the wheat," seitan is a compressed extract of gluten (the protein found in flour). It can be found sold in strips and chunk-style, and can be frozen until ready to use. Seitan can be grilled, roasted, poached, and baked. It adds a chewy texture to dishes in which it is used. If purchased in large amounts, seitan can be frozen until ready to use. Seitan "steaks," marinated in lime juice and onion and grilled is a fast entrée.

Tempeh: is made from cooked, fermented soybeans that are formed into a cake and sometimes mixed with a grain (such as rice or barley) or sea vegetable.

Therefore, there are different flavors of tempeh. You can also find soy-only tempeh, which has the distinctive (and pleasant) bean-nut flavor of soy. Tempeh may have some black spots on the surface. This is the bacterium still working (like the lactobacillus in fermented dairy products). Tempeh is chewy and has the flavor of a smoky mushroom. Tempeh should be refrigerated until used and can be frozen (be sure to thaw in the refrigerator). Tempeh is higher in fiber and lower in fat than tofu and can appeal to people making healthy menu choices. Tempeh can be cut into small pieces and added to soup, stews, stir-fries, or casseroles. It can be grilled and served in a sandwich, too.

Okara: is the solid pulp left after soy milk is strained. It is a good source of protein and fiber. (Please note that commercial soy milk is strained during processing, so there is no need for you to strain it when you bring it home.) Okara is very perishable and must be kept refrigerated until used. It has a neutral flavor and the texture of coconut meat and is a good ingredient for baking and for casseroles.

Soy and rice milk: soy milk is made from boiling soybeans and pressing out the milk. It is available in plain, vanilla, chocolate, and other flavors. Soy milk is available in low- and no-fat and in calcium and vitamin D fortified versions, as is rice milk. Once opened, soy and rice milk is perishable and must be kept refrigerated. Soy and rice milk may be substituted for cow's milk in recipes. A word of caution: soy and rice milk will sometimes appear to "curdle" when put in hot coffee. Just stirring it will usually remedy the situation.

Soy sauce and tamari: soy sauce is made with equal parts of soybeans and wheat that are fermented. Tamari is fermented from soybeans, with no wheat (so tamari is a really a concentrated form of soy sauce). Use both these items for flavoring or as a condiment, remembering the high sodium content. Refrigerate when not being used.

"Fake" or substitute meats and dairy products: Soy yogurt, cheeses of many varieties, sour cream, and cream cheese are available as refrigerated items; check the labels to be sure they are not made with rennet (possibly derived from animals) or casein. Soy cheeses have good texture and flavor, but do not melt easily (great on a veggie burger, a little more challenging in a soup). Soy-based hot dogs and burgers are also available as perishable items (see Chapter 9 for more on this). Depending on the part of the country in which you cook, you may find regional "meat-substitute" products that can range from "sloppy Joe" texture to hot dog texture to a firm, sliceable texture. Again, be sure to check out the label to ensure that only vegan ingredients are included.

Miso: is made from fermented soybeans that are aged for several years. It can be found fresh (and perishable) and dried. Miso can be used for flavoring (like soy sauce or in the place of fish paste) but is very high in sodium.

Soybeans: whole soybeans may be found fresh at farmers' or Asian markets, frozen in the pod, or shelled in a can. Soybeans in the pod make a good appetizer or a garnish (simply steam them; the pods will be fuzzy and the beans green). Canned soybeans (which look beige) go well in soups and stews and can be used as a garnish for salads.

Texturized Vegetable Protein (TVP): be sure to read the label, since some TVP is flavored with meat. TVP is a dry product made from pressed soy flour and is available as a powder, in crumbles, and in chunks. When rehydrated (with water) TVP can give texture to burritos, burgers, stews, and stir-fries.

FIGURE 3.1:
FOODS EXCLUDED FROM VEGAN MENUS

Foods
All meat, poultry, seafood, eggs and egg products, all dairy products and processed products which may contain any of these items. This includes the following items:

- Gelatin (there are alternative vegan jell products)
- Chicken or beef broth (use vegan vegetable broth)
- Margarine with whey or milk proteins (there are vegan margarines)
- Worcestershire sauce containing anchovies (some brands are vegan)
- Soy cheese containing casein (there are vegan soy cheeses)
- Mayonnaise made with eggs (use vegan brands)
- Refined cane sugar (some brands are vegan others are processed through bone char; beet sugar is vegan)
- Honey (insect secretion; see Appendix C)
- Non-veggie wines (some brands are fined with animal products; see Appendix C)

FIGURE 3.2: HANDY GUIDE TO FOOD INGREDIENTS

CLASSIFICATION OF COMMERCIAL INGREDIENTS

Vegetarian means that the ingredient does not contain products derived from meat, fish, or fowl. It may include sources from eggs or dairy. Insect secretions, such as honey, are also classified as vegetarian. **Vegan** means that the item contains no animal products whatsoever. **Non-vegetarian** means that the ingredient (or substance used to process the ingredient) is derived from meat, fish, or fowl. Or, **non-vegetarian** can apply to substances, such as proteins or amino acids, derived from animals (including insects), when the collection of those substances necessitated the intentional death of that animal.

In some cases, a few manufacturers told us that they use vegetarian sources. However, we cannot say with certainty that all manufacturers of a given ingredient produce that ingredient in the same way. Thus, we have classified these ingredients as **typically vegetarian, typically vegan, typically non-vegetarian,** or **may be non-vegetarian**. The classification depends on the degree to which we may conclude from manufacturers' information that a given ingredient may be vegetarian or vegan. Note that a vegetarian or vegan ingredient may have been tested on animals.

Vegetarian

acid casein
albumen
beeswax
calcium caseinate
carbohydrate
casein
cysteine
cystine
honey
L-cysteine
L-cystine
lactalbumin
lac-resin
lactose
royal jelly
shellac
Simplesse
sodium caseinate
Sucanat Granulated
    with Honey

Vegan

Accent
acesulfame K
acesulfame potassium

acetic acid
acid calcium phosphate
acrylate-acrylamide
    resin
acrylic acid
activated charcoal
agar
agar-agar
algin
alginate
alginic acid
alum
aluminum ammonium
annatto
annatto extract
annatto seed
apple acid
arabic
ascorbic acid
aspartame
autolyzed yeast extract
baking powder
baking soda
beet sugar
bentonite
benzoyl peroxide
BHA

BHT
bicarbonate of soda
bioflavinoids
Brewer's yeast
bromelain
bromolin
butanoic acid
butylated hydroxy-
    anisole
butylated hydroxy-
    toluene
butyric acid
n-butyric acid
calcium biphosphate
calcium carbonate
calcium phosphate
calcium phosphate
    monobasic
calcium phosphate
    dibasic
calcium phosphate
    tribasic
calcium propionate
calcium sulfate
calcium sulfate
    anhydrous
candelilla wax

caramel color
carboxymethyl-
    cellulose
carnauba wax
carob bean gum
caroid
carrageenan
caustic soda
cellulose gum
charcoal
Chile saltpeter
chondrus extract
citric acid
CMC
cocoa butter
colophony
corn gluten
corn gluten meal
cream of tartar
cyanocobalamin
DevanSweet
diatomaceous earth
dicalcium phosphate
    dihydrate
distilled vinegar
Equal
erythorbic acid

essential oil
ethanol
ethyl alcohol
ethyl vanillin
fumaric acid
gluten
grain alcohol
grain vinegar
guar flour
guar gum
guaran
gypsum
hesperidin
hexadienic acid
hexadienoic acid
hydrogen peroxide
Irish moss
isoascorbic acid
Japanese isinglass
kieselguhr
light oil
lime
locust bean gum
maleic acid
malic acid
malt
malt extract
malt sugar
maltodextrin
maltol
maltose
mannitol
methyl paraben
methyl-*p*-hydroxy-
  benzoate
mineral oil
molasses
monocalcium phos-
  phate
monosodium gluta-
  mate
MSG
natural sugar
nonnutritive sweet-
  ener
norbixin
Nutrasweet
nutritional yeast
oleoresin
papain
paprika
paraffin
plaster of Paris

polyacrylomite
polydextrose
polyethylene
potash alum
potassium acid tartrate
potassium bitartrate
potassium hydrogen
  tartrate
potassium sorbate
potassium sulfate
precipitaed calcium
  phosphate
1,2-propanediol
propanoic acid
propanoic acid,
  calcium salt
propionic acid
propylene glycol
resin
rice syrup
Rochelle salts
rosin
rutin
saccharin
soda ash
soda lye
sodium acid car-
  bonate
sodium ascorbare
sodium benzoate
sodium benzosulfimide
sodium bicarbonate
sodium carbonate
sodium carboxy-
  methylcellulose
sodium hydrogen
  carbonate
sodium hydroxide
sodium isoascorbate
sodium nitrate
sodium potassium
  tartrate
sodium tartrate
sorbic acid
sorbic acid, potassium
  salt
sorbistat
sorbitan
spirit vinegar
St. John's bread
Sucanat
succinic acid
Sunette

tartaric acid
textured soy flour
textured soy protein
textured vegetable
  protein
tricalcium phosphate
turbinado sugar
turmeric
tumeric
TVP
unmodified food
  starch
unmodified starch
vanilla
vanilla extract
vanillin
vinegar
vinegar, distilled
vital wheat gluten
vitamin B-12
vitamin C
vitamin P complex
washed raw sugar
wheat gluten
wheat isolate
white distilled vinegar
white oil
white vinegar
xantham gum
yeast autolyzates
zein
Zest

Non-Vegetarian

carmine
carminic acid
cochineal
dripping
gelatin
Hi-Vegi-Lip
hydrogenated tallow
isinglass
keratin
lard
lard oil
pancreatin
pancreatic extract
pepsin
pork fat
pork oil
rennet
rennin

suet
tallow
tallow flakes
trypsin
tyrosine

Typically Vegetarian

acidulant
alanine
albumin
alpha tocopherol
antidusting agent
antioxidant
arginine
artificial flavor
aspartic acid
beta-carotene
biotin
butyl lactate
calciferol
calcium pantothenate
caproic acid
caprylic acid
carotenoid
cholecalciferol
coenzyme
color
corn sugar
curing agent
dextrose
drying agent
ethyl lactate
fermentation aid
foaming agent
fructose
fructose syrup
fruit sugar
glucose
glutamic acid
glycine
hexanoic acid
n-hexanoic acid
high fructose corn
  syrup
humectant
hydroscopic agent
isomerized syrup
lactase
lactic acid
leavener
leavening agent
lecithin

levulose
levulose-bearing syrup
malting aid
moisture-retaining
  agent
moisture-retention
  agent
natural sugar
n-octanoic acid
pickling agent
Provitamin A
sodium pantothenate
surface-finishing agent
tocopherol
vitamin B factor
vitamin D
vitamin D-2
vitamin D-3
vitamin E
water-retaining agent
wax
whey
whipping agent

Typically Vegan

amylase
antimicrobial agent
antispoilant
artificial coloring
chelating agent
dough conditioner
dough strengthener
firming agent
lactoflavin
maple sugar
maple syrup
natural coloring
niacin
niacinamide
nicotinic acid
nicotinamide

nutritive sweetener
pantothenic acid
d-pantothenamide
phenylalanine
preservative
pyridoxal
pyridoxamine
pyridoxine
pyridoxine hydro-
  chloride
pyridoxol hydro-
  chloride
reducing agent
riboflavin
riboflavin-5-
  phosphate
sequestering agent
sorbitol
stabilizer
thickener
texturizer
thiamin
thiamine
thiamine hydro-
  chloride
thiamine mono-nitrate
thiamine mono-nitrite
vitamin
vitamin B-1
vitamin B-2
vitamin B-3
vitamin B-5
vitamin B-6
vitamin B-6 hydro-
  chloride
yeast food

May be Non-Vegetarian

activated carbon
adipic acid
amino acid

anticaking agent
capric acid
clarifier
clarifying agent
n-decanoic acid
diglyceride
disodium inosinate
emulsifier
enzyme
fat
fatty acid
fining agent
flavor enhancer
folacin
folic acid
free-flow agent
glyceride
glycerin
glycerine
glycerol
hexanedioic acid
magnesium stearate
modified food
  starch
modified starch
monoglyceride
natural flavor
n-octadecanoic acid
oil
Olean
Olestra
palmitic acid
polyoxyethylene (20)
  sorbitan
  monooleate
polyoxyethylene (20)
  sorbitan mono-
  stearate
polysorbate
polysorbate 60
polysorbate 80
processing aid

protease
protein
pteroyl glutamic
  acid
retinol
sodium steoroyl
  lactylate
sodium stearoyl-2-
  lactylate
stearic acid
sucrose polyester
surface acting agent
surface-active agent
surfactant
vitamin A
vitamin A acetate
vitamin A palmitate
vitamin A propionate
wetting agent
wine

Typically Non-Vegetarian

calcium stearate
cane sugar
colorose
n-hexadecanoic acid
inversol
invert sugar
invert sugar syrup
lipase
myristic acid
cis-9-octadecenoic
  acid
oleic acid
palmitic acid
refined sugar
sucrose
sugar
sugar syrup, invert
n-tetradecanoic acid

This chart is taken from *Vegetarian Journal's Guide to Food Ingredients*.
To receive further information on over 250 ingredients send $4 to VRG, PO Box 1463, Baltimore, MD 21203 or visit our web site at www.vrg.org to order this 28–page guide. Here are two sample entries:
PEPSIN -- Commercial Source: animal (hog- or cow-derived). **Used in:** cheese and cheese products, digestive aids. **Definition:** An enzyme used to break down proteins. Non-Vegetarian
CALCIUM PROPIONATE -- Also known as: propanoic acid, calcium salt. **Commercial Source:** mineral-synthetic. **Used in:** baked goods, stuffing, processed cheese, chocolate products, cakes, pie fillings, artificially sweetened fruit jelly. **Definition:** A preservative that is effective against mold, slightly effective against bacteria, but not effective against yeast. Vegan

BUT WHAT IF IT IS KOSHER?

The kosher industry is a $30 billion per year business and is growing rapidly. Some people, such as Muslims, Jews, and Seventh-day Adventists, purchase kosher foods out of conviction. Others feel that kosher-certified foods are carefully watched and properly prepared.

The kosher dietary laws are explained as being part of the spirituality and holiness of following the Jewish tradition. There are categories of foods that are allowed to be eaten, such as dairy and produce and categories of foods not to be eaten, such as pork and shellfish. For extra added confusion, certain categories of kosher foods can not be combined. Meat and dairy items (even if they are kosher) can not be combined in a kosher kitchen and must be prepared and served in separate containers (kosher kitchens have at least two sets of pots, silverware, dish towels, etc.). The no meat-and-milk-at-the-same-meal rule is explained in humane terms: it would be possible to be eating the offspring of the mother in its own mother's milk. All allowable foods must be produced and prepared according to specific rules. For example, beef is an allowable kosher food, but the animal must be handled in a particular way and only certain parts of the animal may be consumed. Yogurt, as an allowable dairy product must be processed with ingredients (such as added fruit and preservatives) which have been deemed kosher by a certifying agency. For people who adhere to kosher laws, just about everything that goes on you and in you must be kosher; this includes not only food but also soaps, shampoos, aluminum foil, and tooth brushes, to name a few. Kosher classification divides foods into three categories: meat, milk (or dairy), and pareve. Here is an explanation of each category:

Kosher Meat: will not have any pork or other nonkosher animal ingredients (kosher animals, such as cows or lambs, have a cloven hoof and chew a cud) or dairy products in them. Animals to be used for kosher meat must be free of disease and blemishes and must be slaughtered according to certain rituals. Packaged kosher meat must be labeled as kosher. Fresh kosher meat is sold only by kosher butchers.

Kosher Dairy Products: are either directly dairy (such as milk or yogurt), dairy derivatives (casein, whey, lactose, etc.), processed in equipment contaminated by dairy, or dairy by addition (such as butter in croissants, milk solids in margarine, etc.). Kosher labels will indicate that a food is both kosher and contains dairy products (for example, O/U D means "certified as kosher by the Union of Orthodox Rabbis (O/U) and contains dairy products (D)".

Pareve: this category is the tricky one. Its origins are obscure (they are not listed in the Torah or the Talmud), but is generally regarded as the "neutral" category, neither milk nor meat. Many people take this to mean that they will find no animal products in an item labeled "pareve." While there will not be any beef or milk in a pareve item, fish and eggs are considered neutral products. When selecting products you will see that the label may sometimes say "Pareve" and sometimes does not. You will have to look at the package contents and see if the item has meat in it. For example, bottled water has the same kosher certification symbol as a package of kosher bologna or a package of kosher cake mix containing eggs. Once again, do not assume that "pareve" translates into vegetarian.

What does this mean to the vegetarian shopper? If a product is categorized as a meat or a milk product, you can be sure that there are animal-based ingredients in them or that they were processed with animal-contaminated equipment or packaging. This is useful in determining if, say, margarine contains milk solids (would be designated "milk" or "dairy"). Don't be fooled by the pareve designation of "neutral" foods. Remember that pareve means there are no meat or milk ingredients, but there can be ingredients derived from eggs (for example, albumen) or fish (for example, fish oils).

A food manufacturer obtains kosher certification by requesting it. A kosher certifying agency (there are over 200 in the United States with over 1300 different seals or designations, each with slightly different rules) must trace every ingredient in a product to its ultimate source and verify that it is kosher itself and was handled in a kosher way (filters used to screen ingredients are not of animal origin, detergents used in the process were not of non-kosher origin, etc.). If the ingredients and the process are deemed "kosher," a contract is signed between the manufacturer and the kosher agency. As part of the contract, the manufacturer agrees not to change the ingredients or the process without first notifying the kosher agency. An onsite inspector (called a mashgiach) will make sure that the manufacturer is adhering to the kosher agreement.

Just as a side note, there are some basic agreements and some basic disagreements between kosher agencies. For example, pork or shrimp would never be considered kosher by any agency. However, some agencies would say a product was not kosher if all the ingredients were acceptable but were mixed by a non-Jewish person; some agencies rate casein as dairy; and some agencies, who believe casein is so far removed from milk it no longer has the characteristics of milk, rate casein as pareve.

Several of the kosher designations (OU and Chaf-K, for example) are registered servicemarks, and printing them without authorization is a violation of Federal law. Most states have laws about false advertising, and using a kosher designation without permission would fall into that category.

Where do you find the servicemarks? There is no uniform place on the label, so you will have to look carefully. Become familiar with the kosher certifying agencies in your area, as some are very local (if there is one, contact the Jewish Community Center in your town as a starting place). After a while, you will amass a list of products which have the kosher designation (don't assume that all products made under a brandline are kosher; just because the gingerbread mix is kosher, it doesn't mean that the angel food cake will be).

Here are some additional issues to think about when deciding to purchase kosher foods. Fresh produce and some other unprocessed foods (basically foods that were harvested and brought to market without any processing) do not have to be labeled as kosher (which brings to mind the issue of waxes used to coat fresh fruit), so kosher labeling is not a guide for these items. Kosher gelatin can be made from fish bones (considered pareve), kosher animal bones (considered meat), or from vegetable sources. Do not assume that "kosher" gelatin is from a non-animal source; check into the company's sources.

Kosher rennet can be made from kosher animal sources, vegetable products, or microbial sources. So do not assume that kosher cheese contains non-animal rennet; this only means that kosher cheese may contain kosher rennet.

So, to review: kosher products designated "meat" or "milk" will cue you to their animal-contents. Pareve items may not have beef, poultry, or dairy ingredients, but you will have to scrutinize the label for eggs or fish. Prepared kosher foods will not be meat-and-dairy combinations, but can contain meat or dairy in separate items. Whatever you do, be sure to read the labels!

References:
- Kashrus Magazine: published five times a year, call (800) 237-7149; also found at Barnes & Nobles and B. Dalton bookstores.
- Eidlitz, E. Is it Kosher? Encyclopedia of Kosher Foods Facts and Fallacies. Feldheim Publishers: New York, 1992.
- Lipschutz, Y. Kashruth: A Comprehensive Background and Reference Guide. Mesorah Publications: New York, 1988.

SOY 101

Soybeans are a major crop in the United States. What's ironic is that livestock consume more soy than humans do. This is really too bad. Soy is a "user friendly" food "that can save you from heart disease and cancer," says Dr. Mark Messina. Phytochemicals (chemicals of plant origin that have been shown to have beneficial properties) are the nutritional buzzwords of the nineties. Soy is high in phytochemicals, having isoflavones and plant estrogens, which have antioxidant characteristics and properties that seem to inhibit cancer cell growth.

Looking at it another way, eating animal protein encourages the body to excrete calcium and makes the kidneys work overtime. Populations that depend heavily on soy products for their protein have less heart disease (soy has no cholesterol) and less cancer. Research is just showing that soy may also help to inhibit bone loss, thus reducing the risk of osteoporosis. Women not wanting to take pharmaceutical estrogen to decrease menopause symptoms use soy products. If you would like to read more about soy research, the United Soybean Board has updated bulletins. You can contact them at P.O. Box 419200, St. Louis, MO 63141; 800 TALK-SOY.

Soybeans have a make-up of 26% of calories from carbohydrate, 34% protein, and 42% fat (Yes, soy products can be high in fat. If this is a concern, select low- or no-fat soy products.). The fat content is 16% saturated, with 7% being linolenic (the same type found in omega-3 fatty acids, which are touted as reducing heart disease). The amino acids in soy combine to make a high quality protein, which is efficiently used by our bodies. Soybeans contain soluble fiber, which helps to regulate blood glucose levels, important for diabetics.

Okay, so now you're convinced to use more soy products on your menu. Where do you begin? See below for some helpful tips on equivalents, which you can choose from. One serving of protein of various soy foods according to the USDA food pyramid is as follows:

- 1/2 cup cooked soybeans (they're nutty and mild and good in soups, casseroles, chili, or as a side dish on their own)
- 1/2 cup tempeh
- 1 cup textured soy protein
- 1/4 cup soy nuts
- 1/2 cup tofu (available in different textures and fat levels)
- 1/4 cup defatted soy flour
- 1 cup soy milk
- 2 tablespoons miso

Next, let's give you some soy speak. Here are some of the more popular and available types of soy, as well as information on how to use them:

- **Tofu:** soybean curd made from curdling and pressing hot soy milk. Can be found in regular, lowfat, and non-fat varieties. Textures range from thickened milk-like all the way to cutable-with-a-knife. Soft tofu can be used in quiches, puddings, custards, sauces, and cheesecake. Firm tofu can be grilled or stir-fried, used as crumbles in tacos or entrée sauces, and scrambled. Remember, tofu picks up the flavor you cook it with; so the sky's the limit. Use silken tofu instead of sour cream or mayonnaise. Tofu can replace eggs in many recipes. Tofu is available smoked, marinated, and even as a sweet custard. Don't forget that it is perishable and likes moisture; so keep it refrigerated and covered. If you purchase bulk tofu, you will have to change the water it sits in daily until you are ready to use it.

- **Tempeh:** a tender cake of fermented soybeans sometimes mixed with grains. Can be used as the "bite" in entrées. Can stand up to heat and baking. I use it in pasta sauce and chili.

- **Soy milk:** available in various flavors and fat levels. Made by soaking and pressing soybeans. Naturally high in protein, but low in calcium, vitamins A, D, and B12 unless fortified. Use wherever you'd use cow's milk. It's perishable too (unless in unopened asceptic package), so store correctly.

- **Soy sprouts:** growing shoots of soybeans. Soy sprouts are high in vitamin C and protein. Wash sprouts thoroughly before using (but don't let them sit in water because they'll become soggy and lose some of their nutrients). Use in salads, soups, casseroles, and stir-fries.

- **Natto:** made of fermented soybeans, which have been cooked and mashed. Has the texture of cheese and is great for topping soups and casseroles, rice, and veggies.

- **Miso:** is a paste (very salty) of fermented soybeans and grains. Miso has a nutty, smoky flavor. Miso is used for a flavoring (a little goes a long way) in soups, sauces, marinades, and dressings.

- **Textured soy protein:** soybean proteins are extracted and dried. Can be used as a flavor enhancer or as part of the "body" in casseroles. Pretty high in salt. Should not be used for low fiber diets (very high in fiber).

- **Soy cheese and yogurt:** made from soy milk. Different flavors and fat levels are available. Some soy cheeses melt well and can be used in hot or cold sandwiches (in addition to the millions of other ways you use cheese). Use soy cheese or yogurt in place of cream cheese or sour cream. Some soy cheeses contain casein and are not vegan.

- **Soy nuts:** roasted soybeans – they're good! Have a nutty, peanut flavor.

- **Soy grits:** very coarsely ground soybeans. Cooks up just like any hot cereal.

- **Okara:** is soy fiber, a byproduct of soy milk. Tastes a bit like coconut and can be added to baked goods.

SOY EASY: A GUIDE TO SUBSTITUTING SOY PRODUCTS WHEN YOU'RE COOKING (AND REDUCING FAT WHILE YOU'RE AT IT)

INSTEAD OF:	USE:
1 ounce baking chocolate	3 ounces cocoa powder and 1 Tablespoon soy oil
1 cup cow's milk	1 cup soy or rice milk
1 cup yogurt	1 cup soft tofu, blended
1 egg	2-inch square of tofu, blended or 1 Tablespoon soy flour and 1 Tablespoon water
1 cup ricotta cheese	1 cup firm tofu, mashed

As far as nutritive value, for 3-1/2 ounces you get 206 calories from miso, 212 calories from natto, 77 from okara, 173 from whole soybeans, 450 from soy nuts, 33 from whole soy milk, 199 from tempeh, and 145 from firm tofu (the firmer the tofu, the higher the calorie content, because it is more concentrated).

Store dried soybeans in airtight containers in a cool, dry place and they should stay fresh for a year. Soy products can become rancid easily and will absorb flavors and odors, so keep them all stored tightly and separately. Tofu, kept refrigerated, with the water changed, if necessary, should keep for about a week (but no more than that). If you want to prepare dried soybeans, let them soak overnight (discarding the soak water may help to reduce some of the gas-producing qualities). Eight ounces of dried beans cooked in 1-1/2 cups water should yield about 2-1/4 cups cooked beans. Soybeans need long cooking (2-3 hours following soaking) or pressure cooking.

Soy products are versatile, healthy, and easy-to-use. For example, a favorite "throw together" soup of ours is made with firm tofu, soy milk, thawed frozen corn kernels, canned tomatoes, and tomato purée, which is then seasoned with curry powder and garlic. Served as is, it can be used for every diet modification except low sodium and puréed. And you can blend it for that modification. We also make a fast rice pudding with blended tofu, soy milk, leftover rice, dried fruit, cinnamon, ginger, and nutmeg. Start experimenting with soy products now and you'll never believe your kitchen survived without them.

RECIPES
On the next page you will find some recipes to get you started.

DIJON-SESAME DRESSING

Yield: Makes 1-1/2 quarts

Use this recipe as a dressing for salads and as a dip for veggies or bread sticks.

INGREDIENTS	MEASURE	METHOD
Firm tofu	2 pounds	Blend all the ingredients until
Apple juice concen- trate, thawed	4 ounces	creamy. Refrigerate until ready to serve.
Onion, minced	6 ounces	
Prepared mustard	4 ounces	
Vinegar	6 ounces	
Sesame oil	3 ounces	
Sesame seeds	1 ounce	
White pepper	2 teaspoons	
Ginger, powdered	1 teaspoon	
Garlic, powdered	1 teaspoon	

Total Calories per 2 TB Serving: 48   Total Fat as % of Daily Value: 5%   Protein: 2 gm   Fat: 3 gm
Carbohydrates: 2 gm   Calcium: 42 mg   Iron: <1 mg   Sodium: 30 mg   Dietary Fiber: <1 gm

CREAMY CREAM-LESS TOMATO SOUP

Yield: 25 six-ounce servings

Use this smooth recipe as a hot appetizer, as an ingredient in casseroles, or even as a sauce.

INGREDIENTS	MEASURE	METHOD
Vegetable oil spray	to cover pan	Sweat (cook until translucent) onions for about 4 minutes in a kettle or braising pan.
Onions, diced	12 ounces	
Fresh tomatoes, diced	7 each	
Garlic, minced	3 cloves	Add tomatoes, garlic, and pepper; sweat for 2 minutes (until garlic is soft).
White pepper	3 teaspoons	
Soy milk, unflavored	1 quart	
Silken tofu, firm	2-1/2 pounds	Blend in soy milk. Cook and stir for 2 minutes. Remove from heat. Add in tofu and stir (for smooth consistency purée in blender and re-heat). Serve hot.

VARIATIONS: Turn this recipe into vegetable chowder with the addition of diced seasonal veggies, corn, and potatoes.

Total Calories per Serving: 66   Total Fat as % of Daily Value: 3%   Protein: 5 gm   Fat: 2 gm
Carbohydrates: 6 gm   Calcium: 30 mg   Iron: 1 mg   Sodium: 44 mg   Dietary Fiber: 1 gm

BANANA-RAMA

Yield: Serves 20

Try this frozen banana confection in the hot summer months. The lightness and coolness will appeal to everyone. It might be just the thing to please your customers or patients (watch the syrups for diabetics).

INGREDIENTS	MEASURE	METHOD
Bananas, very ripe	10 each	Chunk the bananas into a food processor. Add soy or rice milk and purée thoroughly. Add concentrate and blend again.
Soy or rice milk	30 ounces	
Orange juice concentrate, thawed	3 ounces	
Fresh berries	1 pound	Place a few berries in the bottom of half a 200 steam table pan. Pour mixture over berries. Cover and freeze. Serve garnished with more berries.

Variations: Apple juice concentrate or flavored syrups can be used instead of orange juice concentrate. You can also use flavored soy or rice milk for variety.

Total Calories per Serving: 90   Total Fat as % of Daily Value: 2%   Protein: 2 gm   Fat: 1 gm
Carbohydrates: 19 gm   Calcium: 20 mg   Iron: <1 mg   Sodium: 28 mg   Dietary Fiber: 2 gm

Chapter Four

DOING THE AM SHUFFLE –
BREAKFAST

Breakfast is an important meal during the day, whether it is a grab-and-go quickie or a four-course sit-down.

BREAKFAST BUFFETS

Breakfast buffets can be colorful and bountiful and easy to set up. Think about the season, the audience, and the timing and assemble a buffet that will look good and make everybody happy.

Whether you are serving a breakfast buffet or a sit-down breakfast, you probably already have many items on your menu or in your storeroom that fit into the vegan plan. Cooked cereal (prepared with soy or rice milk and optional margarine rather than milk and butter); cold cereal (just read the label for "hidden" dairy ingredients); many breads and crackers; fresh, canned, and dried fruit; grains (like rice, cornmeal, kasha, or bulgur); fresh, canned, and frozen fruit and vegetable juices; some nondairy creamers; jelly and preserves; peanut and other nut butters; nuts (chopped walnuts and almonds make good cereal toppers); and seeds (think sesame, poppy, pumpkin, etc.) do not have to be a "special order." These items are already vegan. Be sure to include some of them on every morning menu. Here are some sample buffet menus:

Winter Breakfast Buffet:
- assorted hot cereals
- steamed tofu (optional)
- hash browns with sautéed onions and peppers
- steamed brown or white rice
- assorted mini-muffins (carrot, apple, zucchini, etc.)
- assorted bread for toasting
- stewed fruit compote
- fresh whole fruit bowl (apples, pears, oranges, bananas, etc.)
- fruit preserves, peanut butter, and margarine
- assorted vegan milks
- hot cocoa and other hot beverages

For a spicy accent, offer three-bean chili and salsa and tortillas instead of toast. For an Asian flair, include hot miso soup and pickled vegetables.

Note: Vegan milks are available made from soy, rice, nuts, grains, or combinations of these. They may be fortified with calcium, vitamin D, vitamin B12, and/or iron (as they do not naturally contain these). Read the label or ask the manufacturer. Each type of veggie milk has a different taste, so poll your customers to see which they like the best. You can find different flavors in many veggie milks. We've seen vanilla, chocolate, banana, and berry. A word of warning: when put in a hot beverage, vegan milks need to be stirred quite a bit, as they need a little bit of encouragement to stay blended. Let your customers and staff knows this. Strong coffee also can cause vegan milks not to blend well.

Hot Weather Breakfast Buffet:
- assorted cold cereals
- chilled tofu cubes (optional)
- assorted bagels
- fresh fruit salad (cut up apples, pears, oranges, and tangerines tossed with thawed frozen strawberries)
- fruit bowl (grapes, plums, peaches, bananas, etc.)
- melon slices
- vegan cream cheese and sliced cheeses
- margarine, fruit preserves, and peanut butter
- assorted vegan milks
- assorted juices

For a spicy flair, offer breakfast burritos filled with mashed pinto beans, chopped chilies, chopped tomatoes, and chopped cilantro.

HOW MUCH TO MAKE
When figuring out quantities, take into consideration the following:

1. Size of china and paper service ware (don't plan on serving 6 ounces of cereal in an 8-ounce bowl since this makes the customers feel as if they're being scrimped; and servers have a tendency to fill up bowls, so your planned 6 ounces will probably evolve into whatever size bowl is being used).

2. Is the food served or is it self-service? If self-service, then forecast how many times customers will return for particular items. For self-service, use some tricks of the trade such as small serving spoons and placement of less popular items (or less expensive items) first (the psychology of this is that customers

tend to fill up their plates in the order in which they see things, so putting that Swiss chard casserole as the first item might get it more takers).

3. Are free refills given (do you have an "all-you-can-eat" serving line)? Once again, forecast how many refills you will have for the items you think you will be serving. You may find that you are preparing one and-a-half to three times more portions than the actual number of customers served, depending on the popularity of the item.

4. What's the history? Be sure to keep records of what and how much you served; then use these "histories" to forecast how much to prepare.

NOW, LET'S LOOK AT SOME PARTICULARS

1. Coffee – just work backwards. If you have 6-ounce coffee cups and you serve about 75 cups every morning, then you'll need 450 ounces of coffee or about 3-1/2 gallons (450 divided by 128 ounces/gallon). One pound of ground coffee makes approximately 3 gallons of brewed coffee (ask your supplier if you're not certain about the yield of your coffee). The rest will depend on your coffee maker (do you make 16-ounce pots, 1-gallon urns, etc.?).

2. Juice can be figured out in the same way. Decide which glasses you'll be serving in, figure total need, and then decide on the type of juice. Will you be diluting concentrates, purchasing canned and ready to use varieties, purchasing individual juices, etc.?

3. Hot cereals and grains – most expand 2-1/2 times from raw to cooked, so 16 ounces of raw oats should cook up to about 48 ounces of prepared oatmeal. If you want to serve 25 four-ounce portions of oatmeal, then you'll need 100 ounces; divided by 2.5 to figure out the raw amount to cook (you should get about 40 ounces or 2 pounds 8 ounces of raw oats).

4. Fruit – you'll need to take into account the percentage of waste depending on the type of fruit chosen. For example, berries, and grapes don't need to be peeled, so if you buy 20 pounds of them, you can serve 20 pounds. Peeled melons, apples, and oranges will lose some weight during processing, so be sure to order more than you will actually need. Your produce vendor can supply you with a chart that shows the amount of waste from different fruits and vegetables.

Sample amounts for 25 portions:
Coffee (8-ounce cups) – approximately 2 gallons (or 1-1/2 pounds of coffee)
Soy milk (4 ounces, for coffee and cereal) – approximately 3 quarts
Fresh mixed fruit salad (3-ounce portion) – 4 pounds 11 ounces prepared
Toast (1 slice) – 1-1/4 loaves (most commercial loaves have 20 slices of bread, with ends discarded)

MENU IDEAS FOR BREAKFAST

Breakfast in a Cup: You can pre-make and cup up breakfast smoothies or offer a made-to-order "smoothie" bar at your location. Either way, you can make a nutritious meal in a cup. Have one of your more vivacious servers act as a breakfast bartender and make smoothies to order. You can prepare smoothies or breakfast drinks with a minimum of ingredients and equipment, or you can go all out.

Fresh items for smoothies: bananas, grapes, carrots, celery, and seasonal fresh fruit

Frozen items for smoothies: thawed strawberries and/or blueberries, orange and/or apple juice concentrate, frozen soy or rice ice cream

Dried and canned items for smoothies: applesauce, wheat germ, nutritional yeast, dried fruit, cocoa powder, maple syrup, soy or rice milk, assorted juices

Smoothie suggestions: orange juice, wheat germ, banana, and strawberry; apple juice, celery, carrots, nutritional yeast; berries, soy milk, apple sauce, and maple syrup, etc.

SHORT CUT BREAKFAST BEVERAGE BAR

- Equipment: blenders, serving ware
- Ingredients: pre-made juices, soy yogurt, soy/rice/grain milks (offer various flavors and fat-levels), nutritional yeast (for vitamin B12), flavor extracts (vanilla, orange, etc.), wheat germ, bananas, applesauce
- Offer: "Get and Go" drinks consisting of milk, juice or fruit, and nutritional yeast combined; this gives a meal-in-a-cup beverage. For example, combine 4 ounces of rice milk with 1 teaspoon of nutritional yeast, 1/2 banana, and 1/2 teaspoon of orange extract or 4 ounces of soy milk with 1 teaspoon of

nutritional yeast, 2 ounces of orange juice, 1 ounce of applesauce, and 1/2 teaspoon of almond extract.

Here are some other combination suggestions:

1. Creamy Smooth – three ounces fruit-flavored soy yogurt, 1 ounce soy milk, 1/2 banana, 1 Tablespoon nutritional yeast, and 1 teaspoon thawed orange juice concentrate
2. Harvest Apple – four ounces tofu, 2 ounces applesauce, 1 Tablespoon thawed apple juice concentrate, 2 ounces soy milk, and a sprinkle of cinnamon
3. Potassium Plus – three ounces carrot juice, 2 ounces orange juice, and 1/2 banana
4. Sunny – four ounces orange juice, 2 ounces pineapple juice, 1/2 banana or 2 ounces tofu, 3 ounces strawberries, and 1 Tablespoon wheat germ
5. Ginger-peachy – four ounces peaches, 2 ounces orange juice, 1 ounce carrot juice, dash of maple syrup, and a dash of ginger

THE WHOLE ENCHILADA BREAKFAST-BEVERAGE BAR

- Equipment: blenders, juicers, coffee (or espresso) makers, microwave serving ware
- Ingredients: fresh fruit and vegetables (to make juice), assorted vegan milks, nutritional yeast, wheat germ, soy yogurt, extracts, flavored syrups, bananas, applesauce, dried fruit (such as dates and raisins), coffee and espresso beans, cocoa powder, peanut butter
- Offer: hot or cold beverages as described above. Hot beverages could include a café latte (steamed with rice milk) blended with cocoa powder, nutritional yeast, raisins, and peanut butter. You would make the latte, blend the ingredients, and then reheat briefly in the microwave.

Here are some other combination suggestions:

1. Latte with attitude – hot latte blended with banana and dates
2. Chocolate covered cappuccino – hot cappuccino blended with peanut butter and cocoa powder
3. Apples Plus – apple cider blended with applesauce, apple juice concentrate, raisins, and cinnamon
4. Banana Split – steamed soy milk blended with banana, berries, pineapple, and cocoa powder (or chocolate syrup)
5. What the Bunny Knows – carrot juice blended with banana, celery, wheat germ, and orange juice concentrate

ONE DISH WONDERS FOR BREAKFAST

We love a hearty tofu scramble in the morning. It's colorful and tasty and a terrific way to use leftover ingredients. Here are some breakfast entrées that are a meal in themselves.

Tofu Scramble: scramble (in a sauté pan, griddle, or in the oven) crumbled tofu (discussed later in this chapter) with seasonal veggies and spices. Serve on its own or over steamed rice or hash browns. Also, see recipe on page 60.

Breakfast Burrito: fill with mashed or whole beans, tempeh or breakfast strip, or crumbled tofu and serve with salsa and chopped onions, chili, and cilantro. Also, see recipe on page 62.

AM Tofu Quiche: this can be prepared the night before and baked off in the morning.

Morning Bean Pies: use a cornmeal or pastry crust. The filling for these pies can be sweet or savory. Sweet potato pies make a good morning treat as well. Check with ethnic suppliers to see if they have a vegan, ready-to-use version. For a fast version, boil or roast yams, peel and mash with cinnamon, ginger, nutmeg, lemon zest, and margarine, then bake in a pre-made vegan (with margarine or vegetable oil, not butter or animal fat as the moistening agent) crust.

Breakfast Parfaits: this displays beautifully (remember we eat first with the eyes), is easy to make, and is a wonderful way to start the day. Alternate "creamy" ingredients with crunchy and fruity ingredients. "Creamy" ingredients could be 1 pound soft tofu (plain or blended with a teaspoon of vanilla extract and three Tablespoons orange juice concentrate). You can also purchase almond-flavored and sweetened tofu, soy yogurt, or frozen soy or rice ice cream (for the summer!). Crunchy ingredients could be granola, chopped nuts, wheat germ, crushed cold cereal, or chopped dry fruit; and the fruity portion of the parfait could be fresh fruit in season (chopped peaches, apricots, grapes, berries, plums, etc.), thawed frozen fruit, canned fruit, or stewed dried fruit. Breakfast parfaits are quick to make (and fast to sell)!

PUTTING IT ALL TOGETHER

Fashion your breakfast menu for the people you serve. Do they have time for a leisurely breakfast or are they the grab-and-go type? Do your customers go for ethnic or spicy dishes or do they like traditional American morning foods? Vegan pancakes (with fruit and/or nuts) and waffles, vegetable and egg replacer casseroles, chili and rice, tofu crepes or blintzes, breakfast tamales, and tofu and breakfast strips are examples of vegan day starters.

We sometimes think that breakfast can be created out of a string of side dishes including hot cereals such as oatmeal (try Irish or steel-cut for variety), creamed wheat, creamed rice, corn meal, and grits for traditional cereals, and kasha, bulgur, quinoa, barley, and millet for grains. Offer a selection of cold cereals as well (remember the soy, rice, or grain milk). Offer condiments such as raisins, chopped dried fruit, chopped nuts, shredded coconut, wheat germ, chocolate or carob chips, and granola.

Breads can include quick breads that can be made the night before and heated in the morning. They can be made from scratch, mixes, or from frozen batters (muffins and bread loaves can be made from the same batter). Think banana nut, zucchini, lemon-poppyseed, cranberry, mixed berry, carrot, squash, and orange. Cornbread can be made in loaves or muffins and can be plain (think about adding corn kernels for texture) or flavored with chilies, tomatoes, dried fruit, or citrus zest. Bagels, toast, and English muffins are always a hit. Offer breads with margarine, peanut butter, fruit preserves, jams or marmalade, vegan cream cheese, hummus, or sliced, flavored tofu (available ready-made).

The fruit can be fresh, frozen, canned, or dried. Serve whole, sliced, or cut into salads. Use fruit as a topping (thawed frozen strawberries or other berries tossed with a smidgen of orange juice concentrate), as a side dish (melon wedges, grape clusters), or as an entrée (fresh fruit salad with granola and soy yogurt). Fruit can also be cooked into a compote (stew fresh or dried fruit with ginger, lemon zest, and apple juice concentrate) and served as a topping, side dish, or entrée.

Potatoes can be served in many different ways. Try offering traditional hash browns (turn them into O'briens by adding sautéed onion and red and green pepper); baked potatoes (served with chopped veggies, chili, or vegan soy cheese as toppings); steamed potatoes tossed with herbs; scalloped potatoes (sliced, cooked potatoes baked with grated soy cheese, soy milk, and pepper); and dare we mention it French fries (offer seasonings and salsa).

We've already mentioned how to set up a breakfast beverage bar. For simpler presentations, be sure to serve well-brewed coffee (never hold a pot of coffee for more than 30 minutes or higher than 180 degrees, unless you prefer to serve sludge); regular, decaf, and perhaps flavored, as well as a variety of hot and cold, caffeinated and herbal teas (be sure the water is boiling to get the best tea flavor). Beverage condiments should include spice shakers (think nutmeg, ginger, cinnamon, etc.), lemon slices, sweeteners, vegan milk (soy, rice, grain, vanilla, and chocolate), and extracts (vanilla, orange, etc.).

BEYOND EGGS

As much as we don't like to substitute vegan foods for food made with animal products ("hey, this tofu dish tastes just like eggs!"), some textures and flavors are equated with breakfast, therefore, should be available. Get your staff familiar with egg replacers (not egg substitutes, which are usually made with egg whites), such as Ener-G Egg Replacer, available in powder form. We don't recommend serving egg replacers (made from soy products, vegetables, thickening agents, etc.) instead of scrambled eggs; the taste and the texture are not conducive to this. They are useful as an ingredient in breakfast items, such as a breakfast quiche or a baked, filled omelet, and in baking biscuits, muffins, and quick breads.

Explore the properties of tofu. We find that a tofu scramble, using firm tofu with lots of veggies, served with a side of hash browns is both fast and easy to make and very well accepted. Work with different brands and textures of tofu until you find the right one for your facility. We've included several "egg-alternative" breakfast recipes at the end of this chapter.

There are many breakfast convenience items available on the market today. Consider cost, acceptability, and ease of preparation when selecting them. We have sampled and used vegan breakfast strips and "sausages," frozen hash browns, vegan soy cheeses and yogurts, vegan pancake and muffin mixes, and even several frozen vegan breakfast entrées and have been able to select quite a few good products. For example, veggie burgers can do double duty as a lunch and breakfast item. Offer a veggie burger/hash brown breakfast combo, or use the veggie burger as the basis for a breakfast sandwich (served on a biscuit, bagel, or English muffin). The same can be said for vegan breakfast strips. In the morning, serve them as a side dish, chopped in scrambled tofu, or as a tofu "omelet" filling. In the afternoon, use breakfast strips crumbled on top of salads, as a flavoring ingredient in soups, veggies, starches, or casseroles, or even for a vegan "BLT" or club sandwich (tomatoes, lettuce, breakfast strips, and vegan mayonnaise would be the main ingredients; you can add sliced onion, avocado, sprouts, etc. for extra flavor). You may want to use a combination of convenience and from-scratch breakfast items on your menu, depending upon time, employee skills, and budget considerations.

MENU IDEAS FOR BREAKFAST

Quick and Easy:
- Assorted juices, fresh whole fruit (apples, pears, bananas, oranges, tangerines, peaches, nectarines, plums, grape clusters, apricots, etc.)
- Hot oatmeal served with raisins, dates, and dried apricots
- Assorted toast served with margarine, peanut butter, and fruit preserves
- Soy or rice milk

Time to Eat for 25:
- Broiled grapefruit half topped with maple syrup (you'll need 13 grapefruit and 25 ounces or 1 pint plus 9 ounces of syrup)
- Sweet potato pancakes with fruit preserves and orange slices (prepare 50 pancakes; double recipe on page 59)
- Assorted muffins
- Cinnamon applesauce (if serving two-ounce portions, you need 50 ounces or 3 pounds plus 2 ounces)
- Soy or rice milk

Breakfast Banquet for 25:
- Seasonal fresh fruit cup with mint (if serving three-ounce portions, you need 75 ounces of cut fruit, or 4 pounds plus 11 ounces)
- Eggless Asian omelet (see recipe on page 61 and adjust yield) with steamed rice (2 pounds, 2 ounces of raw rice should yield 75 ounces of cooked rice or 25 three-ounce portions)
- Stewed fruit compote (for three-ounce portions, stew about 4 pounds of dried fruit; dried fruit reconstitutes about 1-1/2 times its dried weight)
- Assorted muffins with fruit preserves
- Coffee beverages along with soy or rice milk

Grab and Go Breakfast:
- Fruit smoothie
- Granola and dried fruit mix
- Banana
- Individual rice milk (plain or chocolate)

Breakfast-in-a-Bag:
- Whole-wheat bagel with peanut butter and fruit preserves
- Whole banana
- Granola with dried fruit
- Soy or rice milk (in aseptic packaging)

RECIPES
Here are some terrific recipes to get you started.

LOTS OF GRAINS PANCAKES

Yield: 25 two-ounce (2-inch) pancakes

These pancakes have lots of crunch and flavor. If done carefully, these can be prepared and cooked ahead of time and quickly frozen in single layers. We find this a real time saver when we have large breakfast banquets. Reheat right from the freezer by placing in a pre-heated 400 degree oven (if allowed to thaw, the pancakes become soggy).

INGREDIENTS	MEASURE	METHOD
Whole wheat flour	4 ounces	In mixing bowl, combine flours,
White flour	4 ounces	cornmeal, and baking powder. In
Rye flour	4 ounces	separate bowl, beat milk and oil until
Buckwheat flour	4 ounces	foamy. Add wet to dry ingredients
Cornmeal	8 ounces	and mix until well blended.
Baking powder	1 ounce	
Soy, rice, or grain milk, unflavored	1 pint	
Oil	4 ounces	
Vegetable oil spray	to cover pan	Spray griddle with oil. Heat and drop batter by 2-ounce ladles onto griddle. Cook and turn until browned.

Total Calories per Pancake: 148   Total Fat as % of Daily Value: 8%   Protein: 4 gm   Fat: 5 gm
Carbohydrates: 22 gm   Calcium: 96 mg   Iron: 1 mg   Sodium: 105 mg   Dietary Fiber: 2 gm

TOFU PANCAKES

Yield: 25 two-ounce (2-inch) pancakes

This recipe makes a smooth and luxurious pancake. Don't stop at breakfast! Also use them for a dessert item, topped with fruit preserves and soy or rice ice cream. The batter can be made a day ahead of time and stored, refrigerated. Be sure to stir well before using.

INGREDIENTS	MEASURE	METHOD
Soft silken tofu, mashed	2 pounds	Place tofu, egg replacer, flour, soy milk, optional walnuts, wheat germ, and baking soda in a blender and process until smooth. Heat griddle, spray with oil, and pour batter by 2-ounce ladles. Cook and turn until browned.
Ener-G Egg Replacer*	2 ounces	
Unbleached white flour	4 ounces	
Soy milk, unflavored	8 ounces	
Walnuts, chopped (optional)**	2 ounces	
Wheat germ	2 ounces	
Baking soda	1 teaspoon	
Vegetable oil spray	to cover griddle	
Ground cinnamon	1 ounce	Sprinkle with cinnamon and nutmeg before serving hot.
Ground nutmeg	1 ounce	

*Note: The egg replacer used in the book's recipes is Ener-G Egg Replacer, produced by Ener-G Foods, Inc. They can be reached at (800) 331-5222 or http://www.ener-g.com in Seattle, Washington. The measurement for egg replacer refers to a mixture of the egg replacer and water.

**Note: If you do include walnuts in the pancake batter, be sure to clearly label that the pancakes contain nuts for those that may be allergic to nuts.

Total Calories per Pancake: 55   Total Fat as % of Daily Value: 3%   Protein: 4 gm   Fat: 2 gm
Carbohydrates: 6 gm   Calcium: 27 mg   Iron: 1 mg   Sodium: 70 mg   Dietary Fiber: <1 gm

SWEET POTATO PANCAKES

Yield: 25 two-ounce (3-inch) pancakes

Enjoy these delicious pancakes!

INGREDIENTS	MEASURE	METHOD
Canned sweet potatoes, drained, mashed	4 pounds	In a mixer, combine sweet potatoes, tofu, egg replacer, and vanilla.
Soft tofu	8 ounces	
Ener-G Egg Replacer*	4 ounces	
Vanilla extract	2 ounces	
Unbleached white flour	2-1/2 pounds	Add dry ingredients. Mix until com-
Baking powder	2-1/2 ounces	bined. Preheat griddle; spray with oil.
Cinnamon	2 ounces	Drop batter by 2-ounce ladles and
Nutmeg	1/2 ounce	griddle until golden brown on both
Raisins, chopped fine	6 ounces	sides. Serve warm.
Vegetable oil spray	to cover griddle	

*Note: The egg replacer used in the book's recipes is Ener-G Egg Replacer, produced by Ener-G Foods, Inc. See previous recipe for ordering information. In this recipe, follow box directions to prepare 4 ounces of liquid. If egg replacer is not available, increase tofu to 10 ounces and flour to 2-3/4 pounds.

Total Calories per Pancake: 276   Total Fat as % of Daily Value: 2%   Protein: 7 gm   Fat: 1 gm
Carbohydrates: 59 gm   Calcium: 274 mg   Iron: 4 mg   Sodium: 281 mg   Dietary Fiber: 3 gm

SCRAMBLED MULTI-COLORED TOFU

Yield: 25 two-ounce servings

This dish cooks up quickly and is a great place to use leftover veggies. Use scrambled tofu as part of a traditional breakfast or as a breakfast burrito filling.

INGREDIENTS	MEASURE	METHOD
Vegetable oil spray	to cover pan	Heat sauté pan or griddle and spray
Bell pepper, chopped	10 ounces	with oil. Sauté pepper, mushrooms,
Mushrooms, sliced	12 ounces	and green onions until soft.
Green onions, diced	8 ounces	
Firm tofu, crumbled	2 pounds	Add tofu, tomatoes, parsley, and
Canned tomatoes, diced, drained	9 ounces	black pepper.
Fresh parsley, chopped	2 ounces	Cook only until warmed. Serve
Black pepper	1/2 ounce	immediately.

Total Calories per Serving: 52   Total Fat as % of Daily Value: 3%   Protein: 5 gm   Fat: 2 gm
Carbohydrates: 3 gm   Calcium: 74 mg   Iron: 1 mg   Sodium: 36 mg   Dietary Fiber: 1 gm

EGGLESS ASIAN OMELET

Yield: 10 omelets serving twenty

Slice each omelet into quarters and serve two quarters with steamed rice and vegetables. This recipe is labor-intensive, but worth the effort. Alternate vegetables (such as thinly sliced carrots or green beans) for different flavors.

INGREDIENTS	MEASURE	METHOD
Batter:		
Soft silken tofu	22 ounces	Place tofu, egg replacer, water, and
Ener-G Egg Replacer*	8 teaspoons	pepper in a food processor and blend
Water	1-1/2 cups	until smooth (will be thin). Set aside.
Pepper	1 ounce	
Filling:		
Vegetable oil	1 ounce	Heat sauté pan, add oil, onion, and
Green onion, minced	7 ounces	ginger. Sauté for 2 minutes to flavor
Fresh ginger, minced	2 ounces	the oil. Add sprouts, onions, celery,
Mung bean sprouts	1-1/2 pounds	mushrooms, and soy sauce. Sauté
Onions, chopped	6 ounces	until just tender. Remove from pan.
Celery, sliced thinly	6 ounces	In medium bowl, mix veggies and
Mushrooms, sliced	6 ounces	batter together. Reheat sauté pan
Soy sauce	1 ounce	with oil (adding a bit more oil if
		needed), drop 2 ounces of batter at
		a time onto pan and fry until
		browned.

*Note: In this recipe, the amount of Ener-G Egg Replacer refers to the powder form only.

Serving suggestion: Make a fast sauce for this by combining 2 ounces of diced green onions, 2 cloves minced garlic, and 1 ounce of minced ginger with 6 ounces of soy sauce.

Total Calories per Serving (without sauce): 56   Total Fat as % of Daily Value: 3%   Protein: 4 gm
Fat: 2 gm   Carbohydrates: 6 gm   Calcium: 75 mg   Iron: 1 mg   Sodium: 126 mg
Dietary Fiber: 1 gm

Total Calories per Serving (with sauce): 64   Total Fat as % of Daily Value: 3%   Protein: 5 gm
Fat: 2 gm   Carbohydrates: 7 gm   Calcium: 79 mg   Iron: 2 mg   Sodium: 729 mg
Dietary Fiber: 1 gm

MONGO BREAKFAST BURRITOS

Yield: 25 burritos (with approximately 2 ounces filling)

Use your imagination for the filling. Try leftover cooked and mashed beans, sautéed veggies, cooked and diced potatoes, diced fresh veggies, and/or sautéed tofu. Purchase various "flavors" of tortillas, such as whole wheat, blue corn, or tomato.

INGREDIENTS	MEASURE	METHOD
Texturized vegetable protein (TVP)	1-1/2 pounds	In a mixing bowl combine TVP and hot water and allow to stand until all water is absorbed (about 5 minutes) and TVP is soft. Heat sauté pan and spray with oil. Sauté peppers, onions, and carrots until soft. Add TVP and beans; stir until combined and hot (about 7 minutes). Warm tortillas in steamer or microwave so they can be folded. Place 2 ounces of filling and 1/2 ounce salsa in the center of each tortilla; fold to close. Place on baking sheet and warm in oven (at 325 degrees) for 10 minutes.
Hot water	1 pint	
Vegetable oil spray	to cover pan	
Bell pepper, chopped	9 ounces	
Onions, chopped	8 ounces	
Carrots, minced	5 ounces	
Canned refried beans	1-1/4 pounds	
Flour tortillas, 8-inch	25 each	
Prepared salsa	1-1/2 pints	

Total Calories per Burrito: 225   Total Fat as % of Daily Value: 5%   Protein: 19 gm   Fat: 3 gm
Carbohydrates: 35 gm   Calcium: 155 mg   Iron: 4 mg   Sodium: 485 mg   Dietary Fiber: 6 gm

SAVORY PLANTAINS WITH GARBANZOS

Yield: 25 four-ounce servings

This "taste of the islands" has great texture and is packed with nutrition (don't tell anybody). We use this for a hot breakfast entrée (goes great with scrambled tofu) and as a side dish for lunch and dinner.

INGREDIENTS	MEASURE	METHOD
Ripe plantains	16 each	Preheat oven to 325 degrees. Peel plantains and steam until tender (about 8 minutes). Let cool and cut into 1/2-inch slices. Place in a steam table pan. Add garbanzo beans and toss to combine. Heat sauté pan and spray with oil. Sauté garlic, onions, and pepper until tender. Add to plantains. Add bay leaves and cinnamon. Bake at 325 degrees for 15 minutes. Remove bay leaves and serve warm.
Canned garbanzo beans, drained	2 pounds	
Vegetable oil spray	to cover pan	
Garlic, minced	2 cloves	
Onion, chopped	6 ounces	
Bell pepper, sliced	1/2 pound	
Bay Leaves	5 each	
Cinnamon, ground	1 ounce	

Total Calories per Serving: 181   Total Fat as % of Daily Value: 3%   Protein: 3 gm   Fat: 2 gm
Carbohydrates: 44 gm   Calcium: 18 mg   Iron: 1 mg   Sodium: 89 mg   Dietary Fiber: 5 gm

PEACHY KEEN BREAKFAST CRUMBLE

Yield: 25 three-ounce servings

You can make pans of this ahead of time and freeze it (for up to 2 weeks) or refrigerate it (for up to 3 days), then warm it when ready to serve. Add other cooked fruit as the seasons change (such as apples, pears, dried fruit, and berries).

INGREDIENTS	MEASURE	METHOD
Margarine*	12 ounces	Preheat oven to 350 degrees. Place margarine, chopped raisins, flour, oats, nutmeg, cinnamon, and ginger in a large bowl and combine until crumbly. Place peaches in a shallow steam table pan, one inch deep. Sprinkle topping evenly over peaches. Bake at 350 degrees for 25 minutes or until topping is golden. Serve warm.
Raisins, chopped	1 pound	
Whole wheat flour	1 pound	
Rolled oats	14 ounces	
Nutmeg	1/2 ounce	
Cinnamon	1/2 ounce	
Ginger, ground	1/2 ounce	
Canned peaches, sliced and drained**	9 pounds	

*Note: Please be sure to use vegan margarine (check the label for "dairy" words, such as lactose, whey or whey solids, casein, milk protein, etc.).

**Note: During peach season, this recipe can be made with fresh peaches that have been poached and peeled (toss cooked peaches with apple juice concentrate if extra sweetness is desired).

Total Calories per Serving: 346   Total Fat as % of Daily Value: 18%   Protein: 7 gm   Fat: 12 gm
Carbohydrates: 57 gm   Calcium: 37 mg   Iron: 2 mg   Sodium: 158 mg   Dietary Fiber: 6 gm

COOKIES FOR BREAKFAST

Yield: 25 parfaits

We couldn't decide whether to include this in the kids' recipe section or to share it with adults. We decided that kids of all ages would enjoy this!

INGREDIENTS	MEASURE	METHOD
Applesauce, unsweet-ened	2 quarts	Place 2 ounces of applesauce into a parfait cup or small cereal bowl.
Oatmeal, cooked	3 quarts	Place 2 ounces hot oatmeal on top of
Raisins	1-1/2 pounds	applesauce and stir to combine.
Chopped dates	12 ounces	Sprinkle with raisin, dates, walnuts,
Chopped walnuts	14 ounces	cookie crumbs, and cinnamon.
Oatmeal cookie crumbs*	1 pound	Repeat in all 25 parfait cups.
Cinnamon	5 ounces	
Topping:		Top with more applesauce and
Applesauce	1-1/2 quarts	remaining cookie crumbs and serve
Oatmeal cookie crumbs*	1 pound	immediately.

Total Calories per Serving: 516   Total Fat as % of Daily Value: 25%   Protein: 11 gm   Fat: 16 gm
Carbohydrates: 91 gm   Calcium: 146 mg   Iron: 5 mg   Sodium: 205 mg   Dietary Fiber: 7 gm

*Note: Be sure to use vegan oatmeal cookies to make crumbs in a food processor.

Chapter Five

FEEDING FRENZY –
COOKING FOR KIDS

Kids make eating an experience perhaps unplanned on your part! Depending on the event, the type of service (sit-down versus buffet, for example), age of the children, and time constraints (attention span should always be taken into consideration), design the menu to be easy to eat, relatively quick to serve, and to contain a variety of temperatures, colors, flavors, and textures.

Portion sizes should reflect the children's age. If you are following federal school food lunch guidelines (see Figure 5.1), be sure you have the portion sizes correct for the particular food you have on the menu. For example, peanut butter, beans, and soy cheese (which may be more expensive than dairy-derived cheese) may all be used as a meat alternative, but the portion sizes for each one are different.

At the time of this writing, the USDA's "any reasonable approach" was undergoing field-testing in several school districts. Under this proposal, schools could design menus based on the seven recommendations of the 1995 Dietary Guidelines (limit fat to 30% of calories; limit saturated fat to 10% of calories; choose a diet low in cholesterol; increase intake of fiber-containing foods; eat a variety of foods, etc.). This could be good news for vegans, as the selection and amounts of ingredients would have a wider range. The USDA school lunch program is in a constant state of revision so you should be sure to keep up on current changes (a good source for this is the USDA's Internet site at: mealtalk@nal.usda.gov

FIGURE 5.1: UNDERSTANDING FEDERAL SCHOOL FOOD LUNCH GUIDELINES

The following information is pertinent to those concerned with elementary, middle, and high schools receiving USDA reimbursement. Your school food service program should have access to a copy of the United States Department of Agriculture's (USDA) toolkit, which consists of two notebooks – A TOOLKIT FOR HEALTHY SCHOOL MEALS: RECIPES AND TRAINING MATERIALS and COMMUNITY NUTRITION ACTION KIT. These are current USDA tools for nutrition education and healthy meal preparation in the schools. If your local school food service director does not have these materials, the USDA or appropriate state agency may be contacted.

- The TOOLKIT FOR HEALTHY SCHOOL MEALS notebook contains quantity recipes with several vegetarian (no meat, fish or fowl, but including dairy, honey, and eggs) and vegan (no meat, fish, fowl, dairy, eggs, or honey) options. The recipes have nutritional analyses, state what part of the meal they can be used for (meat alternative, fruit, vegetable, etc.), and there is even a section with photographs of many of the selections, which gives serving and garnish suggestions.

- The COMMUNITY NUTRITION ACTION KIT contains nutrition training materials for the classroom and the community, ranging from how to build and supply a nutrition-kiosk to simple paper and pen activities. Several of the activities, such as "From Seed to You," "Passport to the Fabulous World of Food," and "Pyramid Place" can lend themselves to educating students about being a vegetarian/vegan.

The USDA materials are a good resource to become familiar with because they have been approved by the USDA for use in the schools. For this reason, when working with schools which receive government reimbursement and must follow USDA rules, we suggest you start with the Toolkit. The kits are already being used in many school systems and meet all the requirements outlined by the government. For example, commodity ingredients are incorporated into many of the recipes. Commodities are food ingredients available to the schools through the federal government for free or at greatly reduced prices. Commodities allow school food services to operate within their budgets and to serve healthy meals to more children. In the past, vegetarian commodities have included canned beans, peanut butter, canned fruit, staple items such as flour and corn meal, dried fruit, frozen fruit and vegetables, and dairy products such as cheese and butter. Commodities vary in availability from year to year and from region to region. The school food service director is expected to take advantage of the commodities program whenever possible.

Remember the constraints under which school foodservice personnel must work. They usually have a very short time period (sometimes as little as ten minutes) to feed a large number of children. Their menus and food preparation techniques must follow very precise guidelines. Change is a long and detailed process. For example, in accordance with the old food-based system, there are few ingredient exchanges that can be made without approval. Margarine can be exchanged for butter, but at this time, egg substitute cannot be exchanged for eggs nor can soy crumbles for ground beef. Have patience with your local school food service personnel and understand that they may need assistance in adding vegetarian/ vegan menu options. For example, rather than asking for vegan options in general, have some suggestions (remember, ingredients that are not typically used, such as tempeh or tofu may not be a possibility at first). We have included some vegan recipe names below that appear in the TOOLKIT. You might want to suggest them when speaking with your school food service people.

VEGAN OPTIONS FROM THE USDA TOOLKIT FOR HEALTHY SCHOOL MEALS:

Recipe	Vegan	Meal Component
Quick Baked Potato	x	veg
Thick Vegetable Soup	x	meat/veg/grain
Marinated Black Bean Salad	x (cheese is optional)	meat or veg
Tabouleh	x	veg or grain
Orange Rice Salad	x	grains

New items which are added to school menus must be nutritionally analyzed (consider having this available if you suggest new recipes), must fit into the school's budget, and must be able to be produced on a large scale (and sometimes must be able to withstand freezing, reheating, or being transported). And, most importantly, they must be accepted by the students! Nutrition education is an important part of this; some schools have budgets for nutrition education and some do not. Short meal periods allow little or no nutrition education to occur in eating areas, so classroom teachers must be in tune to nutrition and include it in their lesson plans.

Think about how you can assist in this area; in some locations, chefs' or dietitians' groups may have vegetarian presentations appropriate for the classroom. The Vegetarian Resource Group has materials for children; call (410) 366-8343 or visit our website <www.vrg.org> to find out more about these and how to obtain them.

TYPES OF SCHOOL MEAL SYSTEMS

- **NuMenus**: a nutrient-based approach that enables schools to evaluate menus based on the overall nutritional composition of meals, rather than by food groups.

- **Assisted NuMenus**: a nutrient-based system using ready-made menus that have been provided to the school by another source.

- **Food Based Menus**: this is the old system which calls for specified amounts from the traditional four food groups.

Note: Currently, there are federal school regulations prohibiting the use of foods comprised of over 30% soy. This has made it impossible to introduce soy-based veggie burgers, and the like. The regulation is currently under revision, and if the restriction were lifted, it would allow the use of vegetarian meat analogs in schools.

Introducing vegetarian/vegan changes into the schools is a "do-able" project. You need to be ready to have lots of patience and be prepared to provide information and education for the school personnel responsible for the changes. Stay positive, informed, and enthusiastic and the rest will follow!

NUTRITION NEWS FOR CHILDREN

As children grow, so do their vitamin and mineral needs. Vitamins A, C, E, and the minerals calcium, iron, and zinc may be low, because children who may not care for the foods in which they are contained use these nutrients quite quickly.

Remember that hydration is important for children, as they may become dehydrated without becoming thirsty. Make every ounce count toward good nutrition by offering soy or rice milk (flavor it with puréed fruit or garnish it with an apple slice or an orange wedge), fruit juices, vegetable juices, or even water! Freeze puréed fruit, fruit juice, or chocolate soy or rice milk to create frozen treats that help to hydrate.

The food guide pyramid is a fun learning tool for children and an easy guide for adults to follow. In Figure 5.2 below we have included a vegan kids version.

FIGURE 5.2:
FOOD GUIDE PYRAMID, VEGAN KIDS' VERSION

GROUP	# OF SERVINGS /DAY	SERVING SIZES		
		1-3 YRS	4-6 YRS	7-10 YRS
Bread/Cereal	6-11	1 Tb/yr of age	1/2 cup	3/4 cup
Vegetable	3-5	" "	1/3 cup	1/2 cup
Fruit	2-4	" "	1/3 cup	1/2 cup
Soy and milk alternative	4	1/2 cup	3/4 cup	3/4 cup
Beans, protein	2-3	1 Tb/yr of age	2 oz.	3 oz.

ENTERTAINING THE SMALL FRY

Veggie children's parties are easy to do. Bring on the crispy, crunchy finger foods and the cool desserts. Depending on the setting, you may be able to get children involved with the preparation, from mixing dips to filling snack bags to creating desserts. (One particularly popular preschool treat was the creation of a "beagle pear." On a bed of shredded lettuce, invert a pear half. Use prune or plum halves for ears, raisins for eyes, and a grape for the nose. We couldn't decide if the kids had more fun making them or eating them).

A favorite dessert is a dessert "club." You'll need cookies with a flat surface, softened vegan ice cream or sorbet, and peanut butter which has been combined with granola (the stickier the better). Assemble the club by placing the first cookie on a dessert plate, top with ice cream, add a layer of peanut butter, put on a second layer of ice cream, and top with a second cookie. These can be made ahead of time and frozen (be sure to wrap them, as they will absorb freezer flavors). Kids can help assemble these (and they'll have fun doing it). For an "ice cream" cake, bake larger cookies and go higher on the layers.

ADOLESCENT AGONY

Teenagers may still have the same tastes as younger children, may have moved to more adult selections, or may be on a weird planet all their own. We won't attempt to solve the world of teenagers, but we can give some menu ideas for feeding them.

THE ALL-AMERICAN FIFTIES' THEME:

- **Snack things:** Pretzels, potato and veggie chips (buy them or slice potatoes and carrots thinly, bake off in the oven; use seasonings, like chili or onion powder, if you think your troops will like them), fresh veggie sticks (carrots, celery, zucchini, jicama, cherry tomatoes, radishes, cucumbers) with dips (see the recipes on pages 116, 117, and 135), popcorn
- **Beverages:** Root beer floats (use vanilla or chocolate soy or rice ice cream), fruit punch (color it in unusual colors), sparkling waters, lemonade
- **Entrées:** Veggie pizza (pile on the tomatoes, mushrooms, peppers, onions, etc.), veggie burgers and veggie dogs (remember the condiments: include relish, catsup, vegan mayonnaise, onions, etc.), foot-long (or longer) subs with a base of substitute meats and vegan cheese and heaped with sliced green peppers, cucumbers, tomatoes, shredded lettuce, carrots, and onions
- **Sides:** Baked French-fries, tossed salad, cole slaw, macaroni salad
- **Dessert:** Frozen soy/rice ice cream or sorbet sundaes (have chopped fruit, nuts, and vegan whipped topping available), watermelon wedges, brownies

MAMA MIA, 'ATTA'S GOODA PARTY FOOD:

- **Snack things:** Pizza-flavored veggie chips, assorted olives, pickles, mini-bagel or muffin pizzas
- **Beverages:** Sparkling waters, lemonade, sparkling apple or grape juice
- **Entrées:** Eggplant lasagna (see recipe on page 194), rotini with marinara sauce, assorted ravioli
- **Sides:** Garlic breadsticks, tossed salad
- **Dessert:** Neopolitan soy or rice ice cream (vanilla, strawberry, and chocolate ice cream combo) with chocolate sauce and chopped pistachios, melon balls

MAKE MINE SPICY:
- **Snack items:** Tortillas and veggie chips with salsa (see recipes on pages 115, 183, 250, 251, and 252) and guacamole
- **Beverages:** Iced fruit drinks, horchatas (rice and fruit drinks which can be made by combining rice milk, raspberry or strawberry syrup, and a sprinkle of cinnamon), virgin margaritas (fruit slushes with margarita mix, hold the tequila)
- **Entrées:** Veggie tacos and/or burritos with black bean and red chili sauce, four bean chili (include chopped onions, chopped chilies, chopped bell peppers, chopped fresh cilantro, and shredded vegan soy cheese on the side)
- **Sides:** Steamed and Spanish rice, mini corn cobs (cut corn cobs into 3-inch lengths or purchase frozen, already cut) dusted with chili powder and garlic, steamed tortillas, green salad (to cool off some of the heat)
- **Desserts:** Fruit smoothies, fresh berries, peanut butter bars (see recipe on page 160)

A CAMPING WE WILL GO

There's nothing like a refreshing ten mile hike with children to work up an appetite. Since the days of the chuck wagon are over, camping menus have to be interesting, tasty, nonperishable, and light to transport. We're talking concentrated calories and nutrients that travel well and prepare quickly.

Your camping menu will obviously depend on how long you will be camping, how much everyone can carry, and how much cooking you will want to do. For an overnight trip, prepared sandwiches (we like pita pockets, less seems to fall out), granola, fresh fruit, and lots of water and/or juices can get you through the day. For the evening meal, have some baked beans and veggies burgers pre-cooked. Heat the beans, crumble in the veggie burgers, and serve over bread or buns. The same could be done with a pre-made veggie chili. Bring along some carrot and celery sticks, cherry tomatoes and radishes, and canned bean dip and you will have a fast meal. If you are into building a fire, bring along some white and sweet potatoes and corn on the cob to roast in the flames. The morning meal can consist of cold cereal with soy or rice milk and fruit. Some kids might like to use peanut butter in the morning to "smoosh" into their cereal or spread on apple and banana slices.

We have found the key to camping food is to think "eating constantly." Aim for lots of snacks with meals kept simple. Package everything in as light a container as possible – individually when possible. We mix together several cold cereals, some chopped nuts, and dried fruit, which can double for breakfast food and a quickie granola. Make a fruit "leather" by draining canned fruit (peaches and pears work well), puréeing it in a blender, layering it on sheet pans which have been covered with foil and sprayed with oil in a 1/2-inch layer, and allowing it to dry in a 175 degree oven. After 2 or 3 hours, the fruit is tacky to the touch and ready to be rolled up and wrapped in plastic. Two pounds of fruit usually makes about 16 servings. This is a sweet snack that is easy to carry.

If using individual juice or soy or rice beverage "boxes," freeze them ahead of time. They can be used instead of ice to keep food cold, and when they've done their job, you can drink 'em. (And in a pinch, they can be used as an ice pack for turned ankles or insect bites)! If eaten fairly early in the hike, the tops of the juice boxes can be cut off, and the frozen juice (or chocolate soy or rice milk) can be spooned just like sorbet (yum).

One of our chef friends does a lot of camping, and being a chef, isn't content to just bring along "trail food" for her family. She pre-makes veggie sushi (filled with rice, chopped pickled vegetables and avocado, rolled in sesame seeds and nori [seaweed]); cuts up the "fixings" for stir-fries (marinated portabellos, tofu cubes, diced onions and squash, sliced bell peppers, chopped garlic, and fresh herbs); and prepares vegetable brochettes, ready to be grilled over a campfire. For dessert, she brings along peeled, whole apples or pears, wrapped in plastic, marinating in fruit juice, cinnamon, and ginger. When ready to cook, she wraps the fruit in aluminum and lets it cook down in the coals until soft. The chef's suggestions are a little labor intensive, but if you get your kid crew to pitch in, you could have at least one night of elegance while out on the trail.

RECIPES

We've included some recipes here that we think will be popular with your kid-customers. You might also want to check out the recipes in Chapters 9 (Colleges) and 10 (Fast food) for additional ideas.

YELLOW SOUP

Yield: 25 three-ounce servings

We have "green" salad and "red" fruit punch, why not "yellow" soup? This is mild, full of nutrients (don't tell the kids), and colorful. Makes a good "Jack o'lantern" soup, served out of a pumpkin shell.

INGREDIENTS	MEASURE	METHOD
Fresh yellow squash	3-1/2 pounds	Scrub and chop squash. In a medium stock pot, place squash, corn, and stock. Bring to a boil, lower heat, and allow to simmer until squash is soft (about 15 minutes). Place veggies and spices in a blender or food processor and process until smooth. Reheat and serve hot (garnish with herbed croutons, if desired).
Cut corn, cooked	1-3/4 pounds	
Vegetable stock	3 quarts	
Fresh thyme	1 ounce	
Black pepper	1 ounce	
Fresh parsley, chopped	1 ounce	

Note: If soup is too thin, blend in small amounts of soft tofu until desired texture is obtained.

Total Calories per Serving: 46   Total Fat as % of Daily Value: 2%   Protein: 2 gm   Fat: 1 gm
Carbohydrates: 3 gm   Calcium: 16 mg   Iron: <1 mg   Sodium: 8 mg   Dietary Fiber: 1 gm

STEAMED SQUASH ROLLS

Yield: 25 rolls

This is a recipe with an Asian flair, which has a "secret" filling.

INGREDIENTS	MEASURE	METHOD
Frozen vegan bread dough (approximately 2 pounds)	2 loaves	Thaw bread dough; place in proofer (or in a bowl in a warm place).
Frozen butternut squash, thawed	1-1/2 pounds	Combine squash, garlic, ginger, soy sauce, and pepper in a large bowl and mix well. Roll 2-inch pieces of bread dough into balls. Place on floured surface and roll into 4-inch flat circles. Place a tablespoon of filling into the center of each circle and pinch to close. Place in perforated steam table pans and allow to rise for 30 minutes. Steam in a commercial steamer or in a stock pot with a rack for 15 minutes.
Garlic, minced	2 cloves	
Powdered ginger	1/2 ounce	
Soy sauce	1/2 ounce	
Bell pepper, minced	2 ounces	

Note: When steaming, do not allow rolls to touch or they will stick together. Rolls can be prepared and steamed ahead of time, frozen, and re-steamed when needed.

Total Calories per Roll: 108   Total Fat as % of Daily Value: 3%   Protein: 4 gm   Fat: 2 gm
Carbohydrates: 19 gm   Calcium: 30 mg   Iron: 1 mg   Sodium: 194 mg   Dietary Fiber: 2 gm

MUSTARDY CARROTS

Yield: 25 two to two-and-one-half-ounce servings

The tang of the mustard accents the sweetness of the carrots (and kids love condiments!).

INGREDIENTS	MEASURE	METHOD
Baby carrots	7 pounds	In a medium stock pot combine
Vegetable stock	1 pint plus 1 cup	carrots, vegetable stock, and apple
Apple juice concentrate	5 ounces	juice concentrate. Bring to a boil,
Prepared mustard	7 ounces	then reduce heat and simmer until
Orange juice concen- trate, thawed	5 ounces	carrots are tender (5 minutes in
		commercial steamer, 10 minutes in
		commercial braising pan, and about
		20 minutes in a pot on top of a
		stove). Drain carrots and place in
		steam table pan. In a small bowl,
		blend mustard and orange juice
		concentrate. Toss with carrots. Keep
		carrots warm until ready for service.

Total Calories per Serving: 85   Total Fat as % of Daily Value: <1%   Protein: 2 gm   Fat: <1 gm
Carbohydrates: 18 gm   Calcium: 44 mg   Iron: 1 mg   Sodium: 150 mg   Dietary Fiber: 3 gm

VEGGIE SPRING ROLLS

Yield: 25 each

Great finger food – use as an every day entrée or for party food.

INGREDIENTS	MEASURE	METHOD
Vegetable oil spray	to cover pan	Heat a wok or sauté pan. Spray with oil. Add garlic, ginger, pepper, and onions, and sauté over high heat for 2 minutes.
Garlic, minced	4 cloves	
Fresh ginger, minced	1 ounce	
Bell pepper, minced	2 ounces	
Onions, chopped	10 ounces	
Green cabbage, shredded	3 pounds	Add cabbage and celery, tossing for 2 minutes. Add mushrooms and toss for 1 minute. Add carrots, toss for 1 minute.
Celery, sliced thinly	10 ounces	
Mushrooms, sliced thinly	1 pound	
Carrots, grated	10 ounces	
Mung bean sprouts, rinsed and drained	14 ounces	Add sprouts, toss for 1 minute. Remove from heat and drain in colander. Allow to cool 2 minutes. Separate wrappers and place about 2 ounces of filling on each wrapper. Dampen the edges of the wrappers with cold water to assist in sealing when rolling up. Deep fry spring rolls 45 seconds on 350 degrees in a commercial deep fryer, about 1-1/2 minutes in a commercial braiser, or about 3 minutes in a pan on top of a stove. You can also sauté them briefly and finish them in a 375 degree oven for about 7 minutes.
Eggless spring roll wrappers	25 each	

Note: Cooked spring rolls can be frozen and reheated (do not thaw).

Total Calories per Spring Roll (sautéed): 86   Total Fat as % of Daily Value: <1%   Protein: 3 gm
Fat: <1 gm   Carbohydrates: 19 gm   Calcium: 50 mg   Iron: 1 mg   Sodium: 29 mg
Dietary Fiber: 1 gm

PASTA FAZOOL (PASTA E FAGIOLI)

Yield: 25 three-ounce servings

The kids will have fun deciding how to pronounce the name of this dish. This is a terrific recipe to use up broken pasta.

INGREDIENTS	MEASURE	METHOD
Vegetable oil spray	to cover pot	Heat stock pot, spray with oil, and sauté onions, celery, and carrots until tender. Add sage and red pepper flakes, cook for 1 minute.
Onions, chopped	1-1/2 pounds	
Celery, sliced thin	12 ounces	
Carrots, minced	8 ounces	
Dried sage	1 ounce	
Red pepper flakes	1/2 ounce	Add vegetable stock, pasta, toma-
Vegetable stock	3-1/2 quarts	toes, and beans. Bring to a boil,
Pasta, uncooked	10 ounces	lower heat, and allow to simmer until
Canned tomatoes, drained	2 pounds	pasta is al dente. Serve hot (don't overcook or you will have a stew
Canned white beans, drained*	2 pounds	instead of a soup).

*Note: Can also use dried or frozen, cooked beans.

Total Calories per Serving: 124   Total Fat as % of Daily Value: 2%   Protein: 6 gm   Fat: 1 gm
Carbohydrates: 24 gm   Calcium: 57 mg   Iron: 2 mg   Sodium: 81 mg   Dietary Fiber: 3 gm

ZUCCHINI WRAPS

Yield: 25 servings (approximately 1-ounce filling/wrap)

What a great way to sneak veggies onto the menu.

INGREDIENTS	MEASURE	METHOD
Vegetable oil spray	to cover pan	Heat sauté or braising pan and spray with oil. Add onions and sauté until soft. Add zucchini and cook until soft. Add black beans and heat for 4 minutes or until beans are hot. Spread 1 ounce of filling on each tortilla and fold. Wraps can be heated for service in the oven or can be browned in a sauté pan. Serve with salsa.
Onion, sliced thin	2 pounds	
Fresh zucchini, grated	14 pounds	
Canned black beans, drained	3 pounds	
Flour tortillas, 8-inch*	25 each	

*Note: Make sure you purchase tortillas that do not contain lard.

Total Calories per Serving (without salsa): 235   Total Fat as % of Daily Value: 5%   Protein: 11 gm
Fat: 3 gm   Carbohydrates: 43 gm   Calcium: 10 mg   Iron: 3 mg   Sodium: 176 mg
Dietary Fiber: 5 gm

TAMALE CORN PIE

Yield: 25 three-ounce servings

A favorite for years, this can be made ahead of time, cooked, frozen, and reheated when needed.

INGREDIENTS	MEASURE	METHOD
Topping:		
Cornmeal	2 pounds	In a heavy stock pot, place cold water, cornmeal, and red pepper flakes and cook, stirring until mixture is thick (about 10 minutes) and has come to a boil.
Cold water	1-1/2 quarts	
Red pepper flakes	1 ounce	
Filling:		Preheat oven to 350 degrees.
Pinto beans, cooked or canned and drained	3 pounds	Place beans in a food processor or buffalo chopper and mash until chunky. Heat a stock pot and spray with oil. Sauté onions, celery, bell pepper, and garlic until soft. Add tomatoes, chili powder, and corn and heat, stirring until all items are well-combined and hot. Grease a steam table pan and spread 75% of the cornmeal mixture on the bottom and sides. Fill with the bean mixture and top with the remainder of cornmeal mixture. Bake in an oven at 350 degrees for 35 minutes, or until crust is golden brown and beans bubble.
Vegetable oil spray	to cover pot	
Onions, chopped	8 ounces	
Celery, chopped	6 ounces	
Bell pepper, chopped	6 ounces	
Garlic, minced	3 cloves	
Canned tomatoes, drained and chopped	1 pound	
Chili powder	1 ounce	
Cut corn, cooked	2 pounds	

Total Calories per Serving: 257   Total Fat as % of Daily Value: 3%   Protein: 9 gm   Fat: 2 gm
Carbohydrates: 46 gm   Calcium: 41 mg   Iron: 3 mg   Sodium: 51 mg   Dietary Fiber: 8 gm

SQUASHED PASTA

Yield: 25 three-ounce servings

This dish is colorful and easy to make.

INGREDIENTS	MEASURE	METHOD
Carrots, julienne	2 pounds	Steam carrots and set aside. Steam
Zucchini, julienne	8 pounds	zucchini and squash until firm but
		easily pierced with a fork. Heat a
Yellow squash, julienne	4 pounds	sauté or braising pan with vegetable
Vegetable oil spray	to cover pan	spray. Quickly sauté veggies includ-
Canned tomatoes, drained	1 pound	ing tomatoes.
Cooked pasta	4 pounds	Add pasta and toss quickly to heat.
Fresh parsley, chopped	2 ounces	Add parsley and pepper, toss, and
White pepper	1/2 ounce	remove from heat and serve hot.

Note: For color, add green peas or red or yellow bell pepper. More tomatoes can be added if mixture is too dry. Try different pasta shapes, sizes, or flavors (we like spinach or carrot). To get 5 pounds of cooked pasta, use 2 pounds of uncooked pasta.

Total Calories per Serving: 154   Total Fat as % of Daily Value: 2%   Protein: 7 gm   Fat: 1 gm
Carbohydrates: 31 gm   Calcium: 48 mg   Iron: 2 mg   Sodium: 51 mg   Dietary Fiber: 4 gm

"NOT-MEATBALLS"

Yield: 25 1-ounce servings

Make these ahead of time and freeze on sheet pans until ready to cook.
Experiment with different types of sauces when serving these "meatballs."

INGREDIENT	MEASURE	METHOD
Carrots, chopped	3 ounces	In a food processor, finely chop
Fresh mushrooms, chopped	1 pound	carrots. Add remaining vegetables and garlic and process to a fine
Bell pepper, chopped	4 ounces	paste. Heat sauté pan, spray with
Onions, chopped	2 ounces	oil, and sauté veggies only until soft.
Celery, chopped	4 ounces	In a small mixing bowl, mix tofu and
Garlic, minced	3 ounces	soy milk until frothy. In a mixing
Vegetable oil spray	to cover pan	bowl combine veggies and tofu/soy
Firm silken tofu	3 ounces	milk mixture. Stir constantly, slowly
Soy milk	2 ounces	adding bread crumbs and parsley
Dry bread crumbs	8 ounces	until mixture can be shaped (may not
Dry parsley	1/2 ounce	need all the bread crumbs). Shape into 1-ounce balls. Balls can be baked on a greased baking sheet at 325 degrees for 35 minutes or simmered in a sauce until firm.

Total Calories per Serving: 55   Total Fat as % of Daily Value: 2%   Protein: 2 gm   Fat: 1 gm
Carbohydrates: 10 gm   Calcium: 40 mg   Iron: 1 mg   Sodium: 90 mg   Dietary Fiber: 1 gm

SQUIGGLY NOODLES

Yield: 25 two-ounce servings

Here's another Asian dish. The kids will have fun "slurping" up the noodles.

INGREDIENTS	MEASURE	METHOD
Rice noodles	2 pounds	Boil noodles for 3 minutes, drain, and
Vegetable stock	1 pint	set aside in a bowl with a pint of
Vegetable oil spray	to cover pan	vegetable stock. Heat a wok or sauté
Garlic, minced	3 cloves	pan and spray with oil. Add garlic
Onions, chopped	1 pound	and onions and sauté for 1 minute.
Carrots, grated	1 pound	Add carrots, water chestnuts, and
Canned sliced water chestnuts	8 ounces	pea pods and sauté just until pea pods are barely soft.
Frozen pea pods, cut in half	1 pound	Add 1 quart vegetable stock and soy sauce. Stir to incorporate.
Vegetable stock	1 quart	Drain noodles, add to wok or pan,
Soy sauce	2 ounces	and toss to combine. Serve hot.

Total Calories per Serving: 168   Total Fat as % of Daily Value: <1%   Protein: 3 gm   Fat: <1 gm
Carbohydrates: 39 gm   Calcium: 23 mg   Iron: 2 mg   Sodium: 238 mg   Dietary Fiber: 1 gm

FRUIT AND FUN DESSERT PIZZA

Yield: 1 pizza (serves 12)

This dessert can be easily multiplied and used instead of a cake for celebrations.

INGREDIENTS	MEASURE	METHOD
Crust:		Preheat oven to 350 degrees.
Margarine, cold	4 ounces	Combine margarine, shortening, and
Solid vegetable shortening	4 ounces	flour in bowl or food processor until mixture becomes crumbly.
Unbleached white flour	24 ounces	Add 2 Tablespoons ice water and
Ice water	3 or 4 Table-spoons	continue to mix. Continue to add water, drop by drop, until dough forms a smooth mass. Wrap in plastic and chill for 30 minutes. Roll dough out on floured surface; place on 16-inch pizza form. Flute edges and chill for 30 minutes. Bake at 350 degrees for 15 minutes or until golden. Allow to cool.
Filling:		
Soy cream cheese	3 ounces	Beat cream cheese, concentrate,
Orange juice con-centrate, thawed	1 Tablespoon	milk, and zest until smooth. Add peaches and tofu and whisk until
Soy or rice milk, unflavored	3 Tablespoons	mixture is well combined.
Orange zest	1 teaspooon	
Canned peaches, drained and chopped	2 ounces	Fold in remaining fruit and mix gently. Arrange on crust and chill for
Soft tofu	2 ounces	20 minutes.
Canned apricots, drained and chopped	6 ounces	
Berries	4 ounces	

Variation: Purchase frozen vegan pizza shells and top with fresh or frozen fruit which has been combined with soft tofu and orange juice concentrate. Garnish pizza with chopped fresh or dried fruit, chopped nuts, and shredded coconut. Dough for the crust can be made ahead and frozen (unbaked) until ready to use.

Total Calories per Serving: 398   Total Fat as % of Daily Value: 31%   Protein: 7 gm   Fat: 20 gm
Carbohydrates: 47 gm   Calcium: 18 mg   Iron: 2 mg   Sodium: 142 mg   Dietary Fiber: 2 gm

DON'T TELL THE KIDS
IT'S TOFU CHEESECAKE

Yield: 2 pies (10 slices each)

This recipe is very versatile and can be used for everyday or holidays. Top with seasonal fruit for extra color.

INGREDIENTS	MEASURE	METHOD
Crust:		
Graham cracker crumbs*	2 pounds	Preheat oven to 350 degrees. In a mixing bowl combine crumbs,
Maple syrup	4 ounces	syrup, and orange extract until
Orange extract	1/2 ounce	crumbs are moistened. Divide
Filling:		between two 9-inch layer pans,
Silken tofu	2 pounds	and press firmly into pans.
Orange juice concentrate, thawed	3 ounces	Bake 5 minutes and allow to cool. In blender, combine remaining
Apple butter	2 ounces	ingredients until smooth. Pour into
Orange zest	1/2 ounce	crust and bake for 30 minutes or
Cornstarch (dissolved in 3 ounces soy or rice milk)	1 ounce	until top is slightly browned. Cool and refrigerate until firm and set, about 2 hours.

*Note: Be sure to choose vegan Graham crackers that do not contain honey to make the crumbs.

Variation: If desired, press crust into individual muffin tins to create "personal" cheesecakes.

Total Calories per Serving: 259   Total Fat as % of Daily Value: 9%   Protein: 6 gm   Fat: 6 gm
Carbohydrates: 45 gm   Calcium: 36 mg   Iron: 2 mg   Sodium: 280 mg   Dietary Fiber: <1 gm

CHOCOLATE BANANARAMA

Yield: 25 two-ounce servings

This recipe is cool, creamy, and fun.

INGREDIENTS	MEASURE	METHOD
Ripe bananas, mashed	7 pounds	Put all ingredients in a blender and
Silken tofu	1-1/4 pounds	process until smooth. Portion into
Cocoa powder, unsweetened	3 ounces	individual dishes and chill for at least 1 hour.
Vanilla extract	1 ounce	
Maple syrup	8 ounces	
Orange zest	1/2 ounce	

Total Calories per Serving: 170   Total Fat as % of Daily Value: 3%   Protein: 3 gm   Fat: 2 gm
Carbohydrates: 41 gm   Calcium: 32 mg   Iron: 2 mg   Sodium: 6 mg   Dietary Fiber: 2 gm

Chapter Six

DINNER PARTIES AND ELEGANT DINING FOR ADULTS

FOOD AS ENTERTAINMENT

Dinner parties and elegant events are as much about the ambiance and the service as they are about the menu. There was an intimate French restaurant in Los Angeles for many years that was the most popular place to go for special occasions. The proprietor/host had outfitted the dining area, bar, and even the restrooms as if they were situated in a French country estate, circa 1880's. They always played soft background music (and sometimes featured a harpist, guitarist, or violinist) and the host always had on a dinner jacket and his best Continental manner. The tables were draped in sumptuous linens and attired with elegant centerpieces and lots of china and silver. The waitstaff were starched and polished and attentive to your every need. Complimentary niceties, such as wine, brandy, hors d'oeuvres, and desserts were always offered. The food presentation was always beautiful, with attractive garnishes served on antique china. The food, who noticed? As a food professional, I seemed to be the only person who saw that the menu was not particularly interesting nor was the preparation particularly good.

The moral to this story is not that you should not strive to always serve the best food possible, rather when having an elegant meal be sure to set the stage for its proper presentation. Think of food as theater. When you go to a play, you enjoy the experience the more your senses are being entertained by looking at the scenery, listening to the actors, etc. An elegant meal should delight all the senses, not just taste, but sight, smell, and touch also.

But you don't have a big budget for all the amenities, you say? I'll let you in on a clue: Jean-Louis (our French food-entertainer) made the rounds at thrift shops for his "antique" china and silver, took records and CDs out from the local library, and utilized the heck out of the local colleges and acting societies. Most of his staff were students or aspiring actors, happy to work in a Continental environment (and appreciative of the flexible hours) and his musicians were students or aspiring musicians (working for a meal and tips). A lot of the artwork were posters found at thrift shops or in people's garages and basements and put into "antique" frames. Tablecloths and linen napkins were either run-up by local college students or were found at linen supply houses when they had sales of their extra stock or discontinued colors. Centerpieces could be arrangements of fresh herbs in fifty-cent bud vases or a single flower and a fern leaf in several Perrier bottles. Do these suggestions give you some ideas?

As for the menu, Jean Louis had several core items that could be made to look like many different offerings with the replacement of one or two ingredients. His dishes were simple, but elegant and had been tested many times to ensure success. Jean Louis also made sure to fill up the table. He would present flavored oils and vinegars, crusty breads, an assortment of preserves, pickled vegetables, olives, and crudités (crunchy fresh vegetables) with a variety of dips, chutneys, etc. The eye had a lot to feast on beside the actual food.

A BIT OF THE BUBBLY

For a reception, think about offering a variety of alcoholic (if requested) and non-alcoholic beverages. If it is appropriate, have a bartender mixing drinks as this is part of the showmanship. If it's not appropriate, then be sure to offer a variety of sparkling waters, spritzers (sparkling water or seltzer combined with fruit juice), sparkling ciders (we've seen apple and grape), carbonated beverages, and non-alcoholic wines and beers. In addition champagnes, still and sparkling wines, beers and ales, and mixed drinks can fit into your meal plans. Beverages need a bit of vegan attention. Some wines can be processed with filters containing animal products (see page 230 in Appendix C) and artificially colored sodas or juices may contain carmine or cochineal (a red food color extracted from beetles, considered an animal product). Do some label reading for the artificial colors and ask some questions of your wine supplier, so that you can use the appropriate products. The Vegetarian Resource Group has located two companies that offer vegan organic wines. You can contact Hallcrest Vineyards at 379 Felton Empire Rd., Felton, CA 95018 or at (408) 335-4441. You can also try Frey Vineyards, 14000 Tomki Rd., Redwood Valley, CA 95470 or at (707) 485-5177 or (800) 760-3739. Hallcrest Vineyards does mail order and Frey Vineyards distributes its wine in 42 states throughout the United States and will let you know where their wine can be purchased.

Have fun with party beverages. Freeze fruit juice in ice cube trays and use them as a flavoring and coloring for drinks. Use lots of garnishes such as mini-fruit brochettes (pineapple wedges and strawberries, for example); orange, lemon, and grapefruit wedges; olives, cucumber, and zucchini spears; seasoned celery stalks; bread sticks, etc. If appropriate (and your budget allows), indulge in different types of glassware and in non-edible garnishes, such as swizzle sticks, frilled toothpicks, etc.

CATERING HINTS

In addition to the recipes contained in this book, think about making your own combinations of menu items. This will depend, of course, on your budget, your availability of time, and your staff's knowledge of vegan cooking. For example, appetizers can consist of crudités (crunchy vegetables) such as zucchini and yellow squash sticks, cherry tomatoes, radishes, whole green onions, raw asparagus (use a vegetable peeler to remove the thin, tough layer of skin), broccoli and cauliflower florets, baby carrots, pickled vegetables, as well as various flavors of bread sticks. An accompanying dip could be made of roasted garlic puréed with herbs, such as basil and oregano or cumin and curry powder. If you have access to soy products, then you might include an assortment of vegan soy cheeses and marinated tofu, or use vegan soy cheese or soy yogurt to create a dip.

A grilled tofu or tempeh steak can make a simple, elegant entrée. If soy products are not an option, then think about grilled portabello mushrooms or a savory grain loaf. Side dishes, such as herbed couscous, baked barley pilaf, jasmine rice, grilled vegetables, and fruit compotes can complement the entrée and bring color and interest to the meal.

PASTA-BILITY

Need an elegant cold appetizer or entrée? Look to pasta. Purchase vegan tortellini or miniature ravioli (or make your own if you have the time and the patience). Cook, drain, then cool the pasta and toss lightly with vinegar. Create a dressing of vegan soy sour cream (or you can use vegan mayonnaise instead), prepared mustard, cracked black pepper, chopped fresh grapes, and chopped nuts (hazelnuts or cashews are a good choice). Toss the pasta and dressing together, serve on a bed of fresh spinach or romaine, and garnish with a sprig of fresh basil or some chive flowers. This is easy to prepare and elegant!

Pasta can also serve as an elegant hot appetizer or entrée. Sauté two or three different colors of bell peppers, sliced fennel, minced garlic, baby carrots, and julienned zucchini with olive oil, seasoned with fresh thyme, marjoram, and parsley. Toss with tortellini, orecchiette, or orzo. Fettuccini tossed with sautéed portabellos and spinach is fast, flavorful, and easy on the eye.

BREAD AND CIRCUSES

Interesting breads can be used for appetizers, as side dishes and accompaniments, and even for desserts. If you don't have any time to bake, develop a relationship with a local baker who produces vegan breads, and/or check out the local large-supply store (for example, Smart and Final or Costco) for vegan baked goods. If you have a little time to bake, purchase semi-proofed frozen bakery products such as bread dough, which can be formed and baked into individual loaves or different shapes of dinner rolls and topped with sesame or poppy seeds or ground nuts. Or buy puff pastry sheets (which can be formed into individual shells, used for stuffing with veggies or grains), and dry mixes which are available for dinner rolls, quick breads (such as corn bread), and muffins. Offer a mix of plain and flavored breads and rolls, bread sticks, crackers, and ethnic breads (such as Lebanese cracker bread or Indian naan) on your appetizer and dinner table.

Be sure to match the bread with the menu, allowing it to complement the food. For example, with a French onion tart entrée offer a walnut-green onion loaf. With a couscous and vegetable entrée offer tomato-basil bread, and with a Southwestern portabello entrée offer a hominy and red pepper corn bread. Think about textures and contrasts. Offer crusty, chewy breads with soups and smooth-textured entrées, or offer soft dinner-style rolls and quick breads with crunchy items such as salads and bean and whole grain dishes.

Bread can be used as a conversation-piece serving dish. Order a boule (small, round French bread loaf), hollow out the center (save the crumbs for cooking), and serve soup or casserole-type entrées in the hollowed-out center. Larger loaves can be used as serving vessels for appetizer dips and spreads.

Leftover sweet bread (muffins, raisin bread, etc.) can be used to create bread pudding. For every pound of crumbled bread (figure 4 servings per pound), mix together 1-1/2 pints soy or rice milk, 4 ounces of maple syrup, 2 ounces of apple juice concentrate, 1/2 ounce each of ground cinnamon, ginger, nutmeg, and cloves, and 1 ounce of orange zest. Combine milk and bread (add raisins, chopped dried fruit, chopped nuts, or chocolate chips if you like), and bake at 350 degrees until set. Serve with a creamy brandy sauce (for 1 quart of sauce, use 1 pint of soy or rice milk, 8 ounces of silken tofu, 3 ounces of brandy, 1/2 ounce vanilla extract, and 2 ounces maple syrup; heat and stir until smooth), or a fruit coulis (a coulis is made by puréeing cooked or very ripe fruit with flavorings of your choosing).

A SWEET FINISH

Desserts can be purchased items to which you add ingredients to create a signature dish. Soy or rice ice cream can be served with a fruit coulis (fresh fruit puréed with sweetener and/or liqueurs; remember, some refined cane sugar and honey are not vegan), and a cookie. Check with your local supplier for the availability of prepared vegan cake or cake mixes. Cake served with soy ice cream, fresh berries or a custard sauce (made with soy or rice milk, orange juice concentrate, and spices) will look beautiful on the plate. Sorbets or iced melons and grapes make an elegant warm weather dessert.

A dessert that is vastly elegant and requires minimum preparation (as far as elegant dining goes) is a trio of pears (this can be done with apples or peaches, as well). It consists of a sorbet, a sauce, and a poached pear (peach or apple). You make the pear sauce just as you would an applesauce, just leaving the pears a bit chunky (you can make stewed pears, instead of sauce, which merely entails cooking chunked, cored, peeled pears in a small amount of water with cinnamon, nutmeg, ginger, and raisins). Sorbet is made by puréeing over-ripe fruit with apple juice concentrate (and liqueur, if desired) and freezing. Or you can purchase already-made vegan sorbet. Extra ingredients include ginger snaps or oatmeal cookies and fruit chips (you can buy apple chips already made, or make your own pear or apple chips by peeling, slicing thinly, and baking on a greased baking sheet in a 425 degree oven). Assemble this by starting with a 9-inch dinner plate lined with a doily. Select two glass dishes that will fit on the plate. Place a poached pear in one dish, topped with sorbet. Garnish with a fruit chip. Fill the second dish with sauce and garnish it with a cinnamon stick. Decorate the plate with several cookies and chips – voila! This is elegant and easy to do.

SOME MORE MENU IDEAS FOR DINNER PARTIES

Summertime Dinner:
- Appetizer: Chilled Artichokes with Curried Rice (see recipe on page 104)
- Entrée: French Onion and Olive Tart (see recipe on page 101) with Mango Salsa (see recipe on page 251)
- Sides: Chilled greens (spinach, Swiss chard, etc.) with Lemon Dill Vinaigrette (see recipe on page 95), roasted corn with pimento margarine
- Intermezzo: Sliced melon with cucumber dressing
- Dessert: Chilled Cherry Vanilla Soup (see recipe on page 99) or strawberry-balsamic pie with white and black pepper crust

Winter Dinner:
- Appetizer: Potato-pumpkin ragout or potato-leek soup
- Entrée: Curried Vegetables with Polenta (see recipe on page 143)
- Sides: Barley with ginger and shiitake mushrooms, lemon-tarragon vegetable salad
- Intermezzo: Apple-calvados sorbet (calvados is an apple liqueur)
- Dessert: Rum cake with seasonal fruit compote

And With A Mediterranean Flair:
- Appetizer: Roasted Pepper and Eggplant Dip (see recipe on page 116), served with focaccia and artisan breads
- Entrée: Mushroom-Asparagus Risotto (see recipe on page 124)
- Side: Wilted Greens with roasted garlic, white beans, and sun-dried tomatoes
- Intermezzo: Sliced citrus scented with orange-blossom water
- Dessert: Assorted biscotti and tea cookies

RECIPES
Along with the following recipes, you'll find some of the recipes in Chapter 8 (Occasions) and Chapter 7 (Holidays) also fit into your elegant dining plans.

MUSHROOM STOCK

Yield: 6 quarts or 24 one-cup servings

Mushroom stock can be the base of gravies and soups and can be used as an ingredient in casseroles and stews. Use it as a cooking liquid for rice and grains.

INGREDIENTS	MEASURE	METHOD
Vegetable oil spray	to cover pot	In a stock pot, heat oil spray and add onions. Sauté until soft.
Onions, minced	2 ounces	
Green onions, minced	3 ounces	Add remaining ingredients, bring to a boil, and allow to simmer for 1 hour or until rich flavor develops.
Fresh mushrooms, thinly sliced	3 pounds	
Dried mushrooms	6 ounces	Strain and cool. Store in refrigerator.
Bay leaves	2 each	
Fresh parsley	7 sprigs	
Whole garlic cloves	5 each	
Whole peppercorns	2 ounces	
Water	1-1/2 gallons	

Note: Use several different varieties of fresh and dried mushrooms to enhance the flavor of this stock.

Total Calories per 1 Cup Serving: 39   Total Fat as % of Daily Value: <1%   Protein: 2 gm
Fat: <1 gm   Carbohydrates: 7 gm   Calcium: 7 mg   Iron: 1 mg   Sodium: 4 mg
Dietary Fiber: <1 gm

VEGETABLE STOCK

Yield: 6 quarts or 24 one-cup servings

Vegetable stock adds extra flavor when used as a cooking liquid or an ingredient in soups, stews, casseroles, and sauces. Use this recipe as a base for soups and sauces, and as a flavoring agent for casseroles and stews. Can also be used as a cooking liquid for vegetables and starches (a good cook always attempts to avoid cooking just with water if at all possible).

INGREDIENTS	MEASURE	METHOD
Vegetable oil spray	to cover pot	In a stock pot, heat oil spray and add garlic and onions. Sauté until translucent and soft. Add remaining ingredients. Bring to a boil, reduce heat, and allow to simmer for one hour. Strain and cool. Store refrigerated.
Garlic, minced	1/2 ounce	
Onions, minced	1 ounce	
Cold water	6 quarts	
White wine	4 ounces	
Carrots, sliced	6 ounces	
Fresh mushrooms	9 ounces	
Celery, sliced	5 ounces	
Green onions	4 ounces	
Bay leaves	3 each	
Fresh parsley	5 sprigs	
Whole peppercorns	1 ounce	
Fresh thyme	1 ounce	

Note: Stock can be made in large batches and frozen (for up to three months) until ready to use. Use stock as a cooking ingredient or for the basis of soup or sauce.

Total Calories per 1 Cup Serving: 13   Total Fat as % of Daily Value: <1%   Protein: <1 gm
Fat: <1 gm   Carbohydrates: 2 gm   Calcium: 9 mg   Iron: <1 mg   Sodium: 9 mg
Dietary Fiber: <1 gm

LEMON DILL VINAIGRETTE

Yield: 25 one-ounce servings

Use as a salad dressing or cold savory sauce.

INGREDIENTS	MEASURE	METHOD
Cider vinegar	1-1/2 pints	Place all ingredients in a blender and
Olive oil	10 ounces	combine until smooth and creamy.
Garlic, minced	5 cloves	Refrigerate until ready to serve.
Prepared mustard	1 ounce	
Orange juice concentrate	3 teaspoons	
Fresh dill, minced	2 ounces	
Fresh lemon juice	2 ounces	

Total Calories per Serving: 100   Total Fat as % of Daily Value: 17%   Protein: <1 gm   Fat: 11 gm
Carbohydrates: 3 gm   Calcium: 9 mg   Iron: <1 mg   Sodium: 16 mg   Dietary Fiber: <1 gm

MINT-GARLIC SALAD DRESSING

Yield: 25 one-ounce servings

Use as a salad dressing or a cold sauce. We've tried this with chilled melon and have enjoyed the contrast in tastes.

INGREDIENTS	MEASURE	METHOD
Garlic, minced	8 cloves	Place garlic, mustard, lemon juice,
Prepared mustard	3 ounces	mint, and tofu in a blender and
Lemon juice	6 ounces	process until smooth. Slowly add oil
Fresh mint, minced	5 ounces	and process until well blended.
Soft tofu	1 pound	Serve chilled.
Oil	12 ounces	

Total Calories per Serving: 138   Total Fat as % of Daily Value: 21%   Protein: 2 gm   Fat: 14 gm
Carbohydrates: 2 gm   Calcium: 36 mg   Iron: 1 mg   Sodium: 46 mg   Dietary Fiber: <1 gm

TANGY MUSTARD SALAD DRESSING

Yield: 25 half-ounce servings

Use this as a salad dressing or as a cold sauce for grains or casseroles.

INGREDIENTS	MEASURE	METHOD
Red wine vinegar	9 ounces	Whisk all ingredients together
Prepared mustard	5 ounces	(manually or in a food processor)
Olive oil	8 ounces	until well-blended.
Cracked black pepper	1 ounce	Serve immediately.

Total Calories per Serving: 83   Total Fat as % of Daily Value: 14%   Protein: <1 gm   Fat: 9 gm
Carbohydrates: 1 gm   Calcium: 5 mg   Iron: <1 mg   Sodium: 74 mg   Dietary Fiber: <1 gm

EGGPLANT "CAVIAR"

Yield: 25 one-ounce servings

This recipe can be used as an appetizer dip, thinned with cold tomato sauce and used as a salad dressing, or used as a stuffing for peppers or tomatoes.

INGREDIENTS	MEASURE	METHOD
Eggplant	8 pounds	Preheat oven to 350 degrees. Prick
Vegetable oil spray	to cover pan	eggplant in several places. Bake
Onions, chopped	1 pound	whole eggplant on an oven rack for
Bell pepper, chopped	10 ounces	approximately 40 minutes or until
Canned pimientos, drained and chopped	14 ounces	very soft. Allow to cool. Heat sauté pan and spray with oil. Sauté onions and peppers until very soft.
Lemon juice	3 ounces	Peel and mash eggplant. Combine
Black pepper	1/2 ounce	eggplant, onion/pepper mixture, pimientos, lemon juice, and pepper. Continue to mix until well-combined. Allow to chill for at least one hour.

Note: If mixture is too dry, up to 3 ounces of vegetable oil may be added.

Total Calories per Serving: 54   Total Fat as % of Daily Value: <1%   Protein: 2 gm   Fat: <1 gm
Carbohydrates: 12 gm   Calcium: 17 mg   Iron: 1 mg   Sodium: 9 mg   Dietary Fiber: 1 gm

CHILLED CHERRY VANILLA SOUP

Yield: 25 four-ounce servings

This elegant soup can be used as an appetizer for a cool summer supper, or served as dessert, garnished with fresh cherries and berries. Be sure to make it far enough ahead of time to allow it to cool and have the flavors blend.

INGREDIENTS	MEASURE	METHOD
Fresh cherries, pitted*	12 pounds	Combine cherries, concentrate, water, and cinnamon in a heavy stock pot. Scrape seeds from vanilla bean into pot and then place bean pod into pot also. Bring to a fast boil, reduce heat to medium, and stir occasionally. Simmer until cherries are tender, about 20 minutes.
Apple juice concentrate	1 pint	
Water	3 pints	
Cinnamon sticks	5 each	
Vanilla bean**	1/2 each	
Cornstarch	4 ounces	
Cherry wine***	2 pints	
Lemon juice	3 ounces	

Mix cornstarch with 8 ounces water in a bowl to form a slurry. Pour slowly into soup, stirring to blend. Allow soup to simmer until thickened and clear (about 2 minutes). Remove from heat. Remove cinnamon. Allow to chill overnight. Before serving remove vanilla, and add wine and lemon juice. Serve chilled.

*Note: If fresh cherries are not available, sour (pie) cherries can be used, although the color and flavor will not be as intense.

**Note: Whole vanilla beans can be found in gourmet shops, in the spice section of larger grocery stores, and through mail-order gourmet catalogues. Two ounces of vanilla extract can be used instead of the bean, but the flavor will not be as intense.

***Note: Cherry wine can be found in the dessert wine section of wine shops or package stores. White wine or non-alcoholic wine can be used; there may have to be a correction for sweetness, as cherry wine is very sweet.

Total Calories per Serving: 271   Total Fat as % of Daily Value: 3%   Protein: 3 gm   Fat: 2 gm
Carbohydrates: 54 gm   Calcium: 40 mg   Iron: 1 mg   Sodium: 10 mg   Dietary Fiber: 3 gm

MULTIPLE MASHED POTATOES

Yield: 25 three-ounce servings

Mashed potatoes can range from comfort food to an elegant accompaniment. Experiment with Yukon Gold or Peruvian Purple potatoes for a different look.

INGREDIENTS	MEASURE	METHOD
Boiling potatoes	5-1/2 pounds	Put potatoes in a medium stock pot.
Soy milk, unflavored and heated	1 quart	Cover with water and allow to cook until very soft. Remove from heat
Margarine	4 ounces	and peel. Place peeled potatoes in a
White pepper	1 ounce	mixer bowl. Add milk, margarine, and pepper. Using a paddle attachment, mix potatoes until they are light and fluffy. If too dry, add small amounts of milk until moist.

Variations:

1. Duchesse potatoes: duchesse potatoes are piped through a pastry bag to form large rosettes. They are then brushed with margarine and baked or browned under a broiler. They can be prepared and frozen or refrigerated, and reheated when needed. To prepare duchesse: follow above recipe, whipping potatoes until they are a purée (so smooth that they can be piped). If too thick, additional margarine and soy milk can be added. Place potato purée in a pastry bag with a star tip. Pipe onto greased baking sheets (about 1-ounce portions). Bake for approximately 15 minutes at 375 degrees, or brown under a broiler.

2. Jalapeño mashed potatoes: add 7 seeded, minced fresh jalapeño chilies to recipe above, as they are being processed in the mixer.

3. Garlic mashed potatoes: roast or sauté 12 garlic cloves. Mince and add to potatoes as they are being processed in the mixer.

4. Basil mashed potatoes: shred 6 ounces of fresh basil and quickly sauté. Add to potatoes as they are being processed in the mixer.

5. Horseradish mashed potatoes: add 3 ounces of prepared horseradish to potatoes as they are being processed in the mixer.

Total Calories per Serving: 145   Total Fat as % of Daily Value: 8%   Protein: 3 gm   Fat: 5 gm
Carbohydrates: 22 gm   Calcium: 19 mg   Iron: <1 mg   Sodium: 82 mg   Dietary Fiber: 2 gm

FRENCH ONION AND OLIVE TART

Yield: makes two 9-inch tarts (8 slices from each)

Also called Pissaladiere, this savory tart makes an elegant dinner or brunch entrée, or can be used as a hot hors d'oeuvre.

INGREDIENTS	MEASURE	METHOD
Tart Shell:		
Flour	2 cups	Sift flour and salt into a large bowl.
Salt	1/2 teaspoon	Cut in margarine until mixture is
Margarine, ice cold	6 ounces	crumbly. Roll into a ball, wrap in plastic, and refrigerate for 1 hour. Flatten dough on a floured board and roll to 1/4-inch thickness. Press into two 9-inch tart pans.
Filling:		Preheat oven to 325 degrees.
Olive oil	3 Tablespoons	Heat oil in sauté pan. With low heat,
Sweet onions, sliced thinly	4 pounds	add onions and thyme and cook until onions are soft.
Fresh thyme	2 sprigs	Add pepper, cover, and cook until
White pepper	1/2 ounce	most of the liquid has evaporated
Black olives	5 ounces	(about 25 minutes). Spread onions over pastry, garnish with olives, and bake at 325 degrees for 20 minutes or until pastry is golden.

Total Calories per Serving: 213   Total Fat as % of Daily Value: 20%   Protein: 3 gm   Fat: 13 gm
Carbohydrates: 22 gm   Calcium: 37 mg   Iron: 1 mg   Sodium: 247 mg   Dietary Fiber: 3 gm

SEASONAL VEGETABLE BROCHETTES

Yield: 25 brochettes

Incorporate seasonal vegetables onto your brochettes. Don't forget the fresh fennel, summer squashes, sweet onions, and all the colors of peppers and tomatoes available today. You can make the skewers ahead of time and allow them to marinate overnight.

INGREDIENTS	MEASURE	METHOD
Mushroom caps	50 each	Skewer 2 mushrooms and one of
Cherry tomatoes	25 each	each of the next five veggies onto a
Broccoli florets	25 each	6-inch wood or metal skewer. In a
Cauliflower florets	25 each	large bowl, combine green onions,
Zucchini, cut into chunks	25 pieces	garlic, soy sauce, vinegar, and pepper flakes. Marinate brochettes
Onions, cut into chunks	25 pieces	for at least 2 hours, turning the
Green onions, chopped	12 ounces	brochettes for total coverage.
Garlic, minced	8 ounces	Remove brochettes from marinade
Soy sauce	10 ounces	and grill on char broiler or on hot
Vinegar	6 ounces	griddle or barbecue until vegetables
Red pepper flakes	3 ounces	are soft.

Note: Smoked tofu or "fake meats" may be chunked and added to the brochettes. A separate amount of the marinade may be prepared and served as a sauce. When selecting mushrooms, look for caps that have approximately 2-inch diameters and are about the same size.

Total Calories per Brochette: 62   Total Fat as % of Daily Value: 2%   Protein: 5 gm   Fat: 1 gm
Carbohydrates: 11 gm   Calcium: 51 mg   Iron: 2 mg   Sodium: 819 mg   Dietary Fiber: 2 gm

TOFU-STUFFED EGGPLANT

Yield: 6 eggplant halves, 4 servings each

This recipe can also be done with zucchini, crookneck, or pattypan squash if individual serving "dishes" are desired.

INGREDIENTS	MEASURE	METHOD
Eggplant (1-1/2 pounds)	3 each	Cut eggplants in half (lengthwise), leaving a 1/2-inch shell. Scoop out pulp. Chop pulp and set aside.
Firm tofu, chopped	3 pounds	
Bread crumbs	8 ounces	
Peanuts, chopped	1 pound	Place eggplant shells, face down on an oven rack and roast at 400 degrees, covered with foil, for 10 minutes. Place tofu, bread crumbs, 1 pound peanuts, soy sauce, cilantro, and oil in a food processor and combine until all but the peanuts are smooth.
Soy sauce	1 ounce	
Fresh cilantro	3 ounces	
Oil	1 ounce	
Green onions, chopped	6 ounces	
Peanuts, chopped	6 ounces	
Vegetable oil spray	to cover pan	Heat a large sauté pan, and spray with oil. Quickly sauté eggplant pulp, green onions, and 6 ounces peanuts. Remove from heat. In a large mixing bowl, combine filling and eggplant pulp. Fill each eggplant with filling. Place in a steam table pan and bake, uncovered, at 350 degrees for 20 minutes or until filling is hot and set.

Total Calories per Serving: 220   Total Fat as % of Daily Value: 17%   Protein: 13 gm   Fat: 12 gm
Carbohydrates: 16 gm   Calcium: 152 mg   Iron: 2 mg   Sodium: 169 mg   Dietary Fiber: 1 gm

CHILLED ARTICHOKES WITH CURRIED RICE

Yield: 25 servings

Summer and autumn are a good time to include this dish for your elegant meals.

INGREDIENTS	MEASURE	METHOD
Artichoke hearts, canned	25 each	Drain artichokes, save marinade.
Brown rice, cooked	6 pounds	Allow artichokes to chill. Warm rice slightly. Combine with olives, pepper, tofu, curry powder, cumin, water chestnuts, and reserved marinade (if finished product is too dry). Top each artichoke with approximately 3 ounces of rice mixture.
Green olives, sliced	25 each	
Bell pepper, diced	1-1/2 pounds	
Soft tofu	12 ounces	
Curry powder	2 teaspoons	
Cumin	1 teaspoon	
Water chestnuts, drained and chopped	1 pound	

Notes: The canned artichokes can be hearts, bottoms, or a mixture of both. This recipe can be done with fresh steamed artichokes, split in half lengthwise. Use prepared vinaigrette to replace the marinade. You can also roast your own spices and create a curry blend. If they are in season, you can also steam fresh water chestnuts.

Total Calories per Serving: 170   Total Fat as % of Daily Value: 3%   Protein: 5 gm   Fat: 2 gm
Carbohydrates: 33 gm   Calcium: 52 mg   Iron: 3 mg   Sodium: 295 mg   Dietary Fiber: 4 gm

ROASTED APPLES WITH BRANDY

Yield: 25 servings

This French-inspired dessert takes a bit of handwork and time, but your guests will find it beautiful to the eye and delightful to the taste.

INGREDIENTS	MEASURE	METHOD
Baking apples*	25 small	Core apples but do not cut through to the bottom. Put 1 ounce of sweetener and 1 ounce of brandy in the core of each apple.
Dry sweetener	1-1/2 pounds	
Calvados or dry brandy**	1-1/2 pints	
Frozen phyllo dough	5 sheets	
Margarine, melted	8 ounces	

On a work table or cutting board, place one phyllo sheet (keep remainder moist with a damp towel) and cut into five squares. Brush each square with water. Place an apple in the middle of each square. Bring the sides of the dough up and together to completely cover the apple. Tuck excess dough into the core. Brush each enrobed apple with water. Preheat oven to 375 degrees.
Place on a baking sheet that is either nonstick or lined with parchment. Bake for 10 minutes at 375 degrees, brush with margarine, and continue to bake for 10 more minutes or until apples are soft (can be pierced with a knife) and the phyllo is golden brown.

*Note: Cortland, Macintosh, Rome, and Gala apples work well as cooking apples.

**Note: Calvados is a dry apple brandy; however, any dry brandy can be used. Non-alcoholic brands of brandy are also available.

Total Calories per Serving: 329   Total Fat as % of Daily Value: 12%   Protein: 1 gm   Fat: 8 gm
Carbohydrates: 50 gm   Calcium: 13 mg   Iron: <1 mg   Sodium: 118 mg   Dietary Fiber: 3 gm

MELLOW PLUM TART

Yield: three 9-inch tarts; each tart can serve 7 people

Plums have a tart-sweet flavor and moist texture that make a perfect ending to an elegant meal. You'll find this recipe is not overly sweet.

INGREDIENTS	MEASURE	METHOD
Tart crust:		
Unbleached white flour	1-1/2 pounds	Mix flour and sweetener together.
Dry sweetener	3 ounces	Place in a food processor and blend
Margarine, cubed	12 ounces	in margarine until coarse crumbs are
Apple or cherry brandy*	1 ounce	formed. Add brandy to moisten
		dough. Do not over mix. Divide
		dough into three balls. Place each
		ball in the center of a 9-inch pie pan
		and spread evenly across bottom and
Plum filling:		sides. Refrigerate until ready to use.
Italian plums, pitted	8 pounds	In a large mixing bowl, toss plums,
and quartered**		sweetener, zests, and flour.
Dry sweetener	10 ounces	Preheat oven to 375 degrees.
Lemon zest	2 ounces	Take crust from refrigerator and
Orange zest	2 ounces	brush with orange marmalade.
Unbleached white flour	3 ounces	Arrange plums in a circle on the crust
Orange marmalade***	7 ounces	so they overlap and cover the crust,
		forming a spiral. Bake at 375 degrees
		for 40 minutes or until plums are
		very soft and crust is golden.

*Note: Non-alcoholic brands of brandy are also available.

**Note: Italian plums are a small, firm variety, usually in season in the Autumn. If they are not available, use fresh plums that are firm and not too juicy.

***Note: If orange marmalade is not available, red currant jelly or apricot glaze may be used.

Variation: A similar tart can be made with the same amount of fresh nectarines and 12 ounces of fresh raspberries.

Total Calories per Serving: 466   Total Fat as % of Daily Value: 20%   Protein: 4 gm   Fat: 13 gm
Carbohydrates: 89 gm   Calcium: 31 mg   Iron: 2 mg   Sodium: 177 mg   Dietary Fiber: 5 gm

Chapter Seven

HOLIDAY HINTS

Holidays are usually hectic times. When planning a holiday menu, be sure to include tried-and-true recipes along with new ones. Whatever you do, have a test run of any recipes that you are going to include for an important event. Thanksgiving morning is not the time to find out that the sweet potato casserole recipe just doesn't work.

Veggie holiday menus should be colorful, interesting, and sumptuous. Take advantage of seasonal produce to add color and texture to your holiday meals. Using in-season produce also usually leads to saving money. Many items may be made ahead and refrigerated or frozen to save time on the actual day. Don't feel as if you must make everything from scratch. Become familiar with commercial vegan products that fit your budget and your specifications. For example, you can purchase vegan ravioli and create your own sauce for it. Stuffing ravioli for one hundred people may start out as an act of love, but unless you have a lot of help, it may wind up as an act of lunacy.

In order to plan a successful holiday menu, you have to know your clientele. Are they looking for traditional flavors and colors without the animal products, or will they accept new menu items. Assess what kind of spicing will be popular for the group of people to be served and determine what type of service should be used. Will a festive buffet be okay, or is a sit-down dinner expected? These will all determine how happy everyone will be at the end of the meal. From personal experience, we have found that bounty and variety goes over very well. A meal that is a feast for the eyes and has a little something for everyone is a sure winner. For example, try to have an overflowing crudité (crunchy vegetable) tray with several dips, lots of different breads, rolls and crackers, and fresh and dried fruit for customers to nibble from before and during the meal. This makes the meal look plentiful and allows customers to make independent selections.

Think about the table setting, since this is the stage for your food performance. Centerpieces can be very simple (several candles framed by seasonal flowers) or ornate. Our favorite type is edible centerpieces, such as bouquets of herbs and edible flowers, arrangements of seasonal fruit and vegetables, or if you have the patience and the talent, carved vegetables and flowers. If you are familiar with salt dough (the type of dough used in bread sculptures) you may want to fashion centerpieces out of it. Contact your local bakeries; they may prepare bread sculptures for the holidays. These sculptures last for several months if kept in a cool dry place between uses.

Look through your everyday menus and see what can be "gussied up" for a holiday meal, especially if you have an audience that is not too experimental. For example, your lentil loaf can be encased in puff pastry (buy it frozen) or pie crust and turned into a lentil "Wellington" served with mushroom gravy, garlic mashed potatoes (simply add 1 ounce of sautéed, minced garlic for every pound of potatoes), and curried greens for a holiday meal. Or try baked tomatoes filled with cornbread stuffing (add kernel corn, sautéed onions, carrots, celery, and toasted pine nuts), sweet potato fritters, and braised kale (braised in vegetable stock and seasoned with garlic and white pepper). We once dined on marinated and sautéed portabello "steak" on a bed of a trio of grains (brown rice flavored with onion, couscous flavored with cilantro, and barley flavored with dill). This dish was served with a charred pepper sauce (bell peppers were roasted over a flame, peeled, seeded, puréed, and heated with minced garlic) at a holiday party. We have recreated this menu many times, with great customer satisfaction.

We've included a recipe for torta (see page 126), which works well for a sit-down dinner or on a buffet (pre-slice it for a buffet). Best yet, tortas can be baked ahead of time and reheated when needed. Plan a Mediterranean holiday menu around the torta, with Greek salad or eggplant caviar as an appetizer, and farfalle (bow-tie noodles) tossed with fresh sautéed tomatoes and mushrooms along with broccoli or greens as side dishes. Sorbet and cookies would be a fitting finale for this type of menu.

Many food items are versatile. For example, ravioli can be steamed, sauced, and served as a hot or cold appetizer or entrée. Or you can steam ravioli, drain, and pat dry. Next, dip the ravioli in soy milk, then in seasoned bread crumbs, and finally deep fry them. Serve as a crispy appetizer or as part of a pasta platter (or you can cut to the chase and purchase vegan pre-breaded ravioli that only need to be fried). Cooked and chilled ravioli served with a variety of dipping sauces (think of marinara, pesto, and lemon vinaigrette) makes a festive and fast appetizer. The same goes for veggies. Serve sliced bell peppers (get them in their rainbow of colors), baby carrots, whole green onions, cherry tomatoes or tomato wedges, sliced zucchini and summer squash, and fresh green and wax beans in their natural state (raw, that is) along with dipping sauces as a cold crudité platter. Or go one step further and use the same veggies for hot tempura (you can purchase tempura batter mixes or you can create your own with rice flour and soy milk).

Desserts can be simple, yet elegant for a holiday table, especially if everyone is feeling a little stuffed after a big meal. Here are some fast, yet fancy dessert ideas:

1. Drizzle fresh berries or orange slices with orange liqueur and shredded fresh mint.
2. Serve a small, peeled tangerine with three or four halved dates and some toasted macadamia or hazelnuts.
3. Toss grapefruit sections with pomegranate seeds or sliced fresh grapes, orange juice, and (optional) some rose water.
4. Serve a ripe pear with almond or chocolate biscotti.
5. Serve lemon sorbet topped with fresh or frozen berries and a splash of blackberry liqueur.
6. Serve vanilla soy or rice ice cream drizzled with amaretto and topped with a chocolate cookie wafer.
7. Serve melon slices tossed with fresh shredded mint and chilled champagne.

Holiday catering has to be precisely planned so that the end result looks as if it took no effort at all. When writing your menu, think about the pre-prep time for each item (chopping, marinating, etc.), the needed equipment (if everything needs to be baked in the oven, then you'll have to prepare some things ahead of time), cooking time, and of course color, texture, and flavor blends. With a bit of planning you and your customers can have happy holidays.

For additional recipes, look in Chapter 6 (Elegant Dining) and Chapter 8 (Occasions). There is a tofu-cheesecake recipe in Chapter 5 (Kids) which would fit nicely on any holiday table.

MENU IDEAS FOR HOLIDAYS

Winter Holiday Meal:
- Tomato-lentil soup with herbed croutons
- Assorted ravioli with three-pepper coulis (peeled, puréed bell peppers used as a sauce)
- Torta Rustica (see recipe on page 126)
- Sautéed greens
- Mashed turnip and rutabagas
- Assorted breads and rolls
- Lemon-tofu cheesecake

Thanksgiving:
- Assorted crudités and dips
- Herbed lentil loaf with mushroom gravy
- Baked, candied sweet potatoes with cranberry-walnut gravy
- Broccoli and cauliflower medley
- Tofu Pumpkin Pie (see recipe on page 128)
- Assorted cookies and fresh fruit

Or
- Butternut squash soup with herbed margarine
- Seasonal vegetable pie with mushroom sauce
- Baked sweet potatoes with praline topping
- Garlic Mashed Potatoes (see recipe on page 100)
- Glazed lemon carrots
- Apple-cinnamon pie

(Note: To save time, you can also purchase *Tofurkey*, *Unturkey*, or other pre-made mock turkey entrées)

Happy New Year:
- Holiday hors d'oeuvre platter (assorted olives, radishes, marinated veggies such as asparagus, cauliflower, artichokes, whole green onions, cherry tomatoes, cucumber and carrot sticks, assorted bread sticks, salsas, and dips)
- Black-eyed peas and tofu (black-eyes peas are considered to bring good luck for the New Year)
- Mushroom-Asparagus Risotto (see recipe on page 124)
- Mashed sweet potatoes (seasoned with orange zest and lemon zest, nutmeg, and vanilla)
- Braised greens (braise greens of choice with white wine, minced garlic, and pepper)
- Assorted sorbets and cookies

Fourth of July Grill-Out:
- Assorted veggie burgers (purchased commercially or make your own – see recipes in Fast Food chapter)
- Veggie dogs
- Grilled lemon-herb tofu steaks
- Corn on the cob and baked white and sweet potatoes (cooked right in the coals)
- Potato and pasta salad
- Confetti broccoli slaw (can purchase shredded broccoli or can do it yourself)
- Watermelon wedges and seasonal fresh fruit (served iced)

Passover:
- Crunchy vegetable tray with guacamole
- Matzo balls in carrot-vegetable broth
- Vegetable loaf with gravy
- Fruit compote (stewed fruit sweetened with orange juice concentrate and flavored with ginger and cinnamon)
- Baked sweet potatoes
- Braised greens
- Plum tart (made with matzo meal crust)
- Baked apples with raisins

Halloween:
- Purée of carrot soup served in a pumpkin shell (scoop out pumpkin, toast seeds, and use seeds as a garnish)
- "Monster" sandwich – six-foot submarine bread filled with grilled vegetables, sliced tomatoes, onions, peppers, etc.
- Cole slaw and potato salad (if available, try purple potatoes)
- Assorted veggie chips (bake thinly sliced potatoes, carrots, beets, etc.) with flavored hummus
- "Dirt and worms" dessert – frozen sorbet or rice or soy frozen dessert mixed with cookie and cake crumbs, chopped raisins, and canned fruit cut into strips

Easter:
- Fresh spinach salad with Mandarin orange segments, sliced almonds, and vinaigrette dressing
- Stuffed Tomatoes (see recipes on pages 142 and 154)
- Brown rice pilaf with dates, raisins, and pineapple
- Baby carrots tossed with dill and margarine
- Broccoli and cauliflower florets tossed with garlic and lemon
- Peach upside down cake

Rosh Hashanah:
- Mock Chopped Liver (see recipe on page 135) with assorted crackers
- Mushroom barley soup
- Vegetarian Stuffed Kishke (see recipe on page 139)
- Stuffed baked potatoes
- "Creamed" spinach (use puréed tofu and soy milk to create a "cream" sauce)
- Sliced carrots tossed with apple juice and parsley
- Sliced citrus (slices of oranges, pink grapefruit, tangerines, etc.)
- Assorted fruit breads (carrot, zucchini, pumpkin, etc.)

BETTER THAN HOME FOR THE HOLIDAYS

Everybody wants a feast (or two) during the holiday season! Moving beyond the obvious traditional carnivore centerpiece, you can make your holiday offerings a veritable veggie feast.

Looking at it from a production point of view, it is more energy-, time-, and labor-efficient to produce one form of each dish rather than two or three. Under optimum conditions, you can produce a vegan menu item and serve it to everyone. Under less ideal conditions, the addition of an ingredient or two would change a vegan item into a vegetarian or carnivore item. It still takes less time to divide, say, a batch of vegan fried rice and add ingredients to it, rather than having to make two or three separate batches.

How in the world can I offer vegan items to the non-vegan world, you ask? Think about how really necessary non-vegan ingredients are to a menu item and go from there. For example, pie and pie crusts. Fruit pie fillings contain few non-vegan ingredients; only the sweeteners would be questionable, as many vegans avoid refined cane sugar (it might be processed through a bone char filter) and honey (an animal product). You can use maple syrup or fruit juice concentrate rather than sugar or honey in pie fillings. You'll get a great flavor (more "down-home" style) and an enhanced color. Chances are you'll get comments on how good the pies are this season. Lard or beef fat is sometimes used for pie crusts. I realize that many bakers will scream "heretic," but for health and shelf-life reasons (if you want to make crusts or whole pies ahead of time, freeze, and reheat) doesn't margarine, oil, or solid vegetable oil work better? So, there's an example of one type of holiday vegan fare for everyone.

Soups make a good starter for cold-weather holiday meals. Potage crecy (cream of carrot soup) does not rely on meat products at all for its richness and makes an elegant-looking, lowfat first course. Cook carrots until soft enough to purée (in a food mill, with a Burr mixer or in a blender) and season with tarragon and dill. If the puréed carrots are not thick enough, you can add seasoned mashed potatoes. This is one of the first soups culinary students learn to make, and they are always amazed at how easy it is to prepare and how elegant it looks. Some variations on potage crecy include cooking potatoes in with the carrots for thickness or adding a parsnip or turnip for some "snap."

The same can be done with butternut squash and most hard-shelled winter squash; just change the seasonings for a different flavor. Bean soups can be puréed to create the illusion of a "creamy" texture. Sweet potatoes make a wonderful, colorful soup which can be seasoned savory (think pepper, thyme, or cumin) for a first course or seasoned sweet (think pie spices, like nutmeg or ginger) for a change-of-pace dessert soup.

Speaking of sweet potatoes, what separates "traditional" holiday sweet potatoes from a vegan version of this dish? The answer is usually only the butter and the marshmallows. Consider skipping all the sweet stuff and offering baked sweet potatoes. Your customers who have never tried them will love the natural flavor and texture. If you would like to spiff up the sweet spuds, mash them with a little water (or vegetable broth or heated rice milk), vanilla extract, lemon zest, orange juice concentrate, ginger, and nutmeg. This can be served as a side dish, garnished with candied ginger or citrus peels, or even put into a pie crust and served as a sweet potato pie. For a higher-fat treat, these sweet potatoes can be mixed with some bread crumbs and fried for fritters.

Many side dishes are vegan. Roasted potatoes (tossed with fresh or dried chopped herbs and vegetable or olive oil), sautéed mushrooms, steamed seasonal vegetable medleys, green beans almondine, glazed carrots (made with margarine and orange juice concentrate), cranberry sauce and relishes, fresh fruit salad or fruit compote, dried fruit and nuts, etc., are all vegan. Mashed potatoes and stuffing don't miss the non-veggie ingredients. Use margarine, soy milk, or vegetable stock to moisten the potatoes and toss in some rosemary or garlic for herbed potatoes. Use sautéed mushrooms or vegetables, chopped nuts, dried fruit, and vegetable stock in the stuffing.

Salads can be included on a holiday buffet or served as a starter or inter-mezzo course for a sit-down meal. Tossed fresh lettuce or baby greens, three bean salad, marinated mushroom, fresh fruit salad, and marinated cabbage salad (red and green cabbage and thinly sliced onions tossed with Italian dressing) don't need any vegan adaptation. If making salads using mayonnaise, you can purée tofu or purchase soy mayonnaise (read the label – be sure it is dairy- and egg-free) instead. For a vegan Caesar salad, use nutritional yeast instead of cheese and sliced almonds for flavor and texture.

Salad dressings are vegan-easy. Two of the dip recipes we included in this chapter (Harissa and Roasted Pepper and Eggplant Dip) can be easily made into salad dressing. The harissa is ready to go (caution: this one is hot!), and the eggplant can be thinned with a bit of tomato purée for a salad dressing consist-ency. Salsas and chutneys can serve as salad dressings also, as can oil and vin-egar combos (throw in some fresh herbs, such as parsley or cilantro to flavor).

We have found that accessories are what make a holiday meal really festive. The dishes themselves can be prepared simply, with just enough seasoning to make things interesting. For customers who prefer their food lightly seasoned, you already have a success. For more color and flavor, bring on the condiments. For example, a lentil and mushroom loaf or grilled tofu tastes good. A lentil and mushroom loaf or tofu steak served with walnut gravy, Pineapple-Peach Salsa (see recipe on page 115), mango chutney, freshly made apple-pear sauce, fig-pickle relish, or fruit compote tastes fantastic.

We like to have a condiments platter with sliced sweet and yellow onions, sliced mushrooms, chopped garlic, chopped pickles (sweet and garlic), sliced olives, sliced chilies, and chopped tomatoes on the table so customers can create their own flavor profiles.

Fruit is sometimes overlooked during the holidays (who can see it over all those cookies?). A compote of dried fruit is not labor-intensive and is very versatile. Simply stew mixed dry fruit (try raisins, apricots, apples, and prunes, or peaches, apricots, figs, and apples) with enough water to cover. Season with ginger, cinnamon, and apple juice concentrate until the fruit is soft. This can be used as a hot or cold side dish (it complements savory dishes well), or can be served over soy or rice milk ice cream or custard, or on the side of a slice of pie. As old-fashioned as it sounds, everyone seems to respond to homemade applesauce. You can make your own, or if you don't have the time, purchase unsweetened applesauce and heat it gently with cinnamon. Serve this along side gravy and sauce for variety. Stewed apples and pears make a delicious side dish for savory entrées and also for desserts (think bread pudding with stewed pears).

There are so many options for vegan holiday desserts. We have included a pumpkin-tofu pie that comes out silken and creamy. Serve it with fruit compote or non-dairy whipped topping, although it stands perfectly well on its own. If there's no time for slicing, you could make individual pumpkin tarts with the same recipe. You could also skip the crust altogether and make a pumpkin custard with this recipe. Bake it in a half steam table pan or in individual dishes. Baked apples, fruit tarts, and bread pudding (moistened with vanilla or chocolate soy or rice milk) are easy vegan options.

Vegan holiday meals can be prepared many ways. We have kept the ideas in this chapter close to traditional menu items. Add some ethnic accents, such as Ethiopian vegetable stews, Asian cold noodle salads, and Mediterranean dolmas (rice-stuffed grape leaves) for a twist on the traditional. Most of all have fun!

RECIPES
Enjoy the following recipes.

PINEAPPLE-PEACH SALSA

Yield: 2 pints or approximately 24 one-ounce servings

This salsa can be used as a dip for chips or melon and apple slices. It can also be used as a marinade for tofu or tempeh, or as a salad dressing.

INGREDIENTS	AMOUNT	METHOD
Fresh pineapple	2 pounds	In a large, non-reactive bowl,
Peach nectar	4 ounces	combine all ingredients. Cover and
Chili pepper, chopped, and seeded	8 each	refrigerate until ready to use.
Garlic, minced	8 cloves	
Green onion, minced	6 each	
Fresh cilantro, chopped	4 ounces	

Total Calories per Serving: 28   Total Fat as % of Daily Value: <1%   Protein: 1 gm   Fat: <1 gm
Carbohydrates: 7 gm   Calcium: 12 mg   Iron: <1 mg   Sodium: 3 mg   Dietary Fiber: 1 gm

ROASTED PEPPER AND EGGPLANT DIP

Yield: 2 quarts or approximately 58 one-ounce servings

This recipe can be used with crunchy veggies or chips, as a topping for French bread (use instead of garlic butter), or as a condiment for pita sandwiches.

INGREDIENTS	AMOUNT	METHOD
Red peppers	3 large	Roast peppers over an open flame or in a broiler until charred on all sides (about 5 minutes). Allow to cool. When cool, pull off skin, deseed, and chop. Repeat procedure with egg- plant. In sauté pan, heat oil. Add eggplant and garlic and cook until eggplant is softened. Add onions, oregano, and basil. Continue to cook for 3 more minutes. Remove from heat. Place pepper and eggplant mixture in a blender and combine until almost smooth. Serve immed- iately or refrigerate until ready to use.
Green peppers	2 large	
Eggplant	2-1/2 pounds	
Olive oil	1 ounce	
Garlic, minced	4 cloves	
Red onions, chopped	2 large	
Dried oregano	1 Tablespoon	
Dried basil	1 Tablespoon	

Total Calories per Serving: 13   Total Fat as % of Daily Value: 2%   Protein: <1 gm   Fat: 1 gm
Carbohydrates: 2 gm   Calcium: 3 mg   Iron: <1 mg   Sodium: 1 mg   Dietary Fiber: <1 gm

HARISSA

Yield: 2 pints or approximately 24 one-ounce servings

Harrisa is hot!!! If served as a dip, offer some milder dips to accompany it. Harissa makes a good marinade for tofu and tempeh and for vegetables. It can also be used as a condiment with grains and breads.

INGREDIENTS	AMOUNT	METHOD
Ground red pepper	4 ounces	Combine all ingredients in a large,
Crushed red pepper	4 ounces	non-reactive bowl. Cover and
Garlic, minced	6 cloves	refrigerate for at least 8 hours to
Ground cumin	2 ounces	allow flavors to marry.
Olive oil	16 ounces	
Ground paprika	2 ounces	
Lemon juice	8 ounces	

Variations: If you would like to "cool" off your harissa, you can add tomato paste. For a creamier taste, blend in soft tofu.

Total Calories per Serving: 200   Total Fat as % of Daily Value: 30%   Protein: 2 gm   Fat: 20 gm
Carbohydrates: 8 gm   Calcium: 23 mg   Iron: 1 mg   Sodium: 6 mg   Dietary Fiber: <1 gm

SAVORY MUSHROOM GRAVY

Yield: 25 one-ounce portions

This is a "make ahead" dish, good for entrées, vegetables, grains, and potatoes. Can be made up to two days ahead of time and kept cold until ready to reheat.

INGREDIENTS	MEASURE	METHOD
Dried mushrooms	8 ounces	In a medium bowl, pour 1 pint boiling water over mushrooms. Allow to stand for 15 minutes. Heat sauté pan, spray with oil. Sauté onions until soft. Add flour, mix to form paste. Remove from heat. Strain mushrooms (save liquid) and chop fine. In medium saucepan combine flour with a small amount of stock to form a watery paste. Add stock and mushroom liquid. Cook over medium heat, stirring, until thickened. Add mushrooms, walnuts, and spices. Cook for 5 minutes or until hot.
Vegetable oil spray	to cover pan	
Onions	3-1/2 ounces	
Unbleached white flour	4 ounces	
Mushroom stock*	1-1/2 pints	
Walnuts, finely chopped	8 ounces	
Black pepper	1/2 ounce	
Marjoram	1/4 ounce	
Thyme	1/4 ounce	

*Note: The recipe for mushroom stock can be found in Chapter 6, page 93.

Total Calories per Serving: 105   Total Fat as % of Daily Value: 8%   Protein: 4 gm   Fat: 5 gm
Carbohydrates: 13 gm   Calcium: 8 mg   Iron: 1 mg   Sodium: 1 mg   Dietary Fiber: 2 gm

LENTIL SOUP
WITH SMOKED TOFU AND TARRAGON

Yield: 25 four-ounce servings

Serve this soup with hot bread sticks and an eggplant dip for maximum flavor and interest.

INGREDIENTS	AMOUNT	METHOD
Brown lentils	2-1/2 pounds	Place lentils in a small stock pot, cover with water, and allow to soak for 1 hour. Drain and return to stock pot. Add stock, celery, carrots, mushrooms, and onion to the lentils. Bring to a boil, reduce heat, and allow to simmer for 1 hour or until lentils are soft. Purée the soup (use an immersible mixer or a blender). Return to stock pot, simmer, and add garlic, allspice, tarragon, and tofu. Cook for 10 minutes. Just before serving, stir in parsley and pepper.
Vegetable stock	1/2 gallon	
Celery, diced	1 bunch	
Carrots, diced	1 pound	
Mushrooms, sliced	1-1/2 pounds	
Onion, minced	1 pound	
Garlic powder	1 ounce	
Allspice	1 Tablespoon	
Dried tarragon	2 ounces	
Smoked tofu, cut into 1-inch squares*	2 pounds	
Fresh parsley, minced	3 ounces	
Black pepper	1 Tablespoon	

*Note: Smoked tofu can be found in natural foods stores.

Total Calories per Serving: 216   Total Fat as % of Daily Value: 3%   Protein: 15 gm   Fat: 2 gm
Carbohydrates: 35 gm   Calcium: 168 mg   Iron: 6 mg   Sodium: 83 mg   Dietary Fiber: 4 gm

GRAINS WITH TOMATOES AND GINGER

Yield: 24 three-ounce servings

Serve this grain-based dish with a lentil stew, you can also prepare seasoned black beans and serve them over this dish.

INGREDIENTS	AMOUNT	METHOD
Cooked brown rice or other grains	8 pounds	Combine grain, peas, carrots, and corn in a very large mixing bowl. Set aside, keeping warm.
Peas, steamed	1 pound	
Carrots, steamed and diced	1/2 pound	
Cut corn	1/2 pound	
Fresh ginger, grated	6 ounces	In a medium bowl, mix ginger, toma-
Tomatoes, fresh or canned and chopped and drained	2 pounds and 4 ounces	toes, soy sauce, sesame seeds, miso, and water until well-blended. Toss sauce with vegetables. Serve warm.
Soy sauce	2 Tablespoons	
Sesame seeds	2 Tablespoons	
Brown miso	1 Tablespoon	
Warm water	12 ounces	

Total Calories per Serving: 217   Total Fat as % of Daily Value: 3%   Protein: 6 gm   Fat: 2 gm
Carbohydrates: 43 gm   Calcium: 34 mg   Iron: 2 mg   Sodium: 139 mg   Dietary Fiber: 5 gm

CURRIED GREENS

Yield: 25 two-ounce servings

Serve this as a colorful side dish to complement grain or bean entrées.

INGREDIENTS	MEASURE	METHOD
Vegetable oil spray	to cover pan	Heat sauté pan and spray with oil. Sauté onions and garlic. Add carrots, celery, and stock. Lower heat and simmer for 5 minutes or until carrots are tender. Stir in curry and pepper. Add cornstarch, stir and cook until sauce thickens (about 5 minutes). Add greens; cook until greens are just tender (about 5 minutes in a commercial steamer, 10 minutes in a commercial braising pan, or 20 minutes in a pot on top of a stove). Serve warm.
Onions, minced	1 pound	
Garlic, minced	6 cloves	
Carrots, diced	1 pound	
Celery, diced	8 ounces	
Vegetable stock	1 pint	
Curry powder	2 ounces	
White pepper	1/2 ounce	
Cornstarch	2 ounces	
Frozen greens, thawed*	6 pounds	

*Note: Use frozen mustard, collard, turnip greens, or kale. If using fresh greens, use two times the amount as frozen. Be sure to wash, stem, and coarsely chop (and allow more cooking time) fresh greens.

Total Calories per Serving: 73   Total Fat as % of Daily Value: 2%   Protein: 4 gm   Fat: 1 gm
Carbohydrates: 15 gm   Calcium: 256 mg   Iron: 2 mg   Sodium: 71 mg   Dietary Fiber: 5 gm

TURKEYLESS TETRAZZINI

Yield: 32 four-ounce servings

Serve this tetrazzini with steamed seasonal greens or a baby greens salad. Use Pineapple-Peach Salsa (recipe on page 115) as a dressing.

INGREDIENTS	AMOUNT	METHOD
Filling:		
Mushrooms, sliced	2 pounds	Preheat oven to 325 degrees (convection 300). In a sauté pan, cook mushrooms in wine until soft, about 10 minutes. Cut tofu into small cubes. In a steam table pan, combine mushrooms, tofu, spaghetti, and almonds. Set aside.
White wine	2 ounces	
Firm tofu	2 pounds	
Cooked spaghetti	9 pounds	
Sliced almonds	1/2 pound	
Sauce:		
Flour	8 ounces	Combine flour and margarine over low heat until a paste is formed. In a small stock pot, add broth, a little at a time, to the paste. Stir and incorporate until smooth. Remove from heat and add pepper and soy milk. Pour sauce over spaghetti mixture and toss lightly. Bake for 30 minutes at 350 degrees or until golden on top.
Margarine	8 ounces	
Mushroom or vegetable broth, heated	1 quart	
White pepper	1 Tablespoon	
Soy milk, unflavored and heated	4 ounces	

Total Calories per Serving: 342   Total Fat as % of Daily Value: 18%   Protein: 13 gm   Fat: 12 gm
Carbohydrates: 45 gm   Calcium: 86 mg   Iron: 4 mg   Sodium: 83 mg   Dietary Fiber: 3 gm

SWEET AND HOT GINGER-CARROT TART

Yield: 3 tarts with 6 portions each

This aromatic tart can be served hot or cold. It is a colorful addition to a holiday dessert table. Please note that this recipe is high in fat, an occasional indulgence is okay if you're not on a restricted lowfat diet.

INGREDIENTS	MEASURE	METHOD
Tart crust:		
Unbleached white flour	4 pounds	Mix together flour and sweetener. Place in a food processor and add in margarine until coarse crumbs are formed. Add extract, lemon juice, and water, and process only until dough just holds together. Divide into 3 balls, wrap in plastic wrap, and refrigerate for at least 30 minutes.
Dry sweetener	12 ounces	
Cold margarine, cut into squares	18 ounces	
Vanilla extract	1/2 ounce	
Lemon juice	1 ounce	
Cold water	3 ounces	
Carrot Filling:		
Fresh carrots, peeled and grated	6 pounds	In a medium stock pot or steam-jacketed kettle, combine carrot filling ingredients and cook, stirring occasionally, until reduced to a thick, fruit-preserve-like consistency. This should take about 20 minutes. If mixture becomes too dry, add 1-2 ounces of water. Allow to cool. Preheat oven to 375 degrees. To assemble, roll out dough on a floured board. Place rolled dough onto 9-inch pie plates and press gently into plates. Fill with carrot filling. Bake in a 375 degree oven for 20 minutes or until crust is golden.
Dry sweetener	2 pounds	
Candied ginger, minced	5 ounces	
Fresh ginger, shredded	2 ounces	
Orange zest	1 ounce	

Note: If a closed tart is desired, make a second batch of the dough, cut into strips, and form a lattice work. Tarts can be garnished with additional candied ginger.

Total Calories per Serving: 932   Total Fat as % of Daily Value: 37%   Protein: 12 gm   Fat: 24 gm
Carbohydrates: 169 gm   Calcium: 83 mg   Iron: 6 mg   Sodium: 368 mg   Dietary Fiber: 8 gm

MUSHROOM-ASPARAGUS RISOTTO

Yield: 25 four-ounce servings

The natural creaminess of the risotto (from the starch) gives this dish its luscious texture.

INGREDIENTS	MEASURE	METHOD
Vegetable oil spray	to cover pan	Heat sauté pan and spray with oil.
Onion, chopped	1 pound	Sauté onion, peppers, garlic, and
Bell pepper, chopped	8 ounces	mushrooms. Stir in risotto, 1 pint
Garlic, minced	4 cloves	stock, wine, parsley, and white
Mushrooms, sliced	2 pounds	pepper. Bring to a simmer and cook
Risotto (arborio rice)	1-1/2 pounds	uncovered for 10 minutes, stirring
Vegetable stock, hot	1 pint	constantly.
White wine	6 ounces	
Fresh parsley, chopped	3 ounces	
White pepper	1/2 ounce	Add 1 pint stock and asparagus,
Vegetable stock, hot	1 pint	continue to stir, and cook for 10
Fresh asparagus, cut into 1-inch pieces*	18 ounces	minutes or until risotto is tender. Serve warm.

*Note: If fresh asparagus is not available, use thawed frozen asparagus or omit asparagus and increase mushrooms to 2-1/2 pounds. In order to prepare a successful risotto, you must stir constantly until risotto is thoroughly cooked.

Total Calories per Serving: 130   Total Fat as % of Daily Value: <1%   Protein: 4 gm   Fat: <1 gm
Carbohydrates: 27 gm   Calcium: 19 mg   Iron: 2 mg   Sodium: 7 mg   Dietary Fiber: 1 gm

ASPARAGUS MUSHROOM RAGOUT

Yield: 25 three-ounce servings

Add elegance to your holiday table with this delicate stew (if asparagus spears are not available, julienned zucchini may be used instead).

INGREDIENT	MEASURE	METHOD
Dried mushrooms	4 ounces	In a non-reactive bowl, cover dried
Vegetable oil spray	to cover pan	mushrooms with boiling water and
Garlic, minced	10 cloves	allow to soak for 10 minutes, or until
Fresh mushrooms, sliced	4 pounds	soft. Heat a sauté pan. Spray with oil and sauté garlic and fresh mush-
Red wine or sherry	1 pint	rooms until mushrooms are tender.
Asparagus spears, 1-inch pieces	6 pounds	Add wine, asparagus, pepper, and dried mushrooms (with soaking
White pepper	1 ounce	liquid) and simmer until asparagus
Cornstarch	2 ounces	spears are tender. Dissolve corn-
Water	5 ounces	starch in water. Stir into stew and bring to a boil, stirring until thickened (about 1 minute). Serve warm.

Note: Serve hot over brown rice, herbed couscous, or flavored pasta (spinach or tomato works well).

Total Calories per Serving: 98   Total Fat as % of Daily Value: 2%   Protein: 5 gm   Fat: 1 gm
Carbohydrates: 18 gm   Calcium: 33 mg   Iron: 2 mg   Sodium: 19 mg   Dietary Fiber: 2 gm

TORTA RUSTICA

Yield: 2 tortas (10 slices each)

A "torta" is a savory pie, served as an entrée. Freeze and reheat when needed.

INGREDIENTS	MEASURE	METHOD
Crust:		
Unbleached white flour	2-1/2 pounds	In a mixing bowl, combine flour and salt. Cut in margarine and shortening until mixture resembles coarse crumbs. Stir in just enough ice water so mixture can be rolled into a ball. Wrap in plastic and refrigerate for 30 minutes.
Salt	1 teaspoon	
Margarine	4 ounces	
Shortening	4 ounces	
Ice water	3-4 ounces	
Filling:		
Vegetable oil spray	to cover pan	Heat sauté pan; spray with oil. Add onion and sauté until soft. Add mushrooms and garlic; cook and stir until moisture is 90% evaporated. Add thyme and pepper. Remove from heat and allow to cool. In mixing bowl combine spinach, tofu, nutmeg, and red pepper flakes until well combined. Set aside. Set aside 1/3 of dough. Roll remainder of dough into two 12-inch circles. Press dough in 9-inch pie pan, pressing dough edges to side of pan. Spray dough in pan lightly with oil. Sprinkle with bread crumbs. Fill dough by alternating layers of the mushroom mixture and spinach mixture. End by topping with pepper strips. Roll out remaining dough and top each torta with dough (seal edges of dough and cut several slits in top). Bake at 350 degrees for 55 minutes or until dough is golden brown. Allow to cool for 10 minutes before slicing.
Onions, diced	1 pound	
Fresh mushrooms, diced	3 pounds	
Fresh garlic, minced	5 cloves	
Dried thyme	2 ounces	
White pepper	1 ounce	
Frozen spinach, thawed, chopped, and drained	5 pounds	
Firm tofu, crumbled	2 pounds	
Ground nutmeg	1 teaspoon	
Red pepper flakes	1 teaspoon	
Dry bread crumbs	4 ounces	
Canned red peppers, drained, cut into strips	2 pounds	

Total Calories per Serving: 438   Total Fat as % of Daily Value: 23%   Protein: 17 gm   Fat: 15 gm
Carbohydrates: 62 gm   Calcium: 112 mg   Iron: 5 mg   Sodium: 335 mg   Dietary Fiber: 5 gm

AMAZINGLY RICH
FRUIT AND CARROT CAKE

Yield: Four 4" x 7" loaves (6 slices each)

This is a dense, moist cake that can be baked ahead of time and kept frozen until ready to serve. It is great as a dessert and as part of a gift basket.

INGREDIENTS	MEASURE	METHOD
Fresh carrots, grated	1-1/4 pounds	Place carrots, raisins, cranberries, dates, and zest in a large stock pot. Add water and allow to cook for 10 minutes or until the carrots are just softened. Allow to cool. (There should be a small amount of liquid remaining; you will use this.) In a mixing bowl, combine flour, baking soda, wheat germ, and almonds. Add spices and margarine; stir to combine. Add to fruit and mix until ingredients are just combined. Pour into greased 4" x 7" loaf pans and bake for 40 minutes at 325 degrees or until knife in center comes out clean. Allow to cool on racks before removing from pans.
Raisins, chopped	12 ounces	
Dried cranberries	8 ounces	
Dates, chopped	6 ounces	
Lemon zest	1/2 ounce	
Water	1 pint	
Unbleached white flour	1-3/4 pounds	
Baking soda	2 ounces	
Wheat germ	7 ounces	
Almonds, sliced	7 ounces	
Ground cinnamon	1/2 ounce	
Ground nutmeg	1/4 ounce	
Ground allspice	1/4 ounce	
Ground ginger	1/4 ounce	
Ground cloves	1/4 ounce	
Margarine	6 ounces	

Total Calories per Serving: 351   Total Fat as % of Daily Value: 17%   Protein: 9 gm   Fat: 11 gm
Carbohydrates: 58 gm   Calcium: 55 mg   Iron: 4 mg   Sodium: 736 mg   Dietary Fiber: 4 gm

TOFU PUMPKIN PIE

Yield: four 9-inch pies (8 slices per pie)

Don't save this pie just for the holidays. It's too good! For some extra spice, garnish with candied ginger and lemon peel.

INGREDIENTS	AMOUNT	METHOD
Vegan pie shells (9-inch)	4 each	Preheat oven to 350 degrees.
Firm tofu	4 pounds	Combine all ingredients (except pie
Canned pumpkin	4 pounds	shells) in a blender, until smooth
Vanilla extract	1 ounce	(about 3 minutes). Pour filling into 4
Vegetable oil	9 ounces	frozen pie shells. Bake at 350
Ground ginger	1 ounce	degrees (convection 325) for 50
Ground cinnamon	1/2 ounce	minutes or until set. Let cool. If
Ground nutmeg	1/2 ounce	desired, garnish with additional
Ground cloves	1/4 ounce	cinnamon and ginger.
Apple juice concentrate	1 ounce	

Total Calories per Serving: 238   Total Fat as % of Daily Value: 26%   Protein: 8 gm   Fat: 17 gm
Carbohydrates: 13 gm   Calcium: 119 mg   Iron: 2 mg   Sodium: 104 mg   Dietary Fiber: 2 gm

Chapter Eight

MENUS AND RECIPES FOR SPECIAL OCCASIONS –

WEDDINGS, ANNIVERSARIES, BIRTHDAYS, BAR/BAT MITZVAHS, COMMUNIONS, AND MORE

Eat...

Special occasions call for creative menus. Vegan special occasion menus may include adaptations of traditional recipes, such as wedding cakes or "mock" paté, and may contain original creations with a festive flair.

Identify your customers preferences. Are they more comfortable with traditional foods that have been "made vegan" or will they appreciate new dishes? Does the event call for a four-course sit-down dinner or will a light reception suffice?

Drink...

Beverages are a necessity at all occasions. If you will be serving wine, be sure to have a supply of vegan wine (see Chapter 6), as many non-vegan wines are filtered with equipment containing animal fibers. Soda and carbonated beverages, punch mixes, etc. should be checked for cochineal or carmine red food coloring, as these are derived from insects (and, therefore, are non-vegan). If you're serving hot beverages, be sure to include soy or rice milk for the coffee and tea (non-dairy creamers may do if they do not contain casein or other animal-derived ingredients).

When having a buffet, be sure that vegan foods (cut fruit and veggies, vinaigrette salad dressing, baked potatoes, steamed veggies, etc.) are separate and equal for your vegan guests. Arrange items in such a way that veggie and non-veggie items do not mingle. For example, have a cheese platter and a fruit platter, not a cheese and fruit platter.

Enjoy Dessert...

Desserts are always part of a festive occasion. Depending on your time and budget, you may wish to purchase a variety of prepared desserts and make a display of them. Check your area for bakeries that produce vegan baked goods or check with your purveyor for frozen products. If you have some time, you may want to "speed-scratch" your desserts; that is, use semi-prepared items, such as cake mixes or frozen cookie dough and add your own ingredients to them. For example, use vegan brownie mix and add chopped nuts and dried fruit to the mix.

We like to take the speed-scratch, architectural approach to desserts, especially if we need to produce a lot of desserts in a short amount of time. Dessert displays add a great deal of "sex appeal" to buffets and serving lines. Let's face it, the lentil loaf and the quinoa pilaf taste great, but they're not the most eye-appealing dishes in the world.

Here's an idea of what we do: either bake off or buy two flavors of sheet cake; then marinate fresh or frozen (thawed) berries in liqueur or fruit juice. If you like, you can prepare a whipped topping, flavoring it with liqueur or extracts. You have several choices on how to assemble your creation. If you have cake rings (or want to make them out of 3-inch diameter PVC pipe), you can line them with parchment, cut out 3-inch rounds of cake, and layer cake-berries-cake. Save the cake trimmings, chop them, toss them with liqueur or orange juice, and top the rings with the marinated crumbs. Freeze these for 10 minutes, then serve immediately or refrigerate and serve them at your leisure (and yes, you pull away the rings and the parchment before serving). Top with vegan whipped topping.

As an alternate, make a fruit coulis (purée ripe fruit with a small amount of apple or orange juice concentrate; a pint of sweet fruit, such as ripe peaches or strawberries would use about 2 ounces of concentrate). Place several ounces of coulis on a dessert plate, and place the cake round on top.

If you don't have cake rounds (also called "cake ring" or "ring cutters"), you can assemble this in an ice cream dish or carefully do it free form on the plate on which you will serve it (because it will be hard to move). Let your imagination go. Make several layers, use different types of fruit, whip up a "creamy" tofu sauce, use cake crumbs, fruit, whipped topping, and fruit coulis for a super-dessert, etc. When you have 50 or 60 of these presented on a draped table with a flower centerpiece, it makes quite an impression (and doesn't require a master baker).

And Be Merry...

Be certain to include traditional dishes (or vegan adaptations) along with modern options for special occasions. Discuss the menu with your customers or speak with your staff about "how it's always been done." Matzo ball soup, stuffed cabbage, pasta, soda bread, tamales, and cakes of every variety come to mind for different events. A bowl of black-eyed peas or a slice of pound cake might make all the difference! So, do your research and you'll please your guests (and yourself)!

GUEST-IMATIONS

When you have a light reception or hors d'oeuvre party, you have to do a little forecasting to decide on amounts to prepare. Served or "sit-down" events are a little easier to forecast for than buffets, as you are in charge of the portions. If you are doing a buffet or creating catering platters, here are some simple guidelines:

1. Entrées: estimate by pieces (for individual items, such as enchiladas, cabbage rolls, or corn cakes) or portions (for casserole-type dishes). Assume 2 pieces for adults and 1 piece for children or 8 ounces per adult (for casserole-type dishes) and 3 ounces for children. Multiply the number of portions needed and you will have the amount to prepare, as in 45 tamales or 10 pounds of lentil loaf (see appendix A for amounts held in quantity equipment). Some caterers like to prepare 10% over the anticipated number of guests, for "insurance."
2. Side dishes: estimate 4 ounces for adults and 2 ounces for children for most hot side dishes.
3. Salads: for lettuce salads, estimate 8 ounces (that's volume, not weight; the amount of salad that will fill a measuring cup) for adults and 3 ounces for children along with 3 ounces of salad dressing for adults and 1 ounce for children. For solid salads (fruit, potato, pasta, etc.), estimate 5 ounces for adults and 2 ounces for children.
4. Sauces/gravies: depending on your entrées and side dishes, estimate 2 ounces for adults and 1 ounce for children.
5. Fruit or Vegetable trays: estimate 6-8 pieces (cherry tomatoes, radishes, carrot sticks, etc.) for adults and 2-3 pieces per child or 6-7 ounces per adult and 2 ounces per child.
6. Desserts: This is a little harder to standardize; estimate by the slice (rule of thumb is 96 two-inch slices for a whole cake sheet), by the piece (cupcakes, cookies, etc.), or by the ounce (about 5 ounces of sorbet or ice cream is a standard portion).
7. For the amount of coffee to prepare, see Chapter 3.

MENU IDEAS FOR SPECIAL OCCASIONS

Reception for Non-Vegetarian Friends and Family:
- Vegetable tray with assorted dips (hummus, guacamole, etc.)
- Seasonal vegetable soup with mushrooms and seasoned croutons
- Angel hair or penne pasta with marinara (seasoned tomato) and mushroom sauce
- Italian bread seasoned with rosemary
- Spinach sautéed with garlic
- Assorted olives and pickled vegetables
- Assorted sorbets with fresh berries or melon cubes

Light Reception (for early afternoon dining, such as a late morning wedding or communion):
- Sliced and wedged seasonal fruit with soy yogurt dressing
- Crudités (crunchy vegetables) with garlic vinaigrette and Thai peanut dressing
- Mock "paté"
- Assortment of bread sticks with dipping sauces
- Assorted canapés (cold, marinated tofu on French bread rounds, tofu "egg" salad on Melba toast, chopped marinated vegetables on focaccia, etc.)
- Dolmas (grape leaves stuffed with herbed rice)
- Hot tempura veggies (carrots, cauliflower, sweet potatoes, and green beans) with tamari dipping sauce
- Assorted pastries
- Beverages

Hot and Cold Reception:
To the Light Reception above add –
- Hot hors d'oeuvres such as stuffed mushrooms (and stuffed cherry tomatoes if you have the time and the concentration), vegan egg rolls, and spring rolls
- Light entrées such as vegetable stir-fries and pastas (you can have these pre-set in chafing dishes or set up stations, where your customers can watch the items being prepared)
- Specialty items such as tamales (savory made with chilies or sweet made with raisins and pineapple), enchiladas, Asian steamed buns, mini stuffed cabbage, stuffed zucchini blossoms, filled pastas (such as manicotti, ravioli, or tort-ellini), pierogi (pasta stuffed with potato and sauerkraut or with prune filling), knishes (pastry stuffed with potato or kasha), or blintzes (crepes with fruit filling)

Dessert Reception:
- Fruit including sliced melons (honeydew, cantaloupe, Persian, watermelon, muskmelon, casaba, etc.), grape clusters, fruit brochettes (short skewers of strawberries, pineapple wedges, grapes, etc.)
- Baked goods including assorted vegan cookies, gingerbread squares, assorted fruit tarts (purchase individual puff pastry or tart shells and fill with pie filling), cake rounds (see description above), sliced fruit breads (cranberry, carrot, zucchini, blueberry, persimmon, etc.) served with fruit preserves
- Assorted fruit sorbets or soy or rice ice cream, either garnished with fresh fruit or prepared as mini-sundaes (sundaes can be made ahead of time and frozen until ready to use)

ADDITIONAL SPECIAL OCCASION MENU IDEAS

Sit-Down Wedding:
- Champagne reception with trays of fresh strawberries and grapes
- Ratatouille (eggplant stew with tomatoes, garlic, zucchini, and black olives)
- Crepes with savory filling (for example, marinated, sautéed mushrooms)
- Duchesse Potatoes (see recipe on page 100)/Minted green peas
- Assorted fruit trays
- Assorted crudite trays with dips
- Assorted bread baskets
- Raspberry and lemon sorbet plus wedding cake

Jewish Occasion (Bar or Bat Mitzvah, etc.):
- Matzo ball soup
- Stuffed cabbage with sweet and sour sauce
- Potato pancakes with applesauce
- Glazed carrots/Green beans almondine
- Assorted bread basket including rye and pumpernickel rolls
- Baked apples with cinnamon and ginger
- Mellow Plum Tart (see recipe on page 106)

First Communion:
- Wine reception with fruit kebobs, tofu-cheesecake squares, and assorted cookies
- Finger sandwiches
- Fresh veggie tray with dips
- Antipasto (marinated veggies, olives, pickles, pepperoncini, etc.)

RECIPES
Also see recipes in Chapter 6 (Elegant Dining) and Chapter 7 (Holidays).

TOMATO "CREAM" SAUCE

Yield: 25 one-ounce servings

This can be served hot (with veggies or grains) or cold (as a dipping sauce).

INGREDIENTS	MEASURE	METHOD
Sun-dried tomatoes (dry, without oil)	3 pounds	Combine all ingredients in a blender or food processor and blend until smooth. Can be warmed for service or tossed with hot pasta, rice, or vegetables.
Silken tofu	2 pounds	
Garlic, minced	8 cloves	
Fresh basil, chopped	6 ounces	
Olive oil	4 ounces	
White pepper	1/2 ounce	

Note: One to two ounces of water may be added to blender if sauce is too thick.

Total Calories per Serving: 202   Total Fat as % of Daily Value: 11%   Protein: 10 gm   Fat: 7 gm
Carbohydrates: 32 gm   Calcium: 83 mg   Iron: 5 mg   Sodium: 58 mg   Dietary Fiber: 7 gm

MOCK CHOPPED LIVER

Yield: 25 one-ounce servings

This recipe actually improves with age (up to 2 days). Make ahead of time and refrigerate until serving. For the bakers in the audience, make a vegan paté en croute by encasing the mock liver in pastry dough and baking until golden (the classic French way to serve paté).

INGREDIENTS	MEASURE	METHOD
Lentils, cooked	3-1/4 pounds	Place lentils, 12 ounces onions, and
Onions, chopped	12 ounces	walnuts in a food processor and
Walnuts, chopped	1 pound	process until smooth and well-
Vegetable oil spray	to cover pan	combined. Heat sauté pan, spray
Onions, chopped	1 pound	with oil, and sauté 1 pound onions
Peanut butter	4 ounces	until very soft. Mix lentils, sautéed
White pepper	1/2 ounce	onions, peanut butter, and pepper
Black pepper	1/2 ounce	until well-combined. Refrigerate for
		at least 2 hours before serving.

Total Calories per Serving: 218   Total Fat as % of Daily Value: 20%   Protein: 11 gm   Fat: 13 gm
Carbohydrates: 18 gm   Calcium: 29 mg   Iron: 3 mg   Sodium: 24 mg   Dietary Fiber: 4 gm

WATERMELON GAZPACHO

Yield: 25 two-ounce servings

This recipe is "fire and ice," spicy hot yet cool at the same time.

INGREDIENTS	MEASURE	METHOD
Watermelon, seeded	12 pounds	Purée (in blender or food processor)
Fresh lime juice	2 ounces	melon (without rind) until smooth.
Fresh chili, chopped	2 each	Pour into a large bowl. Return 8
Garlic, minced	4 cloves	ounces of purée to blender and add
Fresh mint, minced	2 ounces	lime juice, chili, and garlic. Blend
Zucchini, diced	1-1/2 pounds	until smooth. Add to large bowl and
Bell pepper	1 pound	mix. Slowly add mint, zucchini, and
		pepper, and mix to combine. Serve
		chilled.

Total Calories per Serving: 82   Total Fat as % of Daily Value: 2%   Protein: 2 gm   Fat: 1 gm
Carbohydrates: 18 gm   Calcium: 30 mg   Iron: 1 mg   Sodium: 6 mg   Dietary Fiber: 2 gm

SPICY BEAN CAKES WITH FRUIT SALSA

Yield: 25 servings of 2 cakes each

These elegant cakes can be made with black or white beans and can be served as an entrée or a side dish. Vary the ingredients in the salsa to match the seasons.

INGREDIENTS	MEASURE	METHOD
Bean cakes:		
Dried black beans, soaked overnight	2-3/4 pounds	Drain and rinse beans. Bring 2 gallons of water to boil. Add beans, lower heat, and simmer until tender (about 40 minutes). Drain beans and cool. Place beans in a large mixing bowl. Add onions, chili, and garlic and toss. Mash beans into a lumpy paste and form into 3-ounce balls.
Onion, chopped	9 ounces	
Jalapeño chili, chopped	3 ounces	
Garlic, minced	4 cloves	
		Flatten, place on a floured baking sheet, and bake at 350 degrees for 10 minutes or until slightly crisp (may have to turn once).
Fruit salsa:		
Vinegar	7 ounces	Combine remaining ingredients in a large bowl and allow to chill for 30 minutes. Serve hot bean cakes garnished with cold salsa.
Lime juice	4 ounces	
Cracked black pepper	1/2 ounce	
Jicama, peeled and chopped	3 pounds	
Fresh strawberries, chopped	1 pound	
Ripe avocado, mashed	3/4 pound	
Fresh green onions, chopped	4 ounces	
Fresh cilantro, chopped	3 ounces	

Note: The bean cakes can be fried in a deep fat fryer or sautéed briefly and then heated in the oven for a different texture (and faster cooking). Different types of beans can be used for variety. For a buffet, place cakes in a chafing dish with the salsa set in a chilled bowl. For table service, line a dinner plate with leaf lettuce then place 2 cakes on the lettuce and garnish with salsa.

Total Calories per Serving: 228   Total Fat as % of Daily Value: 5%   Protein: 12 gm   Fat: 3 gm
Carbohydrates: 41 gm   Calcium: 83 mg   Iron: 3 mg   Sodium: 8 mg   Dietary Fiber: 11 gm

ROASTED SUMMER SQUASH WITH PEPPERS

Yield: 25 two-ounce servings

This recipe is colorful and a welcome addition to a banquet plate or a buffet table.

INGREDIENTS	MEASURE	METHOD
Red bell pepper	7 each	Arrange peppers on a baking sheet. Place peppers under broiler and char until skins are blistered evenly. Remove from heat, let cool, peel, and remove seeds. Spray baking sheets. Spread zucchini and squash on sheets in single layer. Spray with oil and roast at 400 degrees until soft. Let cool. In a small bowl, mix oil, vinegar, olives, and basil. Cut peppers into strips. Place peppers, zucchini, and squash into a large mixing bowl. Add oil mixture and toss lightly. Can be served slightly warm or chilled.
Vegetable oil spray	to cover pan	
Zucchini, cut lengthwise	12 pounds	
Yellow squash, cut lengthwise	7 pounds	
Olive oil	6 ounces	
Vinegar	5 ounces	
Black olives, chopped	5 ounces	
Fresh basil, chopped	2 ounces	

Notes: For the stout of heart, peppers may be charred directly in the stove flame by placing them on a long-handled fork and turning until charred. To make peeling easy, place hot peppers in a plastic bag and refrigerate. When cool, peel will come off easily. This salad can be extended with cooked pasta, such as orzo or rotini, or with steamed, cooled potatoes.

Total Calories per Serving: 121   Total Fat as % of Daily Value: 12%   Protein: 4 gm   Fat: 8 gm
Carbohydrates: 12 gm   Calcium: 63 mg   Iron: 2 mg   Sodium: 47 mg   Dietary Fiber: 4 gm

STUFFED KISHKA

Yield: about 25 slices

Stuffed kishka, also called "derma," was the kosher answer to sausage filling; now we've made it vegan! Roll this dish, cook it, and freeze until ready to use.

INGREDIENTS	MEASURE	METHOD
Carrots, sliced	2 pounds	Place carrots, celery, and onions in a food processor and process until smooth, as in a dough. Add pepper and garlic and mix. Add crackers and margarine and blend until smooth. Shape into "logs" 1-inch in diameter. Wrap tightly in foil and place on sprayed baking sheet and bake in 400 degree oven for 35 minutes. Allow to cool on rack before removing foil. Slice and serve.
Celery, chopped	1/2 pound	
Onions, chopped	1/2 pound	
Black pepper	1/2 ounce	
Granulated garlic	1/2 ounce	
Ritz or matzo crackers	1 pound	
Margarine	2 ounces	
Vegetable oil spray	to cover sheet	

Note: If kishka dough is too dry, add 1 or 2 more ounces of margarine.

Total Calories per Slice: 135   Total Fat as % of Daily Value: 11%   Protein: 2 gm   Fat: 7 gm
Carbohydrates: 16 gm   Calcium: 43 mg   Iron: 1 mg   Sodium: 221 mg   Dietary Fiber: 2 gm

BAKED SWEET ONIONS WITH PEPPER STUFFING

Yield: 25 servings

Serve this recipe as an entrée; use different colored peppers for variety. This recipe can be prepared a day in advanced and stored covered in the refrigerator (uncooked). Please note that this dish is high in fat and should only be eaten occasionally. Those on a restricted lowfat diet might want to avoid this dish.

INGREDIENTS	MEASURE	METHOD
Small sweet onions*	25 each	Preheat oven to 350 degrees. Have a clean rack ready. Peel onions, cut off just enough of the bottom of each onion so it will sit straight. Cut off large slice from tops of onions and save. Scoop out interior of onions until a one-inch shell remains. Save interior and mince.
Margarine	1-1/2 pounds	
Red bell pepper, chopped	3 pounds	
Green bell pepper, chopped	1 pound	Melt margarine in a sauté pan, add pepper and garlic, and sauté until soft. Remove from heat. Add bread crumbs, herbs, and stock and stir until combined.
Garlic, minced	10 cloves	
Fresh bread crumbs	3 pounds	
Dried thyme**	1-1/2 ounces	
Dried marjoram	1 ounce	Fill each onion with about 1 ounce of mixture. Replace top, place on baking sheet, put on rack in 350 degree oven, and bake for 40 minutes or until slightly browned.
Dried sage	1 ounce	
Dried basil	1/2 ounce	
Vegetable stock	1 quart	

*Note: Vidalia or Maui onions are common sweet varieties, and any small, white onion can be used (this requires an onion with a high water content or it will be dry).

**Note: Instead of the listed herbs, an herb de provence mixture may be used for the equivalent amounts.

Total Calories per Serving: 400   Total Fat as % of Daily Value: 38%   Protein: 7 gm   Fat: 25 gm
Carbohydrates: 40 gm   Calcium: 162 mg   Iron: 6 mg   Sodium: 589 mg   Dietary Fiber: 3 gm

EGGPLANT AND PENNE

Yield: 25 three-ounce servings

This recipe is simple and elegant; use different pasta shapes for variety.

INGREDIENTS	MEASURE	METHOD
Eggplant, peeled*	8 pounds	Slice eggplant and place in colander.
Salt	2 ounces	Toss with salt and allow to rest for 20 minutes.
Hoisin sauce**	10 ounces	Mix hoisin, lemon juice, and water in
Lemon juice	6 ounces	a small bowl. Set aside.
Water	6 ounces	Heat oil and sesame seeds in a sauté
Vegetable oil	3 ounces	pan. Add garlic and sauté until soft.
Sesame seeds	1 ounce	Squeeze liquid from eggplant and
Garlic, minced	15 cloves	discard. Add to garlic and sauté for 5
Cooked penne	5 pounds	minutes. Lower heat, add hoisin mixture and toss to combine. Cover and allow to cook for 10 minutes or until eggplant is tender. Remove from heat and toss with penne. Serve hot.

*Note: Salting eggplant removes some of the extra liquid from the eggplant. If you prefer not to add salt, simply allow more cooking time for the eggplant (to remove liquid by cooking).

**Note: If hoisin sauce is not available, the equivalent amount of soy sauce may be used.

Total Calories per Serving: 232   Total Fat as % of Daily Value: 8%   Protein: 7 gm   Fat: 5 gm
Carbohydrates: 41 gm   Calcium: 28 mg   Iron: 2 mg   Sodium: 130 mg   Dietary Fiber: 2 gm

TOMATOES WITH GRAIN STUFFING

Yield: 25 servings

This recipe can be made a day ahead of time and refrigerated until needed. If amaranth is not available, use brown rice, quinoa, or even cooked lentils.

INGREDIENTS	MEASURE	METHOD
Ripe tomatoes, small	25 each	Slice 1-inch top from each tomato.
Vegetable oil spray	to cover pan	Scoop out. Discard tops and pulp (or
Onions, minced	3 pounds	use in stocks). Heat sauté pan and
Garlic, minced	1 pound	spray with oil. Sauté onions, garlic,
Celery, minced	1/2 pound	and celery. Set aside.
Vegetable stock	2 quarts	In a stock pot, bring stock to a boil.
Amaranth*	4 pounds	Add amaranth and veggies. Lower heat, cover, and allow to simmer for 20 minutes or until amaranth is soft and all liquid is absorbed.
Fresh parsley, chopped	12 ounces	Remove from heat, stir in parsley,
Salsa	1 pint	salsa, raisins, and nuts.
Raisins, chopped	8 ounces	Preheat oven to 325 degrees.
Pine nuts	8 ounces	Stuff each tomato with approximately 1-1/2 ounces of stuffing. Bake at 325 degrees for 25 minutes (or until tomatoes are soft but still holding their shape).

*Note: Any grain, such as rice, barley, or quinoa can be used instead of amaranth. If using amaranth, expect the mixture to appear saucy. The cooked amaranth releases a starch which, when combined with liquid, makes a creamy-looking sauce.

Total Calories per Serving: 429   Total Fat as % of Daily Value: 15%   Protein: 16 gm   Fat: 10 gm
Carbohydrates: 74 gm   Calcium: 193 mg   Iron: 8 mg   Sodium: 182 mg   Dietary Fiber: 4 gm

CURRIED VEGETABLES WITH POLENTA

Yield: 25 three-ounce servings

Add a Mediterranean flair to your special meal with this combination of flavorful vegetables and creamy polenta.

INGREDIENTS	MEASURE	METHOD
Sauce:		
Canned coconut milk	18 ounces	In a medium bowl, mix together coconut milk, curry powder, and turmeric. Set aside.
Curry powder	2 ounces	
Ground turmeric	1 ounce	
Veggies:		
Vegetable oil spray	to cover pan	In a sauté pan, spray oil and sauté carrots and celery until soft. Add broccoli, cauliflower, and peppers, and sauté until soft. Reduce heat, add stock, cover, and simmer until very tender. Stir sauce into veggies, simmer for 10 minutes, and set aside.
Carrots, sliced thin	20 ounces	
Celery, sliced thin	14 ounces	
Broccoli florets	14 ounces	
Cauliflower florets	10 ounces	
Bell peppers, chopped	8 ounces	
Vegetable stock	12 ounces	
Polenta:		
Vegetable stock	1 quart	In a stock pot, bring 1 quart stock to boil. Reduce heat, slowly add cornmeal, stirring constantly. Stir for about 5 minutes or until polenta is soupy. Stir in margarine and garlic, simmer, and stir for about 15 minutes or until polenta is thick. Pour into 2-inch deep steam table pan. Let cool. Refrigerate for 2-3 hours, until set. To assemble, spray steam table pans with oil. Cut polenta into large squares and place half on the bottom of the pans. Cover with veggies and top with remaining polenta. Bake at 350 degrees for 15 minutes or until veggies are hot.
Cornmeal	1 pound	
Margarine	4 ounces	
Garlic, minced	3 cloves	

Total Calories per Serving: 174   Total Fat as % of Daily Value: 14%   Protein: 4 gm   Fat: 9 gm
Carbohydrates: 22 gm   Calcium: 44 mg   Iron: 3 mg   Sodium: 85 mg   Dietary Fiber: 3 gm

JUST LIKE GRANDMA'S STUFFED CABBAGE

Yield: 25 cabbage rolls

This is a traditional, sweet-and-sour cabbage recipe. It can be made two days ahead of time (cooked) and reheated when needed.

INGREDIENTS	MEASURE	METHOD
Sauce:		
Canned tomato purée	3-1/2 pounds	Combine all sauce ingredients in a stock pot. Stir and simmer for 30 minutes or until flavors are combined.
Cold water	1 pint	
Apple juice concentrate	7 ounces	
Apple, peeled and diced	4 ounces	
White pepper	1/2 ounce	
Garlic powder	1/2 ounce	Preheat oven to 325 degrees.
Filling:		Steam cabbage leaves 3 minutes.
Green cabbage leaves	25 each	Heat sauté pan, spray with oil, and
Vegetable oil spray	to cover pan	cook carrots, bell pepper, celery,
Carrots, chopped	12 ounces	and mushrooms until browned.
Bell pepper, chopped	6 ounces	Stir into rice and pepper.
Celery, chopped	5 ounces	Place 1 Tablespoonful of filling in the
Fresh mushrooms, chopped	10 ounces	center of each cabbage leaf and roll. Pour half of the sauce in a steam
Rice, cooked	2-3/4 pounds	table pan. Place rolls in sauce and
Black pepper	1 ounce	top with shredded cabbage, raisins,
Raw cabbage, shredded	1 pound	and ginger. Cover with remainder of
Raisins	7 ounces	sauce. Bake, covered, at 325 degrees
Ground ginger	1 ounce	for 1 hour.

Total Calories per Cabbage Roll: 144   Total Fat as % of Daily Value: 2%   Protein: 3 gm
Fat: 1 gm   Carbohydrates: 33 gm   Calcium: 47 mg   Iron: 1 mg   Sodium: 33 mg
Dietary Fiber: 4 gm

VERY BERRY TARTS

Yield: 25 servings

Use a variety of fruit to create a dessert spectacular.

INGREDIENTS	MEASURE	METHOD
Tart shells:		
Flour	2 pounds	Using an electric mixer (or food processor), combine flour and margarine until coarsely mixed. Slowly add water, mixing, until dough forms a ball. Roll onto a floured board; line either three 9-inch tart shells or 25 individual tart shells. Bake at 350 degrees for 10 minutes or until golden brown.
Cold margarine	9 ounces	
Cold water	as needed	
Filling:		
Firm silken tofu	3 pounds	In a colander, place tofu between cheesecloth or a paper coffee filter; weigh down with several dinner plates or pot lids. Allow to press for at least 3 hours.
Vanilla extract	1/2 ounce	Combine drained tofu, extract, sweetener, and zest in a blender and process until smooth. Pour into cooled tart shells. Bake at 350 degrees for about 25 minutes or until tofu is set.
Granulated sweetener	12 ounces	
Orange zest	1 ounce	
Fresh berries*	3 pounds	Allow to cool. Top tarts with berries and brush with glaze. Chill for 1 hour before serving.
Apricot glaze**	1 pound	

*Note: Frozen berries, thawed, may be used in place of fresh berries.

**Note: If apricot glaze is not available, purée fruit preserves, such as strawberry, raspberry, or orange marmalade.

Total Calories per Serving (using blueberries): 373   Total Fat as % of Daily Value: 15%
Protein: 8 gm   Fat: 10 gm   Carbohydrates: 63 gm   Calcium: 31 mg   Iron: 2 mg
Sodium: 134 mg   Dietary Fiber: 3 gm

SOPHISTICATED POACHED PEARS

Yield: 25 pears

Serve this elegant dessert in a brandy snifter or on your best china to show off its shape and color.

INGREDIENTS	MEASURE	METHOD
Red dessert wine*	20 ounces	In a braising pan, combine wine, jam, juice, zests, cinnamon, cloves, and ginger. Simmer. Place pears in poaching liquid and simmer until pears are soft, about 20 minutes. Remove pears and allow to cool. Strain poaching liquid. Can be used as a hot sauce by returning to heat and allowing to reduce until thickened. Can be used as a cold garnish by freezing strained liquid, removing from freezer, and chopping, as a pear "ice."
Strawberry jam**	8 ounces	
Orange juice	4 ounces	
Orange zest	1 ounce	
Lemon zest	1/2 ounce	
Cinnamon sticks	2 each	
Whole cloves	5 each	
Ground ginger	1 ounce	
Pears, fresh (5 ounce)	25 each	

*Note: Port, red Zinfandel, and Muscadet are good wines to use.

**Note: If strawberry jam is not available, apricot glaze, or mixed berry or apple jam may be used.

Total Calories per Pear with Sauce: 147   Total Fat as % of Daily Value: 2%   Protein: 1 gm
Fat: 1 gm   Carbohydrates: 31 gm   Calcium: 20 mg   Iron: 1 mg   Sodium: 3 mg
Dietary Fiber: 4 gm

Chapter Nine

BIG MENU ON CAMPUS – COOKING FOR COLLEGE STUDENTS

Let's move on to college students. Today's college students are more mobile, more intense, and more informed. Menu choices are very serious to them.

Many colleges and universities have successfully incorporated vegan and vegetarian offerings into their meal plans. To network with some of these schools, you may want to contact NACUFS (National Association of College and University Food Services – see Appendix C). The Vegetarian Resource Group also has a list of colleges offering vegetarian and/or vegan options, which you can obtain by sending a self-addressed stamped envelope to VRG, PO Box 1463, Baltimore, MD 21203.

Use your students as a living database for creating or updating vegan menus. School food service directors tell us that they have organized vegan clubs (or are involved in already existing clubs). The members participate in food tastings, menu reviews, and recipe suggestions.

Once you have your vegan menu items in place, be sure that your staff is able to offer information about the items. Here are some of the questions food service directors tell us are most frequently asked:

1. What's in this?
2. What is tofu (or TVP, or seitan or tempeh)?
3. Is this vegetarian or vegan?
4. How was this prepared (i.e., what type of oil was used, which seasonings)?
5. Was this made from scratch or was it purchased (if purchased, can I see the label)?
6. Does this contain any honey or white sugar?
7. Is the soy milk enriched? With what?
8. Is this tofu made with calcium or nigari? What kind of sweetener is it made with?

We can guarantee that you will get questions about vegan menus from both veggie and non-veggie students. Be prepared to be informational! If you serve your students, be sure you have given your staff the background to answer questions about ingredients. If you are self-service, be sure that vegan items are distinctly marked and that, if asked, your staff has all the answers about the items. And, as an aside, educate your staff as to the items that are not specifically vegan but are acceptable to vegan students. For example, are some of your prepared bakery items (crackers, bread, etc.) vegan? Do you steam your vegetables, rice, and pasta without butter or meat stock, etc?

Be aware that you're going to go beyond preparing vegan items for your students. Provide separate serving utensils for vegan items (as you should do for every item, to eliminate cross-contamination). Place vegan items so non-vegan items can't mix with them (for example, think about the placement of vegan and non-vegan salad dressings on the salad bar, pans of vegan and non-vegan pasta on the steam table, etc.). Be careful about the names you assign to vegan items. Just as "mystery meat" is not going to appeal to a carnivore student, "fake meat casserole" (yes, we've seen it!) isn't going to appeal to vegan students.

One of the colleges we spoke to had just implemented a vegan "wrap" bar. A salad bar was set up with a variety of chopped and sliced veggies, dressings, chutneys and salsas, shredded greens (some raw, some steamed), several flavors of steamed and fried tofu strips, cooked beans, steamed and fried rice, several sauces (such as Thai peanut sauce), and canned and marinated veggies. The wraps were regular and over-sized vegan flour, corn, and whole wheat tortillas. Vegan and non-vegan students frequented this station more than any other.

We've always liked the idea of a potato bar. Potatoes are popular with just about everyone, are simple to prepare, and inexpensive. If there are any leftovers (but don't count on it), they are easy to utilize in soups, salads, side dishes, and casseroles. Go beyond the traditional baked potato bar (with chopped fresh veggies, salsas, chopped fresh herbs, flavored tofu or seitan, various types of cooked beans, etc.) and offer a mashed potato bar. Prepare plain and flavored mashed potatoes (we like garlic, rosemary, and horseradish) with the same toppings as the baked potato bar. For a change of pace, offer mashed sweet potatoes (flavored with orange or lemon zest, vanilla extract, cinnamon, and ginger).

Other approaches are to dedicate one serving line to vegan items, to establish a vegan dining room (with its own salad bar, grill, serving lines, etc.), and to incorporate vegan items into the standard menu (which made vegan foods an integral part of every student's dining experience).

Another idea might be to have a "grain bar." In several Aramark (a food service contract company) university accounts, a concept called "the Granary" offers vegetable sautés served over rice, quinoa, wheat berries, and barley, garnished with seasoned croutons. To-go items are served as wraps (flatbread is used for the wrap). Expand this idea with other grains such as amaranth and kasha, and offer some cold grains such as chilled couscous tossed with fresh fruit (think berries and mint) or chopped dried fruit. Toppings could include veggie chili or seasoned soy crumbles.

Vegan students should not have to subsist on the traditional vegan items: peanut butter, French fries or baked potatoes, tossed salad, fresh fruit, cold cereal, and black coffee.

RECIPES

See recipes in Chapter 6 (Elegant Dining), Chapter 5 (Kids Menus), Chapter 7 (Holidays), Chapter 8 (Occasions), and Chapter 10 (Fast food) for additional ideas.

DOWN HOME RED BEANS AND RICE SALAD

Yield: 25 two-ounce servings

Serve this salad with vegetable soup and muffins and you have a complete and colorful meal.

INGREDIENTS	MEASURE	METHOD
Dressing:		
Vinegar	1 pint	In a large bowl, combine all dressing
Oil	12 ounces	ingredients. Set aside.
Garlic, minced	5 cloves	
Dried tarragon	1 ounce	
Black pepper	1/2 ounce	
Tomatoes, diced	8 ounces	
Celery, diced	6 ounces	
Cucumbers, peeled and diced	6 ounces	
Garlic Pickles, diced	4 ounces	
Salad:		
Cooked brown rice	2-1/2 pounds	Toss salad ingredients until com-
Cooked red beans*	1-1/2 pounds	bined. Mix with dressing, cover, and
Bell pepper, chopped	12 ounces	refrigerate until ready to serve.
Green onions, chopped	10 ounces	

*Note: Use either cooked or canned red or kidney beans in the salad.

Total Calories per Serving: 200   Total Fat as % of Daily Value: 21%   Protein: 3 gm   Fat: 14 gm
Carbohydrates: 19 gm   Calcium: 26 mg   Iron: 1 mg   Sodium: 163 mg   Dietary Fiber: 3 gm

RED LENTIL SOUP WITH MANGO RAITA

Yield: 25 three-ounce servings

This soup is hearty enough to be an entrée!

INGREDIENTS	MEASURE	METHOD
Soup:		
Red lentils, rinsed	2 pounds	In a stock pot combine lentils,
Onions, chopped	1/2 pound	onions, bay leaves, spices and stock;
Bay leaves	8 each	bring to a boil. Lower heat and
Cumin, ground	1 ounce	simmer until lentils are tender (about
Tumeric, ground	1/2 ounce	40 minutes). Remove bay leaves.
Coriander, ground	1/2 ounce	Purée soup with a blender or Burr
Vegetable stock	3 quarts	mixer. Return to the pot and simmer
Raita:		for 10 minutes. Add water or stock if
Vegan soy sour cream	1 pint	too thick. Combine raita ingredients
Cucumber, chopped	1/2 pound	in a large bowl and refrigerate for at
Mango purée or	4 ounces	least 30 minutes. Top hot soup with
chopped mango		cold raita before serving.
Fresh cilantro, chopped	1 ounce	

Total Calories per Serving: 156   Total Fat as % of Daily Value: 3%   Protein: 8 gm   Fat: 2 gm
Carbohydrates: 26 gm   Calcium: 115 mg   Iron: 3 mg   Sodium: 26 mg   Dietary Fiber: 2 gm

VEGAN VICHYSSOISE (COLD POTATO CUCUMBER SOUP)

Yield: 25 three-ounce servings

Try this soup to chase away "spring fever" on campus.

INGREDIENTS	MEASURE	METHOD
Vegetable oil spray	to cover pot	Heat oil spray in a large stock pot. Sweat garlic and onions. Add potatoes and 8 ounces water. Stir once, lower heat, cover, and allow potatoes to steam until tender (approximately 15 minutes). Place tomatoes, pepper, and cucumbers in a food processor and chop fine. Add veggies to cooked potatoes. Stir and add juice and dill. Stir to combine and cook for an additional 10 minutes. Serve chilled or hot.
Garlic, minced	6 cloves	
Onions, chopped	1 pound	
Baking potatoes, peeled and diced	4 pounds	
Fresh tomatoes	1 pound	
Bell pepper	1/2 pound	
Cucumber, peeled	1/2 pound	
Tomato juice	1 quart	
Fresh dill, chopped	4 ounces	

Total Calories per Serving: 82   Total Fat as % of Daily Value: <1%   Protein: 3 gm   Fat: <1 gm
Carbohydrates: 19 gm   Calcium: 26 mg   Iron: 1 mg   Sodium: 150 mg   Dietary Fiber: 2 gm

SAVOR THE FLAVOR BLACK-EYED PEAS

Yield: 25 three-ounce servings

This can be served on its own as a side dish, or served over brown rice or corn bread as an entrée.

INGREDIENTS	MEASURE	METHOD
Canned black-eyed peas, drained*	3 pounds	In a large bowl, mix peas, onions, pepper, and chili. Set aside. In a small stock pot, combine vinegar, concentrate, and mustard. Bring to a boil, stirring, until ingredients are well combined. Pour hot mixture over peas and mix. Refrigerate for at least 1 hour before serving.
Onions, chopped	1 pound	
Bell pepper, chopped	10 ounces	
Fresh chili, chopped	3 ounces	
Vinegar	1 pint	
Apple juice concentrate	8 ounces	
Prepared mustard	2 ounces	

*Note: Frozen or dried black-eyed peas, cooked, may be used if preferred or if canned peas are not available.

Total Calories per Serving: 100   Total Fat as % of Daily Value: <1%   Protein: 5 gm   Fat: <1 gm
Carbohydrates: 21 gm   Calcium: 23 mg   Iron: 2 mg   Sodium: 35 mg   Dietary Fiber: 4 gm

GREEN AND RED STUFFED TOMATOES

Yield: 25 servings

Vary the veggies in this stuffing for different flavors; broccoli florets, chopped kale, and chopped green cabbage can be mixed with the spinach or used in place of it.

INGREDIENTS	MEASURE	METHOD
Frozen chopped spinach, cooked	8 pounds	Place spinach in a colander to drain as dry as possible.
Fresh tomatoes	25 each	Slice 2-inch thick tops off tomatoes
Vegetable oil spray	to cover pan	and discard. Scoop out centers (dis-
Onions, chopped	1-1/2 pounds	card pulp or use in stock or soup).
Garlic, minced	5 cloves	Heat sauté pan and spray with oil.
Bread crumbs, dry	1-1/2 pounds	Sauté onions and garlic. Place in
Vegan mayonnaise	10 ounces	a large mixing bowl. Add bread
Dried basil	1 ounce	crumbs, vegan mayonnaise, and
		basil. Mix to combine. Add spinach
		and mix well. Stuff tomatoes with
		spinach mixture. Put on baking sheet
		and bake at 400 degrees for 15
		minutes. Serve hot.

Notes: If vegan mayonnaise is not available, soft tofu may be used (you may want to add a small amount of vinegar or prepared mustard for extra flavor). If vegan soy cheese is available, sprinkle about 2 teaspoons on each tomato before baking. Select small tomatoes (commercial pack; 6x7, 3 layer) so filling amount is adequate.

Total Calories per Serving: 214   Total Fat as % of Daily Value: 8%   Protein: 9 gm   Fat: 5 gm
Carbohydrates: 36 gm   Calcium: 286 mg   Iron: 4 mg   Sodium: 455 mg   Dietary Fiber: 5 gm

VEGETABLE TAGINE

Yield: 25 three-ounce servings

Tagines are flavorful stews, which make the most of seasonal vegetables. This recipe has a Moroccan influence and can be made a day ahead of time.

INGREDIENTS	MEASURE	METHOD
Vegetable oil spray	to cover pan	Heat sauté pan, spray with oil, and sauté onions, garlic, and ginger until soft. Add celery and cinnamon. Sauté for 2 minutes. Place in a stock pot. Add coriander, cumin, and pepper, and cook over low heat for 2 minutes.
Onions, chopped	12 ounces	
Garlic, diced	6 cloves	
Fresh ginger, minced	2 ounces	
Celery, diced	6 ounces	
Cinnamon	2 ounces	
Coriander	2 ounces	
Cumin	2 ounces	
Ground black pepper	1 ounce	Add tomatoes, carrots, green beans, squash, green onions, and cauliflower. Add enough stock to cover veggies and allow to cook for 5 minutes. Stir in saffron. Place in a deep steam table pan, cover, and bake for 40 minutes at 350 degrees or until veggies are tender.
Canned tomatoes, diced	6 pounds	
Frozen carrots, thawed	3 pounds	
Frozen green beans, thawed (optional)	3 pounds	
Fresh zucchini, sliced	4 pounds	
Fresh green onions, chopped	1 pound	
Frozen cauliflower, florets	3 pounds	
Vegetable stock	about 3 quarts	
Saffron (optional)	1/2 ounce	
Canned garbanzo beans, drained	1 pound	Stir in garbanzos, olives, and raisins, and bake for 20 minutes at 325 degrees. Alternately, simmer on very low flame on a stove top for 35 minutes. Serve hot.
Black olives, sliced and drained	1/4 pound	
Raisins	1/4 pound	

Note: Tagine can be served on its own or over couscous. The finished tagine should be relatively dry, not soupy. Don't overcook or veggies will become soggy. Use fresh tomatoes when available, different summer squashes, cut corn, or wax beans as optional ingredients.

Total Calories per Serving: 121   Total Fat as % of Daily Value: 3%   Protein: 5 gm   Fat: 2 gm
Carbohydrates: 24 gm   Calcium: 112 mg   Iron: 2 mg   Sodium: 494 mg   Dietary Fiber: 3 gm

TWO ALARM FOUR BEAN CHILI

Yield: 25 three-ounce servings

A perennial favorite!

INGREDIENTS	MEASURE	METHOD
Vegetable oil spray	to cover pot	Heat a large stock pot and spray with oil. Add red pepper flakes, cumin, and black pepper. Sauté for 1 minute.
Red pepper flakes	2 ounces	
Ground cumin	1 ounce	
Cracked black pepper	1 ounce	
Bell pepper, chopped	1 pound	Add bell pepper, chili, and chili powder. Cook for 5 minutes or until pepper is soft.
Fresh chili, chopped	4 ounces	
Chili powder	4 ounces	
Canned tomatoes, chopped	1 pound	Add tomatoes and beans. Allow to simmer, covered, for 30 minutes or until flavors are well combined.
Cooked white beans, rinsed	3 pounds	
Cooked black beans, rinsed	2 pounds	
Cooked pinto beans, rinsed	1 pound	
Cooked kidney beans, rinsed	1 pound	
Fresh cilantro, chopped	6 ounces	Before serving, stir in cilantro.

Total Calories per Serving: 205   Total Fat as % of Daily Value: 3%   Protein: 13 gm   Fat: 2 gm
Carbohydrates: 37 gm   Calcium: 105 mg   Iron: 5 mg   Sodium: 113 mg   Dietary Fiber: 8 gm

SWEET AND SAVORY LENTIL PILAF

Yield: 25 three-ounce servings

This delicate yet substantial dish can be prepared ahead of time and frozen.

INGREDIENTS	MEASURE	METHOD
Apple juice	8 ounces	In a medium stock pot, bring juice to
Garlic, minced	6 cloves	a boil. Add garlic, onions, carrots,
Onions, chopped	12 ounces	rice, and lentils. Cook and stir for 2
Carrots, chopped	14 ounces	minutes. Add beans and spices, stir
Jasmine rice, raw	1-1/2 pounds	to combine. Add stock, bring to a
Lentils, rinsed	14 ounces	boil, lower heat, cover, and simmer
Canned white beans, drained	14 ounces	until rice is tender (about 15 minutes). Remove bay leaf.
Bay leaf	3 each	Serve hot.
Curry powder	1 ounce	
Ground cumin	1/2 ounce	
Red pepper flakes	1/2 ounce	
Black pepper	1/2 ounce	
Mushroom stock*	1-1/2 quarts	

*Note: See Mushroom Stock recipe on page 93.

Total Calories per Serving: 194   Total Fat as % of Daily Value: <1%   Protein: 7 gm   Fat: <1 gm
Carbohydrates: 40 gm   Calcium: 50 mg   Iron: 4 mg   Sodium: 15 mg   Dietary Fiber: 3 gm

JUMPIN' VEGGIE JAMBALAYA

Yield: 25 three-ounce servings

Make this as "hot" as your customers like it!

INGREDIENTS	MEASURE	METHOD
Vegetable oil spray	to cover pot	Heat a stock pot and spray with oil. Cook onions, celery, carrots, garlic, and peppers until soft (about 5 minutes), stirring. Add tomatoes, purée, file, parsley, and hot sauce. Stir for 5 minutes, reduce heat, and simmer 15 minutes (water or vegetable stock can be added if too thick).
Onions, chopped	2 pounds	
Celery, chopped	1 pound	
Carrots, minced	1/2 pound	
Garlic, minced	10 cloves	
Bell peppers	1/2 pound	
Canned tomatoes, drained and chopped	6 pounds	
Tomato purée	5 ounces	
File powder	2 ounces	
Fresh parsley, chopped	2 ounces	
Hot sauce	1/2 ounce	In a small stock pot or steamer, steam tempeh for 5 minutes. Cut into 1-inch cubes, allow to cool. Heat a sauté pan, spray with oil, and quickly sauté tempeh and sausage to brown. Add tempeh and soy sausage to jambalaya, stir, and cook for 5 minutes. Serve warm.
Tempeh	2 pounds	
Soy sausage, cut	3 pounds	

Total Calories per Serving: 265   Total Fat as % of Daily Value: 12%   Protein: 18 gm   Fat: 8 gm
Carbohydrates: 28 gm   Calcium: 171 mg   Iron: 4 mg   Sodium: 267 mg   Dietary Fiber: 2 gm

RICH AND SWEET FRUIT STEW

Yield: 25 one-and-a-half-ounce servings

Use this as a warm or cold side dish at all meals, as it mixes well with cereal or tops toast and complements sweet potatoes and cooked grains. Can also serve as a dessert on its own or served with cake or ice cream.

INGREDIENTS	MEASURE	METHOD
Dried fruit mixture*	2 pounds	Combine all ingredients in a stock pot. Just cover with water and cook, covered, on low heat until water is absorbed and fruit is soft (more water or apple juice can be added if needed). Serve hot or chilled.
Carrots, grated	8 ounces	
Apples, peeled and diced	8 ounces	
Ground ginger	1/2 ounce	
Ground cinnamon	1/2 ounce	
Lemon zest	1 ounce	
Apple juice concentrate	3 ounces	

*Note: Use any combination of dried fruit except dates. Here are some combinations we like: apricots, prunes, raisins, and dried apples; or dried peaches, apricots, and cranberries; or apricots, dried cherries, dried raisins, and dried pears.

Total Calories per Serving (using apricots, prunes, raisins, and apples): 107
Total Fat as % of Daily Value: <1%   Protein: 1 gm   Fat: <1 gm
Carbohydrates: 28 gm   Calcium: 18 mg   Iron: 1 mg   Sodium: 14 mg   Dietary Fiber: 3 gm

GOOEY, CHEWY PEANUT BUTTER BARS

Yield: approximately 50 balls (serve 2 each)

No cooking is involved in this recipe. You won't be able to keep these in stock!

INGREDIENTS	MEASURE	METHOD
Peanut butter*	1-1/2 pounds	Place peanut butter in a mixing bowl.
Cold cereal, ground**	9 ounces	Add cereal, wheat germ, maple
Wheat germ	2 ounces	syrup, raisins, and chopped nuts.
Maple syrup	3 ounces	Combine until stiff (but not dry).
Raisins	5 ounces	Mixture can be rolled into balls (1/2-
Chopped nuts	4 ounces	ounce each) with the seeds pressed
Toasted sesame seeds	8 ounces	into a sheet pan and topped with the
		seeds. Refrigerate for at least 1 hour
		before serving.

*Note: Either smooth or chunky peanut butter works with this recipe (we actually prefer the chunky); if peanut butter has separated, stir before using. If available, you might want to experiment with almond or hazelnut butter. If the mixture is too thick, add more peanut butter; if it is too thin, add more cereal.

**Note: Use ground flakes, puffs or granola, or a mixture of several cereals.

Total Calories per Serving (2 balls): 318   Total Fat as % of Daily Value: 32%   Protein: 11 gm
Fat: 21 gm   Carbohydrates: 25 gm   Calcium: 110 mg   Iron: 3 mg   Sodium: 256 mg
Dietary Fiber: 4 gm

Chapter Ten

GRAB AND GO FAST FOOD

Fast food is a way of life. Every age group seems to have bought into the idea of food prepared and served quickly. And if it can be consumed while driving a car and speaking on a cell phone, even better!

READY TO USE (RTU) ITEMS

If you are serving fast food, you'll have to make a decision whether to make the products from scratch or to purchase them already made (in the industry jargon, RTU, or "ready to use"). Making items from scratch will involve more labor, but will give more control over the product design. RTU items require less labor and have a consistent quality, but are more expensive to purchase. You may decide to go one way or another or use a combination of both methods.

RTU vegan products are available in both retail (grocery store, health food store) and commercial packs. See Appendix B for a listing of product information. Be sure to read the ingredient line, as some vendors may not be clear on vegan requirements. Look for obvious ingredients (egg whites, cheese powder, milk solids, etc.) and not-so-obvious ingredients (honey, casein, stearic acid, etc.) and take an opportunity to educate your vendors.

Even if you prefer to make everything you serve from scratch, some products are simply easier to purchase. Soy or tofu hot dogs come to mind. While it certainly is possible to make your own vegan sausage, it is a time-consuming process and requires a certain amount of skill and equipment. Depending on the volume you sell, marinated or spicy "fake meats," and usually seitan or tempeh may also be easier to purchase than to prepare yourself.

SPEED-SCRATCH MENU ITEMS

Some products may help you "speed-scratch" menu items. Speed-scratch is a term being used in the food industry to indicate the use of convenience products along with the chef's personal touches to create a "homemade" menu item. Examples of this would be muffin mix to which the chef added dried fruit and chopped nuts; veggie "crumbles" to which sautéed vegetables and spices are added to create a pizza topping; and canned soup to which cooked pasta and herbs are added – you get the idea. Vegan examples of this would be frozen vegan muffin and cookie batter (add fresh or dried fruit, nuts, seeds, fruit juice concentrate, etc.); frozen soups (add veggies, grains, soy cheese, etc.); frozen pie crusts ("build" your own pie with canned or frozen pie filling or defrost crusts and make into savory turnovers with tomatoes, tofu, and veggies); canned refried beans (add your own seasonings); and packaged vegan chili mixes (add your own seasonings, tofu or "fake meats," and chopped veggies).

Then there is the ever-popular vegetarian burger. We have seen vegan RTU burgers made from every conceivable ingredient: textured soy, seitan, okara, beans, corn, mushrooms, grains, potatoes, and whole-grain flour. You will need to do some tastings to see which products your customers would best accept. Many of the RTU veggie burgers must be fried for an acceptable texture (and so they do not fall apart), therefore take this into consideration when choosing. Do you have the equipment to do the frying in the amounts needed in the time needed or is additional fat an undesirable ingredient?

Other points to consider are:
- do the burgers hold up when held in heating equipment for any length of time?
- will the supplier be able to fill orders in the amounts needed?
- are the salt and/or spices at a level acceptable to customers?
- most importantly do the customers like them?

We have included several recipes for from-scratch veggie burgers for you to try.

ETHNIC FOODS
Ethnic foods are quite popular as fast food items. Pizza and pasta, falafel, and stir-fries are easily made vegan. As discussed in the previous paragraphs, you can decide to make these items from scratch or to purchase RTU items.

Fresh or frozen pizza shells can be made into a quick meal. Top shells with tomato sauce (straight from the can or seasoned with tomato purée, fresh or dried basil and oregano, chopped tomatoes, onions, and peppers, etc.). Offer ingredients such as sliced mushrooms, peppers, onions, and garlic, spicy sprouts (try radish or broccoli sprouts), broccoli or cauliflower florets, shredded carrots, capers (the pickled plant, not the fish), artichoke hearts, chopped tomatoes, seasoned tofu, veggie crumbles, and diced pineapple. For variety, make individual calzones (stuffed pizza crust resembling a pizza crust turnover) with the same ingredients; an advantage of a calzone is that it can be pre-made, frozen (uncooked or cooked), and then heated as needed.

Several companies sell vegan pasta entrées such as manicotti, shells, and ravioli. Combined with prepared sauce, this makes a quick (and healthy) meal.

Once again, see Appendix B for product information. Offer pasta with several types of sauce or offer combination pasta platters with bread sticks and tossed salads as side dishes. If you have the time, prepare your own pasta dishes (lasagna, stuffed shells, veggie balls, etc.), freeze and heat as needed.

Falafel (ground chickpea patties) can be purchased frozen and ready to cook, as a dry mix, or can be made from scratch. Depending on the product, falafel can be fried or baked. You should test various products before deciding on a purchase. Offer falafel in pita bread, as a sandwich, or as a combination platter with tabouli (a sprouted wheat and parsley salad, available as a mix or made from scratch), chopped fresh and pickled salad, and hummus. Hummus is a puréed chickpea, garlic, and lemon juice spread, which can be spiced with cumin, pepper, and turmeric. We've seen Southwestern hummus (with jalapeños and cilantro) and Asian hummus (with soy sauce and sesame seeds). Hummus can be purchased RTU or can be made from scratch.

If you would like to do fast food stir-fries, you will have to consider the equipment necessary to do these. Electric woks can be used without making any modifications, but gas-fired woks benefit from specialty gas fittings which bring in more heat (use your local utility companies as resources when researching this). If equipment is an issue, consider offering steamed noodle or rice bowls, rather than stir-fries. Stir-fries are quick to make, but depending on the style of ingredients purchased, the pre-preparation can take a lot of time. Consider your costs to see if you can purchase precut vegetables, marinated tofu, etc.

When designing your Asian fast food menu, take some time to educate yourself about the wide variety of noodles available, both dry and RTU. Exclude the products made with eggs and include wheat, rice, lentil, and bean noodles in every width and length. Noodles topped with steamed, seasoned veggies and tofu, or seitan strips makes a great fast food. Rice (try brown, jasmine, wild, basmati, glutinous, etc.) can be topped in the same way.

OTHER FAST FOOD ITEMS

A discussion of fast food would not be complete without mentioning French fries. Once again, you can buy them frozen and RTU in many shapes, sizes, and flavors. Be sure to read labels, as some commercial fries use animal fat as an ingredient in the coating. We have seen skin-on, skin-off, wedges, rippled, basket weave, and thin- and thick-cut with a variety of seasonings. We have seen sweet potato and eggplant fries and, that cousin to French fries, tempura-style veggies. Tempura batter mix can be purchased or you can make your own with rice flour, spices, and water. Make use of your deep-fat fryer and offer a variety of fries.

Depending on the season and on your clientele, you may want to offer soups-to-go and other easily packaged and eaten foods, such as baked beans or cold salads (think potato or pasta). Remember, with fast food, think about eating your menu items while driving in the car or perched on a park bench – a fact of life in our society.

What's life without dessert? Fast food desserts can be convenience items, such as rice or soy ice cream novelties (we've seen sundaes and sandwiches), scooped sorbet, fruit ices and popsicles, vegan cookies and brownies (make your own or purchase them), and whole fruit or fruit salad.

Fries, veggie burgers, and veggie hot dogs do not stand on their own. They need condiments! Depending on your property, these may be single-serve or large dispensers of ketchup, mustard, and pickle relish (you can purchase or make veggie mayonnaise) or you may offer more exotic flavors. Add some salsa (available RTU or made from scratch), gardiniera (pickled vegetables), chutneys, flavored mustards, satay (Thai peanut sauce), kimchi (marinated, aged, spicy cabbage, available commercially or you can make your own), sauerkraut, soy sauce, tapenade (olive spread), hummus, and sliced veggies if your cost will support it. Your customers will use it. Sliced tomatoes, shredded carrots, sliced cucumbers, and different types of lettuce add color and crunch to the grab-and-go meal. Accessories sometimes perfect the dish!

RECIPES
Here are some fast food recipes to get you started.

VEGAN MAYONNAISE

Yield: 1 pint

You can purchase vegan mayonnaise or you can whip up this quick recipe. Use this vegan mayonnaise in salads or, add your favorite herbs and chopped veggies to create a salad dressing.

INGREDIENTS	MEASURE	METHOD
Silken tofu	2 cups	Place all ingredients in a blender and process until smooth. Keep refrigerated until service.
Oil	1 ounce	
Lemon juice	2 ounces	
Dry mustard	1 teaspoon	
Ground white pepper	1 teaspoon	
Garlic powder	1/2 teaspoon	

Total Calories per 1 Tablespoon Serving: 16   Total Fat as % of Daily Value: 2%   Protein: 1 gm
Fat: 1 gm   Carbohydrates: 1 gm   Calcium: 5 mg   Iron: <1 mg   Sodium: 1 mg
Dietary Fiber: <1 gm

SWEET POTATO BURGERS

Yield: 25 burgers

This slightly sweet and very colorful burger can be made and grilled ahead and then reheated in the oven or microwave. It has a faint taste of India and goes well with eggplant fries or lentil soup.

INGREDIENTS	MEASURE	METHOD
		Preheat oven to 375 degrees (convection 350).
Raw sweet potatoes, peeled	3 pounds	Steam potatoes until tender.
Quinoa	12 ounces	Allow to cool. In a small stock pot,
Low sodium vegetable broth	1-1/2 pints	bring quinoa, broth, and water to a boil. Reduce heat, cover, and
Water	1 pint	simmer until quinoa is fluffy (about
Vegetable oil spray	to cover pan	10 minutes). Allow to cool. Spray
Onions	1 pound	sauté pan and heat. Sweat onions
Garlic	3 ounces	and garlic.
Ground cumin	1/2 ounce	Add cumin and turmeric and
Ground turmeric	1/4 ounce	stir to combine. Remove from
Chopped cashews	2 pounds	heat. In a food chopper, combine
Bread crumbs	6 ounces	potatoes, quinoa, and veggies. Process until well blended. Add cashews and bread crumbs and process again to blend well. Shape into 1/4-inch thick burgers. Put on a sprayed baking sheet and bake for approximately 30 minutes, turning once.

Note: Additional bread crumbs can be used if mixture is too loose to form burgers.

Total Calories per Burger: 356   Total Fat as % of Daily Value: 30%   Protein: 10 gm   Fat: 18 gm
Carbohydrates: 42 gm   Calcium: 66 mg   Iron: 4 mg   Sodium: 74 mg   Dietary Fiber: 5 gm

THYME FOR BURGERS

Yield: 25 burgers

This recipe can be grilled, baked, or broiled. If needed, water can be used to thin the mixture and bread crumbs can be used to thicken. Serve with sliced tomatoes and cucumbers.

INGREDIENTS	MEASURE	METHOD
Potatoes, peeled*	3 pounds	Steam potatoes until tender. Allow to cool. Spray sauté pan and heat. Sweat onions and celery. Add thyme, stir, then remove from heat. In a food chopper, combine potatoes, onions, celery, thyme, and peas and blend until well mixed. Place mixture in a large mixing bowl. Mix in almonds. Shape into 1/4-inch thick patties. Patties can be grilled on a commercial grill at 325 (or medium) for 3 minutes on each side or until browned and heated through; or baked at 400 degrees for 10 minutes or until browned and heated throughout.
Vegetable oil spray	to cover pan	
Onions, chopped	1/2 pound	
Celery, minced	1/4 pound	
Ground thyme	1 ounce	
Canned sweet peas, drained	1-1/2 pounds	
Almond granules**	1/2 pound	

***Note:** Use boiling potatoes for the correct texture.

****Note:** Almond granules are almonds minced very fine.

Total Calories per Burger: 117   Total Fat as % of Daily Value: 6%   Protein: 5 gm   Fat: 4 gm
Carbohydrates: 16 gm   Calcium: 66 mg   Iron: 3 mg   Sodium: 68 mg   Dietary Fiber: 3 gm

BROCCOBURGERS

Yield: 25 burgers

This recipe requires some time in the kitchen to prepare, but we think it's worth it! Bread crumbs can be used for additional thickness.

INGREDIENTS	MEASURE	METHOD
Kasha, fine	1-1/2 pounds	In a small stock pot, bring kasha and broth to a boil. Remove from heat, cover, and let stand until liquid is absorbed. Fluff and set aside. Spray sauté pan and sweat onions and garlic. Set aside. Steam broccoli until tender. Let cool. In a food chopper, combine kasha, onions, garlic, broccoli, and garbanzos until well-blended. Place mixture in a large mixing bowl and add bread crumbs and pepper. Shape into 1/4-inch thick burgers. Burgers can be broiled, grilled, or baked until they reach an internal temperature of 160 degrees. Conduction ovens can be set on 400 and convection on 375.
Vegetable broth	1-1/2 pints	
Onions, minced	8 ounces	
Garlic, minced	4 ounces	
Vegetable oil spray	to cover pan	
Broccoli florets	1-1/2 pounds	
Cooked garbanzos	1-1/2 pounds	
Bread crumbs	6 ounces	
Ground black pepper	1 ounce	

Total Calories per Burger: 167   Total Fat as % of Daily Value: 3%   Protein: 7 gm   Fat: 2 gm
Carbohydrates: 33 gm   Calcium: 54 mg   Iron: 2 mg   Sodium: 181 mg   Dietary Fiber: 6 gm

COLD NOODLES WITH PEANUT SAUCE

Yield: 25 two-ounce servings

This Asian snack can be used as an entrée or a side dish. It's great for hot weather!

INGREDIENTS	MEASURE	METHOD
Soba noodles or rice vermicelli	4 pounds	Boil water in a large stock pot. Add noodles and cook until al dente.
Garlic, minced	7 cloves	Drain and cool. Add remaining
Green onions, diced	8 ounces	ingredients to a blender or food
Fresh ginger, minced	2 ounces	processor canister and process until
Peanut butter	4 ounces	smooth. Place noodles in a large
Soy sauce	2 ounces	bowl, toss with sauce, and chill until
White or rice vinegar	4 ounces	served.
Sesame seeds	1 ounce	

Note: This item should be made ahead of time and will hold well in the refrigerator for three days. Offer as side dish with a veggie burger or as an entrée with sliced tofu.

Total Calories per Serving: 313   Total Fat as % of Daily Value: 5%   Protein: 5 gm   Fat: 3 gm
Carbohydrates: 67 gm   Calcium: 21 mg   Iron: 3 mg   Sodium: 280 mg   Dietary Fiber: 1 gm

FRAGRANT AND FAST TOFU SANDWICH

Yield: 25 servings

You can prepare all the ingredients for this sandwich several hours ahead of time and just keep them refrigerated until ready to use. This filling can be stuffed into a pita, rolled on a lavash or flatbread, or served on whole grain sliced bread, bagels, or rolls. If desired, wrap the sandwich (without the veggies) and heat for three minutes in a hot oven or in a mircowave. Prepare several of these sandwiches and display them, ready-to-go for quick sales.

INGREDIENTS	MEASURE	METHOD
Firm tofu, drained	3-1/2 pounds	Mash tofu in a large mixing bowl.
Fresh basil, minced	2 ounces	Add basil, green onions, and lemon
Green onions, minced	6 ounces	juice. Mix until well combined.
Lemon juice	1 ounce	Place one ounce of mixture on bread
Bread	50 slices	and top with 1 teaspoon each of
Tomatoes, chopped	10 ounces	tomatoes, onions, carrots, pumpkin
Onions, chopped	10 ounces	seeds, and peppers. Sprinkle with
Carrots, shredded	10 ounces	black pepper and garlic. Keep cool
Pumpkin seeds	10 ounces	until service.
Bell peppers, chopped	10 ounces	
Ground black pepper	1 ounce	
Garlic powder	1 ounce	

Total Calories per Sandwich (using whole wheat bread): 283   Total Fat as % of Daily Value: 12%
Protein: 16 gm   Fat: 8 gm   Carbohydrates: 38 gm   Calcium: 173 mg   Iron: 4 mg
Sodium: 306 mg   Dietary Fiber: 6 gm

Chapter Eleven

UN-HOSPITAL FOOD

More and more, hospitals are paying attention to their food offerings. We have seen champagne dinners offered for new parents and spa cuisine classes available to cardiac rehab patients. Special event menus are important for a hospital food service's big picture, but the details of the day-to-day operation are what will keep the patients healthy and well-nourished.

Many patients in the hospital setting are at nutritional risk. Illness, medical tests, and being in a strange environment can create anxieties which do nothing for improving appetite. It is our challenge to offer meals and snacks that will be well received, nourishing, and nurturing. This is the same challenge for veggie and non-veggie patients. Sufficient calorie, protein, vitamin, mineral, and fluid intake are a concern for every patient in the hospital.

SNACKS ARE US

Many hospital patients prefer to eat lots of small meals throughout the day rather than regularly scheduled meals. Make sure the snacks and small meals you offer your vegan patients are packed with nutrition (and are fun and easy to eat). Here are some suggestions:

- popcorn served with cranberry-orange juice
- fresh fruit wedges with herbal tea
- veggie sticks or bread sticks and dip (tofu or vegetable juice based)
- small portions of steamed rice with veggies
- Asian noodles tossed with sesame sauce
- small portions of vegetable or bean soups
- sliced tomato and basil on toast with vinaigrette
- rice or tapioca pudding (made with soy milk)
- soy or rice ice cream served with sliced fresh or canned fruit
- granola tossed with dried fruit and served with a smoothie
- fruit or soy or rice milk shakes
- a mixture of dried fruits and nuts served with orange juice
- peanut butter and fruit preserves served on freshly baked rolls
- baked apple or pear; warm applesauce with cinnamon
- canned fruit with a soy milk custard sauce

DIFFERENT MENUS, DIFFERENT CONSIDERATIONS

The following section will briefly discuss some of the therapeutic modifications that will be ordered in a hospital and how vegan menu items fit into these modifications. In the case of combinations (for example, a calorie controlled, low sodium puréed diet) just integrate all the modifications. Be sure to speak with your dietitian and/or consult your facility's diet manual before implementing any diet change.

REDUCED SODIUM, INCREASED FLAVOR

Sodium is an essential mineral that is responsible for the regulation of normal fluid balance in the body. Before refrigeration and chemical methods of preservation, salt was an important preserver of food. Salt is very desirable in the kitchen for its ability to enhance the flavors of foods and to add that salty "zing" to which we have become accustomed.

We are all born with a taste for salt, and are also taught to like it even more! Today, some commercial baby and toddler foods are still prepared with salt; therefore, you should ask for an ingredient list before purchasing any new product. A certain amount of sodium is necessary in the diet, and this can be obtained from vegetables (tomatoes, celery, and beets are higher than most in sodium) and from drinking water. Americans usually do not lack sodium; we are usually attempting to cut down on it.

Which foods are higher in sodium? All processed foods (canned and frozen) will have sodium in them (except for fruit, which relies on sugar for preservation and taste). So once again, read the labels. Pickled items (cucumbers, chilies, capers, olives, etc.), cold cereals, commercially prepared baked goods, instant hot cereals, and soup bases will all contain sodium unless specifically stated that they do not. Commercially prepared sauces and condiments (ketchup, mustard, salad dressings, soy sauce, hoisin sauce, mirin, etc.), and snack foods (like tortilla chips or microwave popcorn) are also high in sodium.

A big source of anxiety (for the customer or patient) and frustration (for the chef or food service department) is that if the salt is taken out, so is the flavor. If we think about the array of flavors we seek to achieve from each menu item, we can choose the appropriate seasonings to enhance them. Salt is just an easy way out (and if we're in food service, we must not be looking for the easy way out!).

What exactly does "high" in sodium mean? For your healthy customers or patients, the USDA recommends no more than 2500 milligrams of sodium (about one teaspoon) per day. In many facilities this is billed as a "low salt" or "no added salt" diet and may be offered as the house diet. Sodium restriction may be as limited as 250 milligrams per day for critically ill cardiac and renal patients.

Low sodium diets are generally prepared without:

- salt or baking soda
- regular canned veggies
- pickled veggies
- canned tomato products
- sauerkraut
- prepared salad dressings
- instant hot cereal or cold cereal (except Shredded Wheat, which has always been made without salt, or special low sodium products)
- snack foods (like potato chips)
- instant dessert mixes (which can contain monosodium glutamate and sodium-containing preservatives)
- convenience mixes (like an instant rice pilaf mix)

If you decide to purchase specialty products, label terminology is important to know. A "sodium-free" product is to have less than 5 milligrams of sodium per serving; a "very low sodium" product has 35 milligrams or less; and a "low sodium" item has 140 milligrams or less. A "reduced sodium" product is processed to have 75% less sodium than its regular counterpart. "Unsalted" is processed without the normal amount of salt, and "low salt" is made with less salt than the regular variety.

How about salt itself? Regular table salt is sodium chloride and is "harvested" from salt mines or the ocean. It is usually processed to be fine-grained. Iodized salt is table salt with the addition of sodium or potassium iodide, necessary for the health of the thyroid gland. If you prefer to get your iodine from the source, eat vegetables harvested from the ocean. Kosher salt has just sodium chloride and undergoes little to no processing (and is coarse-grained for that reason). Sea salt is the sodium chloride left when ocean water is allowed to evaporate. All of these salts have a high amount of sodium. Light salt or salt replacements will have varying amounts of salt; read the labels.

Make a commitment to learn about the natural flavors in menu ingredients and in fresh and dried herbs and spices. Check your walk-ins and your pantries to be sure you have flavor-ammunition. Savory herbs such as basil, bay leaf, thyme, lemon balm, savory, epazote, and cilantro can jazz up casseroles, soups, and sauces. Chilies and peppers (fresh or dried) add liveliness to ethnic and other dishes, as do fresh or dried ginger, garlic, horseradish, powdered curry blends, paprika, and peppercorns (they come in white, yellow, pink, and red, in addition to basic black). Citrus (lime, lemon, grapefruit, and tangerine) juice, juice concentrates, and zests add the sharpness of salt without the sodium.

So do vinegars and wines. The onion family including leeks, shallots, red, white, and yellow onions, sweet onions, chives, and scallions add aroma and robustness.

Vegan desserts are not usually a sodium dilemma, as soy and rice beverages used in their preparation are much lower in sodium than their animal counterparts. If a stringent sodium restriction is necessary, you may investigate some alternative baking ingredients, such as potassium bicarbonate (instead of regular baking soda). However, you will have to experiment with your current recipes, as the potassium does not act exactly like its salty cousin.

The key to reducing the salt and enhancing the flavor in your menus, as you can see, is to prepare as many items from scratch as possible. Prepared low sodium products are usually more costly and tend to taste flat. You can do a much better job than the big conglomerates. Rely on fresh produce (and properly stored frozen veggies) for optimum flavor. Make a promise to never cook just with water, when a vegetable stock, juice, or herb combination can be used; this would include veggies, grains, and soups.

Put color on the plate (if it looks flat, it's guaranteed it will be perceived as tasting flat) – that ring of red or green bell pepper, slice of pink grapefruit, or orange or tomato wedge will liven up the dish. No salt? No problem!

To flavor specific foods, get a good seasoning chart and post it in the food prep area of your kitchen. Here are suggestions to get you started:

- Flavor beans with chili powder, cloves, dry mustard, and ginger.
- Asparagus comes alive with sesame seeds, basil, and onions.
- Cruciferous veggies (broccoli, cauliflower, Brussels sprouts, etc.) love paprika, onions, marjoram, nutmeg, and onion.
- Cabbage shines with caraway seeds and allspice.
- Tomatoes welcome oregano, basil, and dill.
- Spinach and greens savor savory, thyme, and garlic.
- Carrots go for citrus, ginger, and nutmeg.
- Mushroom soups glow with ginger, oregano, white pepper, bay leaf, tarragon, or chili.
- Onion soup gets a kick from curry, cloves, or garlic.
- Vegetable chowders like fennel (anise), caraway, rosemary, cilantro, or sage (experiment with pineapple or lemon sage).

HOSPITAL PATIENTS NEEDING TEXTURED DIETS

Patients of any age may need a modification in the texture of the food they eat; this can be a temporary or a permanent change. The key is to keep the patient's interest up while conforming to the textural needs of the diet. This is not always easy to do!

There can be many different reasons for textural changes. Physical trauma to the jaw, dental work, stroke, and even psychological diagnoses can indicate an inability to chew or swallow regularly textured foods. As food service professionals we are always hopeful that they will be temporary changes, which means we may have to have a selection of transitional textures. For example, a recent stroke patient may only be able to tolerate thickened liquids, gradually moving to semisolid foods (such as thin mashed potatoes or very soft fruit or vegetables), then onto some solid foods (such as a baked potato), and gradually onto all types of foods.

As food service veterans can tell you, patience with patients is the rule of the day when it comes to textured diets. Puréed and mechanically altered diets may mean different things to different patients. To guarantee that patients will be receiving foods which they can maximally tolerate, be sure to have an open dialogue with the patient and caregivers, including nurses and nurses' aides, speech therapists, and family members (who may be present at mealtime). Be able to individualize diets as much as possible (within the constraints of your department). Be sure that the physicians who are ordering diets have an understanding of what mechanically soft (used for patients who have difficulty chewing solid foods) and puréed (for patients who cannot chew solid foods) mean. Be sure to clarify what types of foods will not be offered with these diets (generally, this means no sticky or chewy items, nuts or seeds, large raw pieces of fruits or veggies, etc.).

FOODS USED FOR MECHANICAL SOFT DIETS

Foods used for mechanical soft diets can be altered by cooking, chopping, mincing, or mashing. Foods for puréed diets can be mashed, blenderized, or puréed. Foods should be altered as little as possible, both for ease of preparation and for patient appeal. For example, a patient receiving a mechanical diet can probably tolerate a soft baked apple or an apple cobbler (with soft topping) and does not need to receive something as soft as applesauce.

A meal pattern (taken from *Simplified Diet Manual,* Iowa Dietetic Association, 6th edition, 1994) for a mechanically altered or puréed diet is as follows (we've adapted for vegan):

- breakfast to include soft fruit or juice, cereal with soy or rice milk, toast or soy or rice milk, toast with jelly, and a hot beverage
- lunch to include soup or juice, soft casserole, soft vegetables, bread and margarine, soft dessert, and soy or rice milk
- dinner to include soft casserole with grain or potato, soft vegetable, soft dessert, hot beverage, and soy or rice milk

DYSPHAGIA PATIENTS

Dysphagia patients may have problems with both food and fluids. If a patient chokes on thin liquids (broth, coffee or tea, water) then thickened liquids will need to be offered. Nectars, sherbets, creamy-style soups, and firm tofu and fruit smoothies may all be better tolerated.

Natural or commercially prepared thickeners can be used for both puréed and dysphagia diets. Commercial thickeners can be purchased which need only to be mixed with thin liquids, such as juice or coffee; read the label, they may have a certain amount of gelatin (a non-vegetarian item), sugar, or salt. Arrowroot and agar are natural thickeners. Arrowroot is neutral in flavor and has twice the thickening ability of flour. Dilute it in water and add at the end of cooking; puddings and sauces thickened with arrowroot have a beautiful gloss. Agar can be used to thicken liquids and gel-like desserts. Agar is derived from ocean vegetables and can be found in powder or flakes. Agar is added at the beginning of cooking and does not need to be diluted before being used.

CREATING SOFT FOODS

Creating soft foods is easy. Making them attractive and interesting is a little more difficult. If you have a large quantity kitchen and an equipment wish list, wish for a Hobart (also called a buffalo) chopper, a vertical chopper, an institutional-size blender, and a hopper attachment (with several blades) for your kitchen. For smaller kitchens, food processors (with several blades) and commercial blenders should do the trick.

Try to select ingredients that lend themselves to being "soft." For example, root veggies (carrots, turnips, beets, etc.), hard-shelled squash, all potatoes, grains, and most fruit tolerate being mashed or puréed. On the other hand, summer squash (like zucchini) or leafy greens (like spinach or collards) are a disaster when altered. Use them as combination ingredients, not stand-alones.

For creamy, soft, pleasant textures, tofu and avocados are a vegan dream. Since both are neutral they can be used to "texture" sweet or savory dishes.

Avocados are higher in fat, but it is mostly unsaturated fat with decent amounts of vitamin A and potassium. Many patients eating modified diets may need the extra calories. You can select the fat content of the tofu you use in your kitchen. Tofu can be used for a binding, a soft thickener, and even a moisturizer in casseroles that are combinations of cooked grains and vegetables.

Make a light dinner entrée (or a heavy dessert) by layering puréed (or chopped) peaches, sweetened tofu (buy it already sweetened or mix in orange or apple juice concentrate), and avocado purée (small cubes) into a parfait glass. Garnish with a spoonful of jelly or preserves. Along the same lines, a breakfast "swirl" of cooked cereal, puréed fruit, and avocado cubes is attractive and packed with nutrition while being easy to swallow.

Bananas, berries, peaches, apricots, apples, and pears can be cooked or mashed into flavorful sauces. Purée some fresh strawberries, sweeten with orange juice concentrate, and use as a sauce for puddings or cakes. Freeze this blend and have a cool, smooth sorbet.

Puréed vegetables, such as carrots or peas, and beans can be cooked or puréed into a smooth, creamy consistency, perfect for soups and sauces. Purée cooked black beans, season with onions and cilantro, heat, and swirl in soft tofu, and you have soup that everyone will like! Potage crecy is a fancy way of saying puréed carrot soup—purée cooked carrots with rice or rice cereal, dill, and parsley; mix in some soft tofu, and you will have a soup that is pretty to look at and great to taste.

How do gingered white beans with butternut squash sound? How about citrus oats or frozen apricot frappe? All can be made for textured diets. The beans are cooked, tossed with cooked squash squares and some mirin. Cook it soft for the mechanicals and serve over rice pilaf, or purée it and serve over seasoned mashed potatoes. Rolled oats (not quick) can be soaked overnight in soy milk with orange and lemon zest, cinnamon, and soft fruit. It can be served, uncooked, for mechanical soft diets and cooked for puréed. Combine canned, drained apricots, soy milk, fresh ginger, and ice cubes in a blender for the frappe; this item can be used for everybody!

The sky is the limit with texturized menus. You may find that you are preparing the same menu items for the whole house!

RENAL MODIFICATONS

Renal diets, usually prescribed for patients with kidney disease, require the teamwork of the dietitian and the food service coordinator. Renal diets cover a wide range of protein, sodium, potassium, and fluid restrictions. So, be sure you work with the medical team to provide the optimal diet for the patient, especially for the vegan patient. For example, potatoes, dried beans, peas, and lentils, all mainstays of a vegan diet, are high in potassium and should be served sparingly. Renal patients sometimes have difficulty getting enough calories because of the nature of their dietary restrictions. Look to carbohydrates and fats to add calories. Your dietitian can help you calculate amounts of protein foods allowable on a renal diet and can assist you in adding extra calories. There are some commercial formulas available designed specifically as renal supplements. Several are vegetable oil-based rather than dairy-based.

Here is an example of a one-day meal plan for a liberal renal diet (60 grams of protein); fluid limits have to be individualized:
- **Morning:** 4 ounces apple juice, 4 ounces oatmeal with maple syrup, 1 slice of toast with 2 teaspoons of margarine and jelly (as desired), 4 ounces soy or rice milk
- **Noon:** 1 ounce egg replacer (prepared), 2 slices bread, lettuce salad (as desired), 1 teaspoon vegan mayonnaise, 4 ounces steamed carrots, 1/2 baked apple
- **Evening:** 3 ounces steamed tofu, 2 ounces herbed rice, 4 ounces broccoli, 1 Tablespoon margarine, 1/2 fresh pear, 1 dinner roll with 1 Tablespoon margarine, 4 ounces canned pineapple
- **Snack:** 4 ounces grape juice, hard candy (as desired)

WHEAT-FREE AND GLUTEN-FREE

Wheat-free eating takes some planning and education. In addition to serving wheat-free meals, be sure to offer informational pamphlets or cooking classes for both wheat-free patients and the community.

"Wheat-free" means that no wheat flour ingredients are used in a food. These would include whole wheat flour, all-purpose flour, or any flour made from wheat. Flours made from other ingredients such as barley, rye, corn, or potato are usually okay. Wheat allergies are among the most common food allergies.

Gluten-free is much more restrictive. Gluten is the protein component in many grains, including wheat, barley, rye, and oats. Gluten-free means that there are no ingredients from these grains used in a food. People who have celiac disease (the old-fashioned term for this was "sprue") are born with an inability to tolerate gliadin, which is contained in gluten. Gluten or gliadin is toxic in their small intestines, damaging the intestines in such a way that nutrients cannot be absorbed. For a celiac person, the smallest trace of gluten can be harmful.

A person with a wheat allergy could eat a gluten-free product, but a person with celiac disease or gluten intolerance could not eat just a wheat-free product, because other grains contain gluten. Some common foods that contain gluten include bouillon, some soy sauce, vinegar, and some extracts which contain alcohol. See Figure 11.1 for a more extensive list.

If you are preparing foods from scratch, using unprocessed ingredients, then you will know if a menu item is gluten- or wheat-free. The patient should tolerate arrowroot, cornmeal, soy, rice, tapioca, and potato products. If you use any processed items such as spice blends, mashed potato mix, soup bases, etc., then you will need to read the labels very carefully or even contact manufacturers about their products.

When working with vegan products, be sure to read the label. Some items may be wheat or gluten-containing. For example, a soup mix may use flour as a thickener and some prepared tofu products (such as soy ice cream) may have wheat or gluten added. Remember that seitan is made from gluten and some "fake meats" may also have flour or gluten as ingredients.

FIGURE 11.1:
FOODS TO ELIMINATE FROM GLUTEN-FREE MENUS
- Commercial chocolate beverage and other drink mixes
- Malt powder
- Cooked or dry pasta made with wheat, rye, oat, and barley; also macaroni and noodles
- Cooked or dried cereals made from grains listed above
- Bread or bread products (crumbs, croutons, bread sticks, etc.) made from grains listed above
- Convenience items (soups or soup mixes, cake mixes, pudding mixes, salad dressings, frozen entrées, etc.) which may have the grains listed above as an ingredient
- Beer and ale, cereal beverages (such as Postum or grain milk), root beer

SUGGESTED GLUTEN-FREE MENU
- **Morning:** assorted fruit or fruit or vegetable juices, rice or corn cereal, muffins made with rice or corn flour, margarine or peanut butter (check the label for gluten; some peanut butter has it), and fruit preserves
- **Evening:** tofu stir-fried with seasonal veggies, potatoes steamed with fresh herbs, green salad with chutney, fresh fruit slices, and sorbet.
- **Snack:** rice cakes with salsa and guacamole or seasoned popcorn with vegetable sticks

FIGURE 11.2: ALLERGY AND VEGAN FOOD REPLACEMENTS

ALLERGY/ANIMAL FOOD	SUGGESTED REPLACEMENTS
Some brands refined cane sugar	fruit juice, rice or maple syrup, molasses
Eggs	tofu, vegan egg replacer (a packaged dry product), puréed fruit (in baked goods)
Milk and dairy	soy, rice, or grain milks (look for enriched or fortified versions), soy cheese and yogurt, soy and rice ice cream
Wheat	Alternate flours such as oat, corn, millet, lentil, rice, chickpea, buckwheat, and potato used as an ingredient in baking and cooking
Gluten	Baked goods prepared with rice, soy, potato, tapioca, or corn flours
Yeast	Replace vinegar with citrus juice (vinegar is often made with yeast); replace yeast breads with unleavened breads (matza, flat bread) and quick breads (leavened with baking powder and soda)
Chocolate	carob

Note: The allergy replacements may not have the same nutritional value as the original food. In the case of therapeutic need, consult a medical professional. Allergy replacement foods may not translate equally for cooking needs (for example, tofu has some of the cooking properties of eggs, but 1 ounce of tofu may not replace 1 ounce of egg). Work with the replacements to learn about their properties.

RECIPES

Here are recipes that should appeal to hospital patients. Of course, some patients may be feeling fine and for them you should offer a restaurant-level menu (it can be done!). You will find that these vegan ideas will appeal to everyone. Look at recipes included in Chapters 7 and 8 for holiday and special occasion recipes, in Chapter 4 for breakfast ideas, and in Chapter 12 for recipes designed for the senior set.

MARMALADE VINAIGRETTE

Yield: 25 one-ounce servings

Use this recipe as a salad dressing or as a marinade or glaze for vegetables, tofu, or seitan.

INGREDIENTS	MEASURE	METHOD
Orange juice	12 ounces	In a blender process all ingredients until smooth. Store refrigerated until service.
Oil	4 ounces	
Orange marmalade	9 ounces	
Orange juice concentrate	2 ounces	
Prepared mustard	2 ounces	
Black pepper	1/2 ounce	

Total Calories per Serving: 77   Total Fat as % of Daily Value: 6%   Protein: <1 gm   Fat: 4 gm
Carbohydrates: 10 gm   Calcium: 7 mg   Iron: <1 mg   Sodium: 31 mg   Dietary Fiber: 1 gm

CURRIED GRAPEFRUIT CREAM SALAD DRESSING

Yield: 25 one-ounce servings

This salad dressing goes equally well with vegetable and fruit salads.

INGREDIENTS	MEASURE	METHOD
Vegan mayonnaise	1 pint	In a blender, process all ingredients until smooth. Store refrigerated until service.
Frozen grapefruit juice concentrate, thawed	4 ounces	
Lemon juice	3 ounces	
Silken tofu	4 ounces	
Apple juice	2 ounces	
Curry powder	1/2 ounce	

Total Calories per Serving: 58   Total Fat as % of Daily Value: 6%   Protein: <1 gm   Fat: 4 gm
Carbohydrates: 4 gm   Calcium: 6 mg   Iron: <1 mg   Sodium: 136 mg   Dietary Fiber: <1 gm

CRANBERRY SALSA

Yield: Makes 48 one-ounce servings (3 pounds)

This is a low-sodium salsa.

INGREDIENTS	MEASURE	METHOD
Whole, raw cranberries	3 pounds	In a food processor, combine all
Fresh lemon juice	3 ounces	ingredients and process until just
Orange juice	3 ounces	combined. A chunky texture is
Fresh lime juice	2 ounces	desired. (Note: This salsa can be
Apple juice concentrate	1 ounce	stored for 3 days.)
Scallions, chopped	4 ounces	
Bell pepper, chopped	1 ounce	
Fresh cilantro, chopped	1 ounce	
Fresh parsley, chopped	1 ounce	
Black peppercorns, cracked	1 Tablespoon	

Total Calories per Serving: 18   Total Fat as % of Daily Value: <1%   Protein: <1 gm   Fat: <1 gm
Carbohydrates: 5 gm   Calcium: 5 mg   Iron: <1 mg   Sodium: 1 mg   Dietary Fiber: 1 gm

TOFU SOUR CREAM

Yield: approximately 1 pint or 32 half-ounce servings

Use this recipe as a base for salad dressings and sauces and as an ingredient or topping for soups and casseroles.

INGREDIENTS	MEASURE	METHOD
Soft tofu	14 ounces	Boil 1 pint plus 1 cup of water. Drop uncut tofu into water and allow to boil for 1 minute. Remove from heat. Allow to stand for 3 minutes or until cool. Drain water. Place tofu, lemon juice, and salt in a blender and process until smooth.
Lemon juice	1 ounce	
Salt	1/2 teaspoon	

Total Calories per Serving: 10   Total Fat as % of Daily Value: 2%   Protein: 1 gm   Fat: 1 gm
Carbohydrates: <1 gm   Calcium: 13 mg   Iron: 1 mg   Sodium: 37 mg   Dietary Fiber: <1 gm

VERSATILE WHITE SAUCE

Yield: About 1 quart or 32 two-Tablespoon servings

This sauce can be used as is, as a base for soups, or as an ingredient in a casserole or side dish. Flavor it with puréed vegetables (for a savory dish) or with puréed fruit (for a sweet dish) and fresh herbs (chopped or ground).

INGREDIENTS	MEASURE	METHOD
Margarine	1 ounce	In a saucepot, melt margarine. Add
White, soy, or whole wheat flour	1 ounce	flour to form a roux (a paste used for thickening). Over low heat, slowly
Soy milk, unflavored	1 quart	add soy milk, stirring constantly until sauce thickens to desired texture. Can be stored, covered, and refrigerated for two days.

Total Calories per 2 Tablespoon Serving: 30   Total Fat as % of Daily Value: 3%   Protein: 1 gm
Fat: 2 gm   Carbohydrates: 2 gm   Calcium: 10 mg   Iron: <1 mg   Sodium: 22 mg
Dietary Fiber: <1 gm

OH-SO-ADAPTABLE VEG-MED SAUCE

Yield: 60 three-ounce servings

INGREDIENTS	MEASURE	METHOD
Vegetable oil	6 ounces	In a steam jacketed kettle (or in a double boiler) heat oil and sweat (cook until they glisten) carrots, onion, garlic, celery, and peppers. Add mushrooms, broccoli, and squash and continue to cook until the veggies are soft.
Carrots, diced	16 ounces (1 pound)	
Onions, diced	16 ounces (1 pound)	
Garlic, minced	4 ounces	
Celery, diced	1 pound	
Bell peppers, diced	1/2 pound	
Mushrooms, sliced	2 pounds	
Broccoli, chopped	1 pound	
Soft-shelled squash (zucchini, crookneck, etc.), chopped	1 pound	
Tomatoes, canned, diced (not drained)	2 pounds	Add tomato products and spices. Reduce heat, cover, and allow to simmer until flavors have married and desired texture is achieved (about 30 minutes).
Tomato purée	1 pound	
Tomato paste	1 pound	
Dried oregano	2 Tablespoons	
Dried basil	2 Tablespoons	
Black pepper, ground	1 Tablespoon	

Low salt: Simply use fresh tomatoes and/or low sodium canned products.
Low fat: It is!
Diabetic exchanges: If served with 1/2 cup cooked grains, approximately 1 bread exchange and 2 vegetable exchanges (+ 1/2 fat exchange).
Garnish suggestions: Chopped fresh herbs, such as basil and oregano, crumbled; seasoned tofu (marinated in Italian, Spanish, or Greek herbs for 2 to 3 hours before crumbling); sliced olives or seasoned croutons.
To prepare as a casserole: Combine sauce with 6 pounds of cooked pasta (rotini, shells, and penne are good shapes) or cooked grains. Will yield one full 400 steam table pan (12" x 20" x 4").
Freezing: Sauce can be frozen (be sure to chill and thaw properly) for up to one month.

Total Calories per Serving: 55   Total Fat as % of Daily Value: 5%   Protein: 2 gm   Fat: 3 gm
Carbohydrates: 7 gm   Calcium: 25 mg   Iron: 1 mg   Sodium: 85 mg   Dietary Fiber: 2 gm

ORANGE AND WILD RICE SALAD

Yield: 25 three-ounces servings

Use this recipe as a change from pasta or potato salad.

INGREDIENTS	MEASURE	METHOD
Mandarin oranges	3-1/3 pounds	Drain oranges; save syrup. Place
Wild rice, uncooked	18 ounces	syrup in a stock pot, add one pint
Snow peas*	2 pounds	water, and bring to a boil. Reduce
Italian salad dressing	1 pint	heat, add rice, cover, and cook for
Orange juice	8 ounces	20 minutes or until rice is tender.
Almonds, chopped	8 ounces	Drain. Mix in snow peas and allow to
Fresh parsley, chopped	4 ounces	cool. Add remaining ingredients and
Orange zest	1 ounce	toss gently to combine.
Green onion, minced	8 ounces	

*Note: Snow peas may be fresh or frozen (thawed, blanched). Cut snow peas into small pieces for easier service.

Variations: To increase the protein, add seasoned soy crumbles or diced, firm tofu. For calorie controlled diets, use mandarins packed in juice, unsweetened orange juice, and calorie-controlled salad dressing. For restricted sodium diets, use low-salt salad dressing (or make a vinaigrette of oil and vinegar). For mechanical-soft diets, use steamed white rice rather than wild and use tofu to replace almonds.

Total Calories per Serving: 308   Total Fat as % of Daily Value: 28%   Protein: 7 gm   Fat: 18 gm
Carbohydrates: 34 gm   Calcium: 66 mg   Iron: 2 mg   Sodium: 310 mg   Dietary Fiber: 2 gm

"CHICKEN" SALAD WITHOUT THE CHICKEN

Yield: 25 two-ounce servings

Be sure to allow prep time for this recipe. It can be made up to two days ahead of time and kept refrigerated until ready to serve.

INGREDIENTS	MEASURE	METHOD
Tempeh	4 pounds	Chop tempeh into 1-inch pieces and steam 5-7 minutes in a commercial steamer or 10-12 minutes on a stove top steamer. Drain and cool.
Tamari	3 ounces	
Lemon juice	2 ounces	In a large bowl, mix tamari, lemon juice, vegetable stock, and poultry seasoning. Add tempeh and allow to marinate for at least 4 hours. In a medium bowl, mix mayonnaise, mustard, vinegar, garlic, and pepper. Chill. Remove tempeh from marinade and place a single layer on a baking sheet. Bake for 10 minutes at 325 degrees or until golden. Allow to cool. Toss cabbages, carrots, and bell pepper together. Mix in dressing and gently mix in tempeh. Serve chilled.
Vegetable stock	18 ounces	
Poultry seasoning	2 ounces	
Vegan mayonnaise	1 pint	
Prepared mustard	1 ounce	
Vinegar	1 ounce	
Granulated garlic	1/2 ounce	
Black pepper	1/2 ounce	
Green cabbage, shredded	1-1/2 pounds	
Red cabbage, shredded	12 ounces	
Carrots, shredded	6 ounces	
Bell pepper, diced	4 ounces	

Variations: For a Southwestern flavor, omit poultry seasoning and use red pepper flakes; for a Mediterranean flavor, omit poultry seasoning and add dried basil and oregano in equal parts; and for an Indian flavor, omit poultry seasoning and add curry powder and cumin in equal parts.

Total Calories per Serving: 217   Total Fat as % of Daily Value: 15%   Protein: 15 gm   Fat: 10 gm
Carbohydrates: 19 gm   Calcium: 114 mg   Iron: 3 mg   Sodium: 408 mg   Dietary Fiber: 1 gm

SWEET POTATO SOUP

Yield: Makes 2 gallons or 32 two-cup servings

Enjoy this low-sodium soup.

INGREDIENTS	MEASURE	METHOD
Vegetable oil	2 ounces	In a small steam-jacketed kettle, heat oil. Add garlic, celery, onions, and carrots and sweat. Add stock, peppers, and potatoes. Bring to a boil. Reduce to simmer and cook until potatoes are very tender. Purée soup in a blender or food processor. Return to the kettle and add cinnamon, nutmeg, ginger, and concentrate and bring to a boil.
Garlic, minced	4 cloves	
Celery, minced	12 ounces	
Onions, chopped	12 ounces	
Carrots, chopped	6 ounces	
Vegetable stock (low sodium)	4 ounces	
Bell pepper, chopped	6 quarts	
Sweet potatoes, peeled and chopped into 1-inch cubes	5 pounds	
Cinnamon sticks	2	Serve hot or store, refrigerated and covered, for up to 2 days.
Nutmeg	2 teaspoons	
Ground ginger	1 teaspoon	
Orange juice concentrate	4 ounces	

Total Calories per 1 Cup Serving: 149   Total Fat as % of Daily Value: 3%   Protein: 3 gm
Fat: 2 gm   Carbohydrates: 32 gm   Calcium: 40 mg   Iron: 1 mg   Sodium: 24 mg
Dietary Fiber: 6 gm

HARVEST SOUP

Yield: 25 four-ounce servings

Take advantage of vegetables in season for this savory soup. Mechanically-altered diets can have the soup as is; process in a blender or food processor for puréed diets. Use hard-shelled squash such as hubbard, banana, or butternut. Vegetable juice may be used for all or some of the stock.

INGREDIENTS	MEASURE	METHOD
Spray oil	to cover pot	Spray a medium stock pot or small steam-jacketed kettle with enough spray oil to cover the bottom and heat. Sweat onions and garlic until they glisten. Add carrots, sweet potatoes, and squash and continue to sweat for about 5 minutes.
Onions, chopped	3 large	
Garlic cloves, finely diced	4 large	
Carrots, chopped	5 large	
Sweet potatoes, peeled and chopped into 1-inch cubes	4 large	
Hard-shelled squash, peeled and cubed	1-1/2 pounds	
Canned diced tomato	1 pound	Add tomatoes, peppers, millet, and stock and bring to a boil. Reduce heat and allow to simmer until vegetables are soft and millet is cooked. More stock may be added if soup is too thick. Serve hot, garnished with fresh herbs or chopped vegetables.
Bell peppers, seeds removed	2 large	
Millet, toasted, washed, and drained	12 ounces	
Vegetable stock	2 quarts	

Total Calories per Serving: 110   Total Fat as % of Daily Value: 2%   Protein: 3 gm   Fat: 1 gm
Carbohydrates: 23 gm   Calcium: 34 mg   Iron: 1 mg   Sodium: 74 mg   Dietary Fiber: 4 gm

FRUIT AND NUT BREAD

Yield: 2 loaves, 10 slices each

This recipe is gluten and wheat free. Use seasonal fruit for different flavors. The bread can be baked and frozen until ready to use

INGREDIENTS	MEASURE	METHOD
Potato flour	1 cup	In a large bowl, combine flours, baking powder and salt.
Soy flour	1-1/2 cups	
Rice flour	1-1/2 cups	In a blender, combine soy milk,
Baking powder	1-1/2 Table-spoons	bananas, oil, sweetener, tofu, and extract until smooth. Mix flour and
Salt	1/2 teaspoon	tofu mixtures together until just
Soy or rice milk	1 cup	combined (do not over mix). Add in
Ripe bananas	8 ounces	raisins and walnuts and mix only
Oil	1/2 cup	until combined. Bake in greased loaf
Dry sweetener	1 cup	pans in a preheated oven at 350
Silken tofu, pressed	1 cup	degrees for 40 minutes or until a
Vanilla extract	2 teaspoons	toothpick inserted in the middle
Raisins	2 cups	comes out clean. Cool before
Walnuts, chopped	1 cup	serving.

Total Calories per Slice: 297   Total Fat as % of Daily Value: 15%   Protein: 6 gm   Fat: 10 gm
Carbohydrates: 49 gm   Calcium: 118 mg   Iron: 3 mg   Sodium: 159 mg   Dietary Fiber: 2 gm

NEW ENGLAND BAKED BEANS

Yield: 25 two-ounce servings

This recipe is worth the cooking time and can be made ahead (up to three days ahead of time).

INGREDIENTS	MEASURE	METHOD
Dried Navy beans*	2 pounds	Soak the beans for at least 2 hours (can be soaked overnight, if desired, or not soaked at all and cooked for a longer time). In a stock pot, add beans and enough water to cover beans at least 4 inches. Bring beans to a boil, reduce heat, and allow to simmer about 35 minutes until tender. Drain. In a small bowl, mix onion, mustard, ginger, pepper, vinegar, tomato purée, molasses, and syrup and stir to combine. Place beans in a deep steam table pan and mix in sauce. Add enough water to cover beans by one inch. Cover and bake at 350 degrees for 3 hours (if liquid cooks off, add water to keep beans soupy). Uncover and bake for 30 more minutes or until sauce is thickened.
Onions, chopped	12 ounces	
Dry mustard	1 ounce	
Ground ginger	1 ounce	
Black pepper	2 ounces	
Cider vinegar	5 ounces	
Tomato purée	3 ounces	
Molasses	4 ounces	
Maple syrup	5 ounces	

***Note:** 6 pounds drained canned beans can be used instead of dried beans.

Total Calories per Serving: 160   Total Fat as % of Daily Value: 2%   Protein: 8 gm   Fat: 1 gm
Carbohydrates: 32 gm   Calcium: 86 mg   Iron: 3 mg   Sodium: 9 mg   Dietary Fiber: 9 gm

TOFU TETRAZZINI

Yield: 25 three-ounce servings

This recipe becomes a favorite wherever it is served! For a change of flavor, try some smoked tofu. If tofu is not available, use an equivalent amount of sautéed, thickly sliced and cubed portabello mushrooms.

INGREDIENT	MEASURE	METHOD
Filling:		
Mushrooms, sliced	1 pound	In a nonstick sauté pan (or braising
White wine	6 ounces	pan), sauté mushrooms and wine
Firm tofu, diced	4 pounds	until mushrooms are soft. Gently toss
Pasta, cooked	5 pounds	mushrooms, tofu, pasta, almonds,
Almonds, slivered	1/2 pound	and peas together. Place in a steam
Green peas, cooked	1 pound	table pan.
Sauce:		
Flour	7 ounces	Combine flour and margarine
Margarine	7 ounces	(making a roux) over low heat until a
Vegetable stock	1-1/2 pints	paste is formed. Add stock, little by
Soy milk, unflavored and warmed	10 ounces	little, stirring to form a smooth sauce. Remove from heat and stir in
White pepper	1 ounce	soy milk and pepper. Pour sauce over pasta and mix. Bake at 325 degrees for 20 minutes or until casserole is firm and browned on top.

Notes: Any type of mushrooms may be used. For a shortcut, use vegan canned mushroom soup (prepared according to package directions) rather than making the soup from scratch. Use plain tofu or purchase smoked tofu for a change of flavor. For color and crunch, top with chopped red and green bell pepper and sliced almonds. Pasta shapes for this recipe should be bite-size, such as spaghetti, which has been chopped to short lengths, gemilli (twists), penne (flutes), or small shells.

Total Calories per Serving: 379   Total Fat as % of Daily Value: 25%   Protein: 18 gm   Fat: 16 gm
Carbohydrates: 40 gm   Calcium: 174 mg   Iron: 4 mg   Sodium: 114 mg   Dietary Fiber: 4 gm

EGGPLANT LASAGNA

Yield: 25 three-ounce servings

Use zucchini instead of eggplant for a change of flavor. This recipe can be prepared ahead of time and frozen until ready to use.

INGREDIENTS	MEASURE	METHOD
Lasagna noodles cooked and drained	60 each	Spray baking sheets, place eggplant in a single layer, and sprinkle with oregano and basil. Cover and bake for 40 minutes at 350 degrees or until eggplant is soft. Heat sauté pan, spray with oil, and sauté peppers, onions, and garlic until tender. In a mixing bowl, toss tofu with marinara sauce. Assemble lasagna by alternating layers of noodles, eggplant, tofu, and mushrooms, ending with noodles.
Eggplant, peeled and sliced	6 pounds	
Dried oregano	2 ounces	
Dried basil	2 ounces	
Vegetable oil spray	to cover pan	
Bell peppers, diced	10 ounces	
Onions, diced	10 ounces	
Garlic, minced	5 cloves	
Firm tofu, cubed	4 pounds	
Marinara sauce	2-1/2 pints	
Canned mushrooms, drained and chopped	2 pounds	
Canned tomatoes, diced and drained	1-1/2 pounds	Top with diced tomatoes and herbs. Bake covered at 375 degrees for 45 minutes or until heated through. Serve warm.
Fresh basil, chopped	4 ounces	
Fresh parsley, chopped	3 ounces	

Total Calories per Serving: 380   Total Fat as % of Daily Value: 12%   Protein: 19 gm   Fat: 8 gm
Carbohydrates: 58 gm   Calcium: 184 mg   Iron: 5 mg   Sodium: 502 mg   Dietary Fiber: 4 gm

PUT IT ALL IN THERE:
POTATO, SPINACH, AND LENTIL STEW

Yield: 25 two-ounce servings

This flavorful stew is low in fat and sodium and high in flavor.

INGREDIENTS	MEASURE	METHOD
Dry lentils, rinsed	3 pounds	In a stock pot bring lentils, stock,
Vegetable stock	3 quarts	and water to a boil. Reduce heat and
Water	1 pint	simmer covered until lentils are tender (about 15 minutes on a stove top or 8 minutes in a commercial steamer).
Vegetable oil spray	to cover pot	Heat a second stock pot and spray
Onions, chopped	18 ounces	with oil. Sauté onions and celery
Celery, minced	6 ounces	until soft. Add lentils and liquid,
Frozen chopped spinach, thawed and cooked	3 pounds	spinach, and potatoes. Cook over low heat until potatoes and lentils are soft. You should have
Red rose potatoes, thinly sliced and cooked	2-1/2 pounds	enough liquid to be stew-like; if liquid has evaporated, add more stock or water. Stir in juice, zest, and
Lemon juice	7 ounces	mint just before service.
Lemon zest	1 ounce	
Fresh mint, chopped	8 ounces	

Total Calories per Serving: 247   Total Fat as % of Daily Value: <1%   Protein: 14 gm   Fat: <1 gm
Carbohydrates: 48 gm   Calcium: 178 mg   Iron: 6 mg   Sodium: 78 mg   Dietary Fiber: 6 gm

MINI-CASSEROLES (TIMBALES) OF VEGETABLE RICE

Yield: 25 servings

Use as a side dish or serve over a mixture of cooked beans as an entrée. This is a low-sodium dish.

INGREDIENTS	MEASURE	METHOD
Fresh cranberry beans*	1-1/2 pounds	Cook beans in boiling water until they are tender (about 10 minutes on a stove top or 5-8 minutes in a commercial brazier). Drain and mash.
Vegetable stock (low sodium)	1 pint	In a small pot, sweat onions and garlic in 1 ounce of stock until onions are translucent.
Onions, minced	3 ounces	
Garlic, minced	4 cloves	
Long-grain rice	1 pound	Add rice and toss until rice is coated.
Tomato paste (low sodium)	1 ounce	Add remaining stock, paste, vinegar, chili, cumin, pepper, and paprika. Stir until combined and allow to simmer, covered, until rice is soft.
Vinegar	2 Tablespoons	
Chili, roasted, deseeded, and minced	1 whole	
Cumin, ground	2 teaspoons	
Black pepper, ground	2 teaspoons	Remove from heat. Fold in vegan soy cheese and corn. Serve scooped onto plates or pack into small molds to shape. Unmold on plates and garnish with chilies or chopped tomatoes.
Paprika	2 teaspoons	
Soy cheese, grated	4 ounces	
Corn kernels, cooked and drained	4 ounces	

*Note: You can also use fresh or frozen baby lima beans instead of cranberry beans.

Total Calories per Serving: 121   Total Fat as % of Daily Value: 2%   Protein: 4 gm   Fat: 1 gm
Carbohydrates: 22 gm   Calcium: 63 mg   Iron: 1 mg   Sodium: 57 mg   Dietary Fiber: 2 mg

VERY-VEGGIE VEGETABLE CURRY

Yield: 25 servings

Serve over couscous, basmati rice, or a barley pilaf. Garnish with fresh peas, pepper rings, and chopped tomatoes and onion. This is a low-sodium dish.

INGREDIENTS	MEASURE	METHOD
Vegetable oil	2 ounces	In a small steam-jacketed kettle,
Onions, sliced thinly	2 pounds	heat oil. Add onions and garlic and
Garlic, minced	4 cloves	sauté until brown.
Celery or fennel, sliced	8 ounces	Add celery, potatoes, and beans and
New potatoes, raw, peeled, and cubed	2 pounds	sauté until veggies are tender.
Green or wax beans, blanched	2 pounds	
Green onions, sliced	1 bunch	Add green onions, curry, cumin, and
Curry powder	2 ounces	coriander. Sauté briefly.
Ground cumin	1 teaspoon	
Ground coriander	2 teaspoons	
Vegetable stock	1-1/2 pints	Add stock and tomato products and
Tomato paste (low sodium)	1/2 pound	allow to simmer until veggies are tender.
Tomato sauce (low sodium)	8 ounces	If not thick enough, use a paste of arrowroot and cold water to thicken.

Variations: Try bias-cut zucchini or yellow squash, fresh fennel, greens, or cubed turnips.

Total Calories per Serving: 96   Total Fat as % of Daily Value: 5%   Protein: 3 gm   Fat: 3 gm
Carbohydrates: 17 gm   Calcium: 49 mg   Iron: 2 mg   Sodium: 23 mg   Dietary Fiber: 3 gm

QUINOA CASSEROLE

Yield: 25 servings

This casserole can be made with soft vegetables for the patient needing a mechanically altered diet or with mashed beans or mashed vegetables for puréed diets. Use frozen and thawed or fresh steamed carrots. For more flavor, mashed potatoes may be seasoned with garlic, onions, or pepper. The quinoa and the fresh herbs will chase the blahs away from any one!

INGREDIENTS	MEASURE	METHOD
Spray oil	to cover pot	Spray a medium stock pot or small steam-jacketed kettle with enough oil to cover the bottom and heat. Sweat garlic until it glistens. Add stock and bring to a boil. Add carrots and quinoa and return to a boil. Lower heat and allow to simmer for 5 minutes. Add beans and herbs and allow to simmer until quinoa is soft and mixture has started to thicken. Remove from heat. Stir in mashed potatoes and scale into half 200 pans. Bake in a 325 degree oven for 15 minutes or until casserole is firm. Garnish with chopped tomatoes and peppers.
Garlic cloves, minced	5 large	
Vegetable stock	3 quarts	
Carrots, small dice	1 pound	
Quinoa, rinsed	1-1/2 pounds	
Red beans, cooked	1 pound	
Ground cumin	1 Tablespoon	
Fresh oregano, chopped	2 ounces	
Fresh cilantro, chopped	1 ounce	
Prepared mashed potatoes	8 pounds	

Total Calories per Serving: 264   Total Fat as % of Daily Value: 3%   Protein: 8 gm   Fat: 2 gm
Carbohydrates: 55 gm   Calcium: 44 mg   Iron: 4 mg   Sodium: 24 mg   Dietary Fiber: 5 gm

CINNAMONY BAKED APPLES

Yield: 25 apples

This recipe can be used as a side dish or as a dessert and can be served hot or cold. For extra calories and nutrients, serve with soy ice cream.

INGREDIENTS	MEASURE	METHOD
Baking apples, cored and top half peeled	25 each	Place apples in a steam table pan. Fill pan with 1 inch water. Drizzle syrup over each apple. Sprinkle each apple with cinnamon, ginger, nutmeg, and zest. Cover and bake at 350 degrees for 30 minutes or until apples are tender (do not overbake).
Maple syrup	1 pint	
Ground cinnamon	3 ounces	
Ground ginger	2 ounces	
Ground nutmeg	2 ounces	
Orange zest	2 ounces	

Total Calories per Apple: 171   Total Fat as % of Daily Value: 2%   Protein: 1 gm   Fat: 1 gm
Carbohydrates: 42 gm   Calcium: 43 mg   Iron: 1 mg   Sodium: 5 mg   Dietary Fiber: 3 gm

SAVE SOME ROOM FOR RICE PUDDING

Yield: 25 two-and-half ounce servings

This is an old-fashioned dessert and a real comfort food. If pudding does not thicken, stir in 4 ounces of flour (to avoid lumps, remove a small amount of the pudding, mix with flour and then return to pot, stirring until combined). The pudding can also be finished by baking. After adding the syrup, zest, etc., place pudding in a greased steam table pan and bake, at 350 degrees for 10 minutes or until thickened. Serve with a vegan topping.

INGREDIENTS	MEASURE	METHOD
White or Basmati rice, uncooked*	8 ounces	Bring rice and water to a boil in a stock pot. Lower heat, cover, and allow to simmer. When rice is "soupy" (most of liquid is absorbed), stir in milk and raisins.
Water	1-1/2 pints	
Rice or soy milk**	1-1/2 quarts	
Black or golden raisins	8 ounces	
Maple syrup	6 ounces	Bring to a boil again. Lower heat, cover, and allow to simmer for 15 minutes or until slightly thickened. Stir in syrup, extract, and zest. Stir constantly for 5 more minutes or until thick.
Vanilla extract	1/2 ounce	
Orange zest	1 ounce	

***Note:** Brown rice can be used, decrease amount by 2 ounces. Brown rice will require a longer cooking time.

****Note:** You can use plain or vanilla flavored rice or soy milk.

Total Calories per Serving: 112   Total Fat as % of Daily Value: 2%   Protein: 1 gm   Fat: 1 gm
Carbohydrates: 26 gm   Calcium: 19 mg   Iron: 1 mg   Sodium: 24 mg   Dietary Fiber: 1 gm

MELON MELANGE WITH SPICY WINE SAUCE

Yield: 25 servings

This elegant menu item can be served as cold soup or as a summery dessert. Use ripe melon, cut in very small pieces, for mechanically altered texture and purée for softer diets.

INGREDIENTS	MEASURE	METHOD
Dessert wine (i.e. sauterne)	2 quarts	In a small sauce pot, mix wine, concentrate, ginger, and vanilla.
Apple juice concentrate	4 ounces	Bring to a boil, reduce heat, and allow to simmer for 5 minutes.
Fresh ginger, peeled and sliced	3 ounces	Remove from heat, remove ginger, and allow to cool.
Vanilla extract	2 Tablespoons	
Ripe melon, cut into 1-inch cubes	20 pounds	Place melon in full 400 pans (or large mixing bowls) and pour cooled sauce over. Refrigerate for at least 1-1/2 hours.

Total Calories per Serving: 254   Total Fat as % of Daily Value: 2%   Protein: 3 gm   Fat: 1 gm
Carbohydrates: 42 gm   Calcium: 48 mg   Iron: 1 mg   Sodium: 41 mg   Dietary Fiber: 3 gm

Chapter Twelve

SENIORS

Becoming veggie is getting to be quite popular among seniors. Wherever we go, we hear "my eighty-year-old aunt just became veggie" or "I need to bring veggie meals to my 95-year-old grandmother." Many active seniors have told me that they are embracing the veggie life style; they are participating in 10K's, playing tennis, swimming, and are members of the Sierra Club. These individuals find that veggie eating makes them feel better and gives them more energy.

Seniors may turn to a veggie life style for other reasons. Medications may make some foods "taste funny" or the aging process may just alter taste perception in some people. Many of my former senior patients turned away from meat and dairy and relied on produce and grains when they weren't feeling well. Economic and mobility issues may also come into play. Many veggie foods are less costly than animal-based products and they may also have longer shelf-lives (for those seniors who don't have the ability to shop regularly, this is very important).

Incorporating vegan foods into senior menus is as easy as for any other population segment. If you are designing menus or preparing meals for a funded senior program, be sure you comply with regulations pertaining to portion sizes, ingredients, etc.

Know your audience – does your group like spicy or mild food? Do they like lots of little portions or good square meals? What ethnic foods go and which don't ? Can you coordinate special events with your menus? Are you able to get seniors to participate in the menu planning (beyond the suggestion box!)?

If you are offering home delivered meals, be sure that your veggie-requesting participants are familiar with the foods you are sending (train your drivers or volunteers about the menu and develop informational flyers or pamphlets). We once had a whole day's worth of black beans and rice returned because our veggie-seniors (who had requested more bean dishes) had never seen black beans. The drivers weren't familiar with the menu and the seniors took one look at the gray rice with a mound of black mush and rejected it. After we did some educating and counseling, black beans became one of our more popular items. The Vegetarian Resource Group has created a 4-week vegan/vegetarian meal plan in collaboration with the National Meals on Wheels Foundation. To receive this handout, send a self-addressed stamped envelope with four first-class stamps to VRG, PO Box 1463, Baltimore, MD 21203.

Even menu wording can make or break you when it comes to seniors. For example, we attempted to offer tortellini and gnocchi (stuffed with veggies and potatoes) in our area where the seniors were very non-ethnic but had asked for more "noodle dishes." When billed by their Italian (and correct names) the dishes were a flop. When renamed "home-style, home-made stuffed noodles," they were a hit! (And they still are!)

Be sure to follow food safety guidelines (see Chapter 2 and Appendix E) and to provide clean and sanitary containers for delivery and storage.

SENIOR NUTRITION

As mentioned in Chapter 1, good nutrition is important through the entire life span, with various nutrients needed in varying amounts at different times of life. It is difficult to establish senior nutrition needs, as they are such a diverse group. For example, the needs of a wheelchair-bound eighty-year-old will differ from an eighty-five-year-old who plays tennis and swims every day. We can make some generalizations about the nutrition needs of people over sixty-five and you will have to fill in the blanks, depending on your customers. Remember to consider the chewing and swallowing ability, the dexterity (can they use a knife easily), and the flavor preferences (do they like spices) of your seniors.

Energy (calorie) needs are reduced in the elderly, as lean body mass (muscle) declines with age. Therefore, seniors need to select foods that are concentrated in nutrients while low in calories. It is estimated that after the age of 51, men should reduce their intake by 600 calories a day and women 300 calories a day (Smolin, 1997); of course, this will vary depending on the level of exercise.

The need for protein does not decrease with age; adequate protein is important for a healthy immune system, for repair and maintenance of skin, muscle, and blood, and for synthesizing nutrients. Vegan sources of protein for seniors can be soups or casseroles made with beans and legumes and rice or grains, whole wheat breads served with bean salads, and tofu combinations (such as a tofu scramble served with potatoes or rice). If your seniors go for ethnic foods, bean burritos or falafel and pita bread are good protein sources.

Vitamin D and calcium are both of concern to seniors, as the need for them is high and intake can be low. Good vegan sources are tofu processed with calcium, broccoli, kale, Asian greens (such as bok choy), orange juice fortified with calcium, soy milk fortified with calcium and vitamin D, legumes, and fortified bread and cereal products.

Vitamin B12 is of concern for vegans in every age group, as it is important for a healthy blood supply. Vitamin B12 can be gotten from fortified soy beverages, fortified cereals, and nutritional yeast (Red Star's Vegetarian Support Formula), which can be added to casseroles, soups, and dressings.

Iron and zinc are important for senior nutrition for the maintenance of healthy eyesight and for a healthy blood supply, to name a few. Vegan seniors can get their iron and zinc from legumes, tofu, whole grains, and fortified cereals. Additional sources of iron are dried fruit and green leafy veggies.

Hydration is very important to seniors, as they may not think about drinking and can become dehydrated quite easily. Dehydration can result in disorientation and confusion, a change in blood pressure, and can even lead to renal and cardiac abnormalities. Offer fruit and vegetable juice "cocktails," sparkling waters, chilled and flavored soy and rice milk, and hot or cold herbal teas. Remember that caffeine- and alcohol-containing beverages do not replenish, but deplete the body of fluid.

Unfortunately, in the United States there are a large number of seniors who are malnourished or at risk of being malnourished. The digestive system works less efficiently as we age, so even a healthy, active senior must be aware of good nutrition. Add economic problems, decreased mobility, multiple medications (and drug and medication interactions), dental problems, and changes in taste, smell, or vision to this and you may have someone who is not eating very well.

In summary, your task is to prepare meals that are nutrient dense, balanced, and appeal to a broad spectrum of seniors. Senior menus should be varied to prevent boredom and to stimulate interest. Are you up to the challenge?

SENIOR MENU IDEAS

Morning meal: Apple-cranberry juice, raisin bran with sliced bananas, cinnamon toast with fruit preserves, and soy or rice milk
Or
Baked apple, oatmeal with sliced peaches, carrot muffin with margarine and fruit preserves, and soy or rice milk

Snacks: Seasonal fresh fruit and popcorn, stewed fruit and corn bread, graham crackers with peanut butter and grape juice, mixed fruit juice cocktail and pretzels, rice pudding (see Chapter 11 for recipe) and orange slices, strawberry sorbet, and peanut butter cookies

Main meal: Ravioli with marinara sauce, tossed green salad with dressing, steamed, herbed broccoli, citrus fruit salad, garlic bread, and orange sorbet
Or
Lentil-tomato soup with a whole grain roll, baked potato with tofu sour cream (see Chapter 11 for recipe) and chopped veggies, steamed carrots with dill, vegetable juice cocktail, and tapioca pudding (made with rice or soy milk)
Or
Veggie loaf with mushroom gravy, mashed potatoes, applesauce with cinnamon, steamed yellow squash, sliced beet salad, and peanut butter cookies
Or
Minestrone soup, pasta salad (with chopped veggies and vinaigrette dressing), carrot and raisin salad (with vegan mayonnaise), corn bread, and butterscotch pudding (made with rice or soy milk) topped with chopped dried fruit or chopped canned apricots

MENU WRITING IDEAS FOR SENIORS

Breakfast ideas: Pancakes (add fruit and/or nuts), waffles, cold cereals, hot cereals (wheat, rice, cornmeal, kasha, oats, etc. served with canned or stewed fruit)

Fruit: Baked apples; applesauce; canned, dried or fresh apricots; bananas sliced in fruit juice; fresh or frozen berries; canned cherries; fresh, canned or dried figs; fresh or broiled grapefruit; grapes; fresh, canned or dried peaches; fresh, canned or dried pears (can also be baked or made into sauce); sliced or crushed canned pineapple; fresh, canned or stewed prunes; fresh plums; sliced or diced melons; stewed rhubarb

Fruit juice: Apple, apricot, cranberry, grape, grapefruit, pineapple, orange, prune, tomato, and blends

Vegetables: Fresh, canned or frozen asparagus, green beans, wax beans, lima beans, broccoli, beets (pickled, with orange sauce), cabbage (sautéed, sweet and sour), Brussels sprouts, carrots (glazed, orange juice), cauliflower (creamed, au gratin – with soy cheese and soy milk), collard greens, corn (baked, creamed), eggplant (stewed, baked), kale (braised, steamed), okra (stewed, fried), spinach (sautéed with garlic, creamed, steamed), zucchini, crookneck squash, winter squash (baked with cinnamon), spaghetti squash, tomatoes (stewed, fried), turnips (mashed, baked)

Soups: Cream of broccoli, asparagus, carrot, mushroom, cauliflower, celery, tomato ("cream" is made by cooking veggies until soft, puréeing, and adding mashed potatoes and heated soy milk. Some cooked veggies, such as sweet potatoes, squash, and carrots have a creamy appearance with puréeing – no additional ingredients needed). Navy bean, corn chowder, green pea, split pea, lima bean, vegetable, lentil, white bean, black bean, barley, minestrone, tomato vegetable

Main dishes: Lentil stew, Tofu Tetrazzini (see recipe on page 193), veggie burgers, veggie loaf, ravioli, tortellini, spaghetti and not meat balls (see Chapter 5 for recipe), vegetable stir-fry, vegetable lo mein, stuffed cabbage, peppers or tomatoes, tomato strata, veggie baked sandwiches, tamale or shepherd's pie (bean casserole topped with corn bread or mashed potatoes), veggie lasagna

Desserts: Fresh fruit kebobs, fruit pies, Tofu Cheesecake (see recipe on page 85), assorted cookies, sorbet, soy or rice ice milk, puddings made with soy or rice milk, shortcakes (biscuits served with peaches or strawberries), baked apples or pears, fruit crisps and cobblers, quick breads (carrot cake, zucchini or banana bread), frozen or canned fruit garnished with vegan whipped topping or served with sorbet

RECIPES

See Chapters 4 (AM Shuffle), 7 (Holidays), and 11 (Un-hospital Food) for additional recipes that suit your needs.

TORTELLINI AND VEGGIE SALAD

Yield: 25 five-ounce servings

This cold pasta salad makes an excellent entrée.

INGREDIENTS	MEASURE	METHOD
Frozen vegan tortellini, cooked, drained, and cooled	6 pounds	Place pasta in a large mixing bowl and toss with dressing, lentils, and vegetables.
Vinaigrette dressing	3 pints	
Lentils, cooked, drained, and cooled	3 pounds	Line dinner plates with romaine.
Carrots, shredded	1 pound	Place 5 ounces of pasta on each leaf.
Green onions, chopped	5 ounces	Serve chilled. Garnish with cherry
Olives, sliced	8 ounces	tomatoes, fresh basil, or chopped
Tomatoes, chopped	8 ounces	broccoli.
Cucumbers, chopped	8 ounces	
Romaine leaves, washed and drained	25 leaves	

Variations: Use cooked kidney or garbanzo beans for color variety. If your clientele will accept it, used cubed firm tofu instead of beans. Mini-ravioli can be used instead of tortellini.

Total Calories per Serving: 332   Total Fat as % of Daily Value: 17%   Protein: 17 gm   Fat: 11 gm
Carbohydrates: 52 gm   Calcium: 121 mg   Iron: 4 mg   Sodium: 770 mg   Dietary Fiber: 4 gm

CREAM OF CARROT SOUP

Yield: 25 six-ounce servings

Potage Crecy (Cream of Carrot to us!) has a natural beauty in its taste and texture. It can be prepared a day ahead and reheated.

INGREDIENTS	MEASURE	METHOD
Vegetable oil spray	to cover pot	Spray a stock pot and heat. Add carrots and onions and allow them to cook until just soft. Add stock and potatoes. Bring to a boil, reduce heat, and allow to simmer (covered) until vegetables are very tender, about 15 minutes.
Carrots, finely diced	4-1/2 pounds	
Onions, finely diced	1 pound	
Vegetable stock	5 quarts	
Potatoes, peeled and diced	1-1/2 pounds	
Ground ginger	1/2 ounce	Stir in spices. Purée in a blender or food processor until smooth. Place soup back in pot to heat. Serve hot.
White pepper	1/2 ounce	

Variations: If soup is too thick, it can be thinned with a small amount of heated carrot juice or soy milk. For a change of thickeners, white rice can be used instead of potatoes.

Total Calories per Serving: 76   Total Fat as % of Daily Value: <1%   Protein: 2 gm   Fat: <1 gm
Carbohydrates: 17 gm   Calcium: 36 mg   Iron: <1 mg   Sodium: 37 mg   Dietary Fiber: 3 gm

CHESAPEAKE CORN CHOWDER

Yield: 25 six-ounce servings

This soup can be prepared as is or diced seasonal vegetables can be added for color and flavor. Add a baked potato or hearty whole grain bread and a vegetable salad for a fast lunch or light supper menu.

INGREDIENTS	MEASURE	METHOD
Vegetable oil spray	to cover pot	Heat a stock pot and spray with oil.
Onions, medium diced	14 ounces	Sauté onions, celery, and garlic
Celery, finely diced	6 ounces	(don't brown). Add flour and stir
Fresh garlic, minced	1 ounce	well for 2 minutes (don't brown).
Flour	6 ounces	This is your thickener.
Vegetable stock	3-1/2 quarts	Add stock and potatoes, stirring
Potatoes, peeled	4 pounds	constantly until smooth.
Cut corn, thawed*	3-1/2 pounds	Add corn. Allow to simmer until
Unflavored soy milk,	3 pints	all vegetables are tender. Heat milk.
White pepper	1 ounce	Stir in milk, pepper, and onion
Onion powder	1 ounce	powder. Allow to simmer for 2 minutes. Serve hot.

*Note: Used thawed frozen cut corn or drained canned corn. If using canned corn, a portion of the stock can be replaced with the liquid from the drained corn. For a smoother chowder, use canned creamed corn (reduce stock by 3 cups).

Total Calories per Serving: 211   Total Fat as % of Daily Value: 5%   Protein: 8 gm   Fat: 3 gm
Carbohydrates: 29 gm   Calcium: 51 mg   Iron: 1 mg   Sodium: 81 mg   Dietary Fiber: 3 gm

PASTA WITH VEGETABLE-MARINARA SAUCE

Yield: 25 servings (four ounces sauce and five ounces pasta)

Make the sauce one or two days ahead of time to allow the flavors to "marry."

INGREDIENTS	MEASURE	METHOD
Olive oil	3 ounces	Heat a stock pot. Add oil. Sauté onions and spices until onions are soft. Add tomato paste, tomatoes, and juice. Allow to boil, reduce heat, and simmer for 15 minutes. Add squash and mushrooms. Cook only until squash is soft. Serve hot over pasta.
Onions, diced	1 pound	
Garlic powder	1/2 ounce	
Dried basil	1 ounce	
Ground oregano	1/2 ounce	
Black pepper	1 ounce	
Tomato paste	12 ounces	
Canned tomatoes, chopped and drained	2 pounds	
Tomato juice	2-1/2 quarts	
Zucchini, chopped	2 pounds	
Summer squash, chopped	1 pound	
Canned mushrooms, drained and sliced	1 pound	
Pasta, cooked and drained	2-1/2 pounds	

Variations: If fresh squash is not available, you can use thawed, frozen squash. Allow more cooking time as the frozen has more liquid, which will have to cook off. Fresh mushrooms can be used, just blanch them (steam briefly) before adding to sauce.

Total Calories per Serving: 157   Total Fat as % of Daily Value: 6%   Protein: 5 gm   Fat: 4 gm
Carbohydrates: 27 gm   Calcium: 78 mg   Iron: 4 mg   Sodium: 530 mg   Dietary Fiber: 4 gm

VERY VEGGIE CHOW MEIN

Yield: 25 four-ounce servings

This is an American spin on Asian flavor. Serve over steamed brown or white rice, rice noodles, angel-hair pasta, or use as a filling for egg rolls or won ton wrappers (to do this, you'll need to chop the vegetables rather than slice them).

INGREDIENTS	MEASURE	METHOD
Bell peppers, sliced thinly	4 ounces	Steam all vegetables until just soft.
Celery, sliced thinly	2 pounds	Place vegetables in a stock pot, add
Green onions, chopped	8 ounces	stock, and allow to heat.
Onions, sliced thinly	1 pound	In a small bowl, mix cornstarch and
Mushrooms, sliced thinly	2 pounds	water and stir until a paste is formed.
Fresh bean sprouts	2 pounds	Stir soy sauce into paste.
Vegetable stock	1 quart	Add paste into vegetables, stirring
Cornstarch	4 ounces	constantly for smoothness. Allow to
Cold water	5 ounces	cook until thickened. Serve hot.
Soy sauce	5 ounces	

Notes: The key to this dish is to keep the veggies crisp, so have all your ingredients ready and cook minimally. Reduced-salt soy sauce may be used if desired. If fresh bean sprouts are not an option, drain and rinse canned bean sprouts and add after paste has been incorporated. Garnish with fresh pepper strips, baby corn, sliced almonds, or crisp noodles. If desired, steamed tofu or seitan can be added to this recipe (approximately 2-1/2 pounds)

Total Calories per Serving: 59   Total Fat as % of Daily Value: 2%   Protein: 3 gm   Fat: 1 gm
Carbohydrates: 12 gm   Calcium: 33 mg   Iron: 1 mg   Sodium: 440 mg   Dietary Fiber: 2 gm

SOUTHWEST TOMATO RICE

Yield: 25 six-ounce servings

This colorful dish can serve as an entrée, a side dish, or as stuffing for baked tomatoes or bell peppers. If desired, 2 pounds of soy crumbles or TVP can be mixed in before baking (or used as a topping). Crumbled cooked veggie burgers can also be used.

INGREDIENTS	MEASURE	METHOD
White rice, cooked*	6 pounds	Keep rice warm until ready to use.
Vegetable oil spray	to cover pot	Heat a stock pot, spray oil, and
Mushrooms, sliced	2-1/2 pounds	sauté mushrooms. Add onions,
Onions, chopped	10 ounces	pepper, and celery and cook until
Red pepper flakes	1 ounce	soft.
Black pepper	1/2 ounce	
Celery, chopped	8 ounces	
Canned tomatoes, chopped	3 pounds	Add remaining ingredients (except rice) and allow to simmer for 5
Tomato paste	8 ounces	minutes. Mix in rice. Place in steam
Chili sauce**	2 cups	table pans, top with chopped fresh tomatoes (2 pounds) if desired, and bake at 350 degrees for 45 minutes.

*Note: You can make this recipe also with pastina pasta or couscous.

**Note: Fresh salsa can be used instead of chili sauce.

Total Calories per Serving: 198   Total Fat as % of Daily Value: 2%   Protein: 5 gm   Fat: 1 gm
Carbohydrates: 43 gm   Calcium: 32 mg   Iron: 3 mg   Sodium: 382 mg   Dietary Fiber: 2 gm

SPARKLING APRI-PINE PUNCH

Yield: 25 six-ounce portions

Fluids are important – make them fun!

INGREDIENTS	MEASURE	METHOD
Apricot nectar	1-1/2 quarts	Combine all ingredients and serve
Pineapple juice	1-1/2 quarts	chilled.
Frozen lemon juice, thawed, not diluted	6 ounces	
Cold water	1-1/2 pints	
Cold ginger ale	1 quart	

Total Calories per Serving: 80   Total Fat as % of Daily Value: <1%   Protein: <1 gm   Fat: <1 gm
Carbohydrates: 20 gm   Calcium: 12 mg   Iron: <1 mg   Sodium: 6 mg   Dietary Fiber: <1 gm

ORANGE NUT FILLING

Yield: 1 quart or 28 one-ounce servings

Use this hearty filling as a topping for fruit tarts, make cookie "sandwiches" with it, or layer it on cakes.

INGREDIENTS	MEASURE	METHOD
Margarine	3 ounces	In a small stock pot, melt margarine.
Walnuts, chopped	1 pound	Add nuts and toss and cook until
Dry sweetener	6 ounces	toasted. Add sweetener and
Cinnamon	1 ounce	cinnamon. Heat thoroughly. Add
Orange marmalade	1 pound	marmalade, remove from heat. Mix well. Use warm or refrigerate until ready to use.

Variation: Finely chopped dried apricots or dates can be added when the marmalade is added.

Total Calories per Serving: 185   Total Fat as % of Daily Value: 18%   Protein: 4 gm   Fat: 12 gm
Carbohydrates: 19 gm   Calcium: 16 mg   Iron: 1 mg   Sodium: 35 mg   Dietary Fiber: 1 gm

HOMESTYLE MOLASSES COOKIES

Yield: 6-1/2 dozen one-ounce cookies

These aromatic cookies are reminiscent of gingerbread.

INGREDIENTS	MEASURE	METHOD
All purpose flour	2 pounds	Mix together flour, spices, and soda. Set aside. Add shortening and sweetener in a mixer bowl. Beat on medium speed for 4 minutes, using paddle.
Ground cinnamon	2 ounces	
Ground nutmeg	1/2 ounce	
Ground ginger	1/2 ounce	
Ground cloves	1/2 ounce	
Baking soda	2 ounces	
Vegetable shortening	12 ounces	
Granulated sweetener	6 ounces	
Egg replacer*	7 ounces	Add egg replacer, slowly, beating well. Add molasses slowly, beating well. Combine dry and wet ingredients. When combined, put mixer on low speed and mix well. Preheat oven to 350 degrees. Drop by 1-ounce spoonfuls onto greased baking sheets. Bake at 350 degrees for 8 minutes or until crisp around the edges, but soft in the center.
Molasses	6 ounces	

*Note: Read the directions for the egg replacer you choose; you need 7 ounces of liquid egg replacer for this recipe. If egg replacer is not an option, substitute 5 ounces of puréed silken tofu.

Total Calories per Cookie: 100   Total Fat as % of Daily Value: 6%   Protein: 1 gm
Fat: 4 gm   Carbohydrates: 14 gm   Calcium: 33 mg   Iron: 1 mg   Sodium: 201 mg
Dietary Fiber: <1 gm

WEIGHTS AND MEASURES

VOLUME (LIQUID MEASURE)
1 gallon = 4 quarts or 128 fluid ounces
1 quart = 2 pints or 4 cups or 32 fluid ounces
1 pint = 2 cups or 16 fluid ounces
1 cup = 8 ounces
1 ounce = 2 Tablespoons
1 Tablespoon = 3 teaspoons

WEIGHT (SOLID or DRY)
1 pound = 16 ounces

MISCELLANEOUS
1 fluid ounce = one solid ounce
1 pint of water = one solid pound

CAPACITY OF QUANTITY EQUIPMENT
Full 200 pan = 12-15 pounds or 8 quarts
Full 400 pan = 24-30 pounds or 14 quarts
Half 200 = 6-7 pounds or 4 quarts
Half 400 = 12-15 pounds or 6 quarts
Half 600 = 18 pounds or 10 quarts
Quarter 200 = 60 ounces
Quarter 400 = 96 ounces
Quarter 600 =146 ounces

SCOOPS (the number on the tine of a scoop indicates the number of servings per quart; for example, a # 8 scoop holds 4 ounces {32 ounces/quart divided by 8 = 4} here is a reference chart to save time on the math):

32 = 1 ounce (used for margarine, soy cream cheese, etc.)
16 = 2 ounces
12 = 2-1/2 - 3 ounces
10 = 3-3-1/2 ounces
8 = 4 ounces

COMMON COMMERCIAL CAN SIZE

Number	Size
Number 10	6 pounds 9 ounces or approximately 3 quarts; the largest can size, used for fruit, vegetables, beans, peanut butter, jelly
46 ounce	cylindrical, used for juice
Number 2-1/2	3-1/2 cups, used for fruit and veggies, tomato products
Number 303	2 cups, cylindrical, used for vegetables, sauces
Number 300	1-3/4 cups, used for specialty items such as cranberry sauce
Number 1	1-1/4 cups, cylindrical, used for condensed soups

PRODUCT RESOURCES

Please note: the following list is to get you started. Today there are countless vegan items available for food service. For more product information visit The Vegetarian Resource Group website at: www.vrg.org

APPLE CIDER VINEGAR

The Hain Food Group, Inc. vegan product line for food service includes Apple Cider Vinegar in cases of twelve 32-ounce containers. For more information on this product call (800) 434-4246 or (516) 237-6200.

BEANS, REFRIED

Hunt-Wesson Foodservice, Fullerton, CA 92833 distributes Rosarita vegan refried beans, as well as other vegan Mexican food items. Call (800) 633-0112 for more information.

BEVERAGES, NON-DAIRY

The Hain Food Group, Inc. vegan product line for food service includes both soy milk (plain and vanilla flavor) and rice milk (plain and cinnamon flavor) in cases of twelve 32-ounce containers. For more information on these products call (800) 434-4246 or (516) 237-6200.

5-pound and 20-pound packages of organic lowfat soy milk powder are available from Sunorganic Farm. For more information call (888) 269-9888 or write to Sunorganic Farm, PO Box 2429, Valley Center, CA 92082 and request their catalog. Also visit their website at www.sunorganic.com

BREAD

Tortilla wraps are great for breakfast and lunch sandwiches. Fill with chopped vegetables and hummus, black beans and chopped onions, crumbled veggie burgers, and salsa, or even fresh fruit and soy yogurt for a dessert wrap (we've seen dessert wraps baked with syrup or deep-fried and sprinkled with chopped nuts). Tumaro's offers gourmet tortillas in various flavors including Sun Dried Tomato and Basil, Jalapeño and Cilantro, Whole Wheat, and more. All flavors are available in 6-inch, 8-inch, 10-inch, and 12- to 13-inch sizes. These can be used for vegan wraps. For information call (800) 777-6317 or write to Tumaro's, 5300 Santa Monica Blvd., Suite 311, Los Angeles, CA 90029. You can also visit their website at www.tumaros.com

CHILI

Birch Hill Country Foods is offering a natural chili base made from fresh peppers to be used with beans, veggies, or grains to build your own chili. Call (978) 297-1783 or visit them online at www.masy.com/birchhill

Ridgefield's offers a pre-made vegan chili for food service. You can contact them at (800) 800-2269.

CHIPS

Readers may recall seeing Terra Chips made out of taro, sweet potatoes, and other vegetables. These beautiful looking and absolutely delicious gourmet chips are available now to food service only in a julienne rendition. Cut into matchstick size, these chips can be used as an alternative to croutons in salads, as a colorful garnish alongside entrées, tossed in with popcorn to add color, or as a side to sandwiches. Each case contains four 16-ounce bags. For further information contact Hain Food Group at (800) 434-4246.

DRIED BEANS, ORGANIC

Eden Foods, Inc., 701 Tecumseh Rd., Clinton, MI 49236 is now offering on the east coast of the United States 25-pound bags of packaged organic dried beans including: aduki beans, black soy beans, black turtle beans, dark red kidney beans, green lentils, green split peas, navy beans, pinto beans, and red small beans. For further details call (517) 456-7424 or (800) 248-0301.

Sunorganic Farm offers organically grown dried peas and beans in both 5-pound and 20-pound bags. For more information call (888) 269-9888 or write to Sundance Country Farm, PO Box 2429, Valley Center, CA 92082 and request their catalog. Also visit their website at www.sunorganic.com

DRIED FRUIT, NUTS, AND NUT BUTTERS, ORGANIC

Sundance Country Farm offers organically grown dried fruit and nuts. They can be ordered in 5-pound and 20-pound bags. Nut butters come in 15-pound buckets. For more information call (888) 269-9888 or write to Sunorganic Farm, PO Box 2429, Valley Center, CA 92082 and request their catalog. Also visit their website at www.sunorganic.com

ENTRÉES

Alle Processing Corporation manufactures Mon Cuisine food service products, which include several vegan entrées such as stuffed shells, burgers, "meatballs." "beef steak" in cherry sauce, breaded chicken-style cutlets in mushroom sauce, and more. Call (800) 245-5620 for information or write to them at 56-20 59th Street, Maspeth, NY 11378.

Cuisine Solutions offers ready-to-use entrées for the chef. All products are made to fit upscale menus, as if a chef had been preparing them. Among the vegan offerings are Penne with Fire Roasted Red Pepper Sauce, Penne with Dijon Mustard Sauce, and Medley of Lentils and Vegetables with Chili Spices. Entrées come frozen in four 3-pound pouches. All products are immersed in boiling water (or placed in a steamer) for preparation and are very easy to prepare. Cuisine Solutions is an international company with headquarters in France, Norway, and the USA. For more information contact Cuisine Solutions, 85 S. Bragg Street, Suite 600, Alexandria, VA 22312; (888) 285-4679 or (703) 751-8600. You can also visit their website at 222.cuisinesolutions.com

FLOURS, ORGANIC WHOLE GRAIN

Eden Foods, Inc., 701 Tecumseh Rd., Clinton, MI 49236 is now offering on the east coast of the United States a number of their products in food service size packaging including the following organic whole grain flours in 50 pound bags: buckwheat flour, yellow corn meal, blue corn meal, rye flour, toasted soy flour, whole wheat pastry flour, whole golden amber durum wheat flour, whole hard red spring wheat flour, and whole hard red winter wheat flour. For further details call (517) 456-7424 or (800) 248-0301. Their website is www.eden-foods.com

FRUIT

Amber Foods offers a wide selection of fruit sections and fruit salad for food service. For information call (559) 591-4782 or write to Amber Foods, 42637 Road 114, Dinuba, CA 93618.

GRAINS

Fantastic Foods offers a wide range of vegan products for food service that are simple to prepare. In the grain category they offer 11# Arborio Rice; 11#, 22#, and 44# Basmati Rice; 44# Brown Basmati Rice; 50# Couscous; 50# Jasmine Rice; and 50# Whole Wheat Couscous. For further information call the Food Service Manager at (360) 855-2722.

Sundance Country Farm offers organically grown grains in both 5-pound and 20-pound bags. For more information call (888) 269-9888 or write to Sunorganic Farm, PO Box 2429, Valley Center, CA 92082 and request their catalog.

ICECREAM, SOFT-SERVE VEGAN

Looking for a vegan product to put in your soft-serve machine? Oatscream is made from oats, water, and natural flavors (such as coffee, Dutch cocoa, vanilla extract, and fruit concentrates) and calcium carbonate. It has no sugar, fat, emulsifiers, or preservatives. There are 120 calories in a 4-ounce serving. Flavors available include chocolate, vanilla, black cherry, pumpkin pie, and mango. The manufacturer suggests that you can make you own flavors by mixing, for example, chocolate with cherry or mango with vanilla.

Oatscream comes frozen in 1 gallon pails, 4 gallons to the case. It must be thawed in the fridge and can be used in any standard soft-serve machine. The thawed mix has a 4 week shelf life in the fridge. Use Oatscream to create smoothies, shakes, sundaes, and frozen cakes and pies.

For further information contact American Oats, Inc., 18338 Minnetonka Blvd., Wayzata, MN 55391; (612) 473-4738; or www.OatsCream.com

ITALIAN FOOD ITEMS

Master Food Services a division of Uncle Ben's, Inc. distributes Seeds of Change's organic pasta sauces including Spicy Roasted Garlic and Tomato Basil. For more information call (800) 432-2331. Their website is www.masterfoodservices.com

The Pastene Companies, Ltd., PO Box 256, Canton, MA 02021 offers a wide range of Italian food service items. For example, they offer balsamic vinegar, wine vinegar, Italian peeled tomatoes, ground peeled tomatoes, tomato paste, olive oil, sundried tomatoes, pasta, marinated peppers, and marinated vegetables. For more information call (888) 727-8363. Visit their website at www.pastene.com

MEAT ALTERNATIVES

Worthington Foods, Inc. now offers two vegan products under the Morningstar Farms label. Better'n Burgers come frozen in 4 packages of 12 burgers per case. These burgers are fat-free and their shelf life is approximately 12 months. The burgers are manufactured on certified Kosher/dairy equipment. According to the company, Better'n Burgers may be baked or grilled. They can be prepared and held in a covered heated container up to 30 minutes prior to serving. For savory vegan "meatballs" you can defrost these burgers and roll them into bite-size pieces. Bake the "meatballs" and serve them with barbecue sauce. They're absolutely delicious!

The Foodservice IQF Burger Crumbles come in two 5-pound bags per case. A serving size is considered 2/3 cup. This product is primarily made from textured vegetable protein and can be used in recipes calling for browned ground beef such as tacos, sloppy Joes, chili, lasagna, pasta dishes, pizza toppings, and salads. The Crumbles should thaw in the refrigerator 24-36 hours prior to use. For information call (800) 243-1810 ext. 301.

Gardenburger (formerly Wholesome and Hearty) now offers 2 vegan burgers for food service. One is both fat-free and cholesterol-free. The primary ingredients for this burger are soy protein concentrate and modified wheat gluten. The burger can be placed frozen on a lightly oiled griddle and heated for approximately 3-5 minutes on each side before serving. The burger can also be prepared over a grill. Each case contains forty-eight 2.5-ounce burgers. For information call Gardenburger at (800) 636-0109.

Vegi-Deli's Vegetarian Slice of Life meatless deli rolls contain fewer than 3 grams of fat per serving. These meat alternatives are made from wheat protein, nutritional yeast, and seasonings. Two 3-pound deli rolls come in each case. A 3-pound deli roll contains sixteen 3-ounce servings. Refrigerated, shelf life for this product is 3-6 months depending upon the product. For further details call (888) 473-3667 or visit their website at www.vegideli.com

Lightlife Foods, Inc., 153 Industrial Blvd., Turner Falls, MA 01376; (413) 774-6001 continues to offer a wide range of delicious meat alternatives suitable for food service settings. Their Smart Dogs come in cases containing 3 packages of 32 dogs (for a total of 96). Smart Dogs are pre-cooked and simply need to be warmed in boiling water for 2-3 minutes. These veggie dogs should be served in a chafing dish containing warm water.

Lightlife also offers a wide variety of veggie hamburgers including their soy-based Lightburger which come in cases containing 3 packages of 16 hamburgers (for a total of 48). Lightburgers should be pan-fried in oil for 2 minutes per side, until brown. You can also heat the burgers on high for 60 seconds per burger in a microwave, or grill, broil, or bake them until hot. In addition to serving veggie burgers the traditional way (buns, lettuce, and tomato, etc), try layering them in steam table pans and creating sloppy Joe casseroles, individual "Salisbury steaks," or tamale pies.

Lightlife offers Grilles Tamari and Barbecue tempeh burgers. Cases contain 3 packages of 18 (for a total of 54 burgers). Both products can be fried in a lightly oiled pan for 2 minutes on each side or grilled.

Chia's Classic Chili comes in cases containing 4 five-pound containers (totaling 20 pounds). You simply heat this product and serve as you would a meat-based chili. This product is delicious served over Lightlife's Smart Dogs.

Lightlife's Lean Links Italian are terrific served on a roll with peppers and onions for lunch or tossed with pasta and marinara sauce for dinner. This product comes in cases containing 3 packages of 35 links (totaling 108). Lean Links Italian can be heated on an oiled griddle for 6-8 minutes, turning frequently or microwaved 1 minute per 2 links.

Smart Deli Slices Turkey come in cases of 3 packages that are 4 pounds each. Smart slices can be served like traditional cold cuts. Portion sizes are 3 slices. Traditional Seitan comes in cases of four 2.5-pound packages. Seitan can be used in place of meat in many recipes including stir-fries, kabobs, stews, sandwiches, and more. The seitan can be pan fried, microwaved, or grilled.

Lightlife's Gimme Lean Beef product comes in cases containing 3 packages weighing 4 pounds each. Use as you would ground beef to make meatballs, burgers, meat loaf, pizza topping, casseroles, and more. To use this product, you simply form it into patties or make "crumbles" by chopping with a spatula while cooking. Brown Gimme Lean Beef in oil for 3-5 minutes. Several of Lightlife's products are fat-free. For information visit their website: www.lightlife.com

Vegan Epicure, Rebecca Hall Kitchen, 1251 Trumansburg Rd., Ithaca, NY 14850; (607) 272-0432 offers seitan (gluten) in various flavors in 8-ounce to 5-pound packages. Seitan is an excellent alternative to meat in stew recipes.

Spice of Life from Golden Light Health offers 5-pound and 25-pound institutional packs of its vegan meatless meats (texturized vegetable proteins). These products are wheat-free, cholesterol-free, high in fiber and protein, and have the look, taste, and texture of a wide range of meats. Varieties include beef, ground beef, Mexican beef, Teriyaki beef, chicken, chicken mince, Italian sausage, pepperoni, smoked ham, unflavored, and unflavored mince. To prepare you simply boil these items in water for 10 to 12 minutes (6 to 8 minutes if you are microwaving on high). Every 8 ounces makes about 1 pound of meat after reconstitution. This company also offers delicious meatless jerky in 5-pound and 25-pound packages. For further information call (800) 256-2253 or (818) 909-0052 or write to Spice of Life Company, 15445 Ventura Blvd., Suite 115, Sherman Oaks, CA 91403.

Boca Burger offers a vegan burger for food service, as well as ground Boca Burger, which can be used in casseroles, chili, etc. For information visit their website at www.bocaburger.com or call (312) 840-8560.

MIDDLE EASTERN FOOD ITEMS

Zanontian & Sons Import-Export Corporation offers a wide variety of Middle Eastern items appropriate for food service. Items include rice-stuffed grape leaves and more. For further information write to PO Box 9901, Fresno, CA 93794 or call (559) 248-0151.

Grecian Delight offers vegan hummus for food service. It comes frozen and simply has to be thawed to use in sandwiches, etc. The hummus is sold in half-gallon containers, three per pack. Grecian Delight also sells falafel for food service. For further details you can write to Grecian Delight at 1201 Tonne, Elk Grove Village, IL 60007 or call (800) 621-4387.

MIXES

Fantastic Foods sells several of their bulk mixes in quantities of 10# and 25# including Falafel, Hummus, Instant Black Beans, Instant Refried Beans, and Tabouli Salad. They also produce their Tofu Burger mix, Nature's Burger Original Flavor, Nature's Burger Sausage, and Vegetarian Chili in 10# and 25# packages. For further information call the Food Service Manager at (360) 855-2722.

MUSHROOMS

Giorgio Fresh Division offers a wide variety of mushrooms including shiitake, oyster, portabella, and crimini for food service. Package sizes are between three and 10 pounds. The mushrooms can be purchased sliced, too. For more information call (610) 939-9400 or write to Giorgio Fresh Division, PO Box 96, Temple, PA 19560.

Marinated Portabello Mushrooms are available from Phillips Foods, Kennett Square, PA. The mushrooms have a ninety-day shelf-life (refrigerated) and are available as caps or slices. They come 2/8-pound tubs packed to a case. These mushrooms work well as a main entrée ingredient and in salads, soups, stir-fries, and pastas. Use these portabellos for elegant entrées (grill with garlic and basil) and for cold entrée salads (served on a bed of chilled couscous tossed with chopped cilantro). Call (610) 925-0520 or visit www.phillipsfoodservice.com

OILS

The Hain Food Group, Inc. vegan product line for food service includes Canola, Safflower, Sunflower, and Peanut Oil in cases of twelve 32-ounce containers. For more information on these products, call (800) 434-4246 or (516) 237-6200.

1-gallon and 3-gallon jars of organic oils are available from Sunorganic Farm. For more information call (888) 269-9888 or write to Sunorganic Farm, PO Box 2429, Valley Center, CA 92082 and request their catalog.

PASTA

Costa Macaroni Company has egg-free pasta in a variety of shapes and sizes (the gemilli, a short-braided pasta, and the orecchiette, which looks like miniature snail shells are terrific) in 10- and 20-pound boxes. Add this semolina-based pasta to soups, stews, casseroles, and salads.

Remember when preparing dried pasta such as this that raw product yields 2-3 times its weight when cooked (so for every pound of raw pasta cooked, you'll get between 2 and 3 pounds of cooked pasta). Try to rinse pasta lightly, so as to preserve as many nutrients as possible. For more information call (800) 433-7785.

You can order 5-pound and 20-pound bags of organic whole wheat pasta and organic wheat-free pasta from Sunorganic Farm. For more information call (888) 269-9888 or write to Sunorganic Farm, PO Box 2429, Valley Center, CA 92082 and request their catalog.

If you prefer fresh pasta, Florentyna's offers several egg-free fresh pastas, including fettuccini (try the tomato or the lemon pepper flavor) or angel hair. This fresh pasta has a refrigerated shelf life of 30 days. Custom packaging is available (they may pack to the size you need). You know the drill with fresh pasta: have the water at a rolling boil, add the pasta, and allow to cook for only three or four minutes. Don't rinse it and do serve immediately. Fresh pasta has a chewy texture and a milder flavor than dried pasta. Also, fresh pasta does not expand as much as dried pasta, so take this into consideration when ordering. Fresh pasta only expands about half its weight. For Florentyna information call (800) 747-2782 or visit their website at www.freshpasta.com

PRODUCE, PRE-CHOPPED AND/OR ORGANIC

Tanimura & Antle's Fast n' Fresh product line is sure to make food service personnel's life easier. Items available include fresh cut salad mixes (American Mix, European Mix, Salad Mix, and Cole Slaw Mix); fresh cut broccoli florets and carrots (shredded or whole peeled mini carrots); and head lettuce including trimmed iceberg, trimmed green leaf, trimmed red leaf, and trimmed romaine. They also offer both red and green cabbage shredded and fresh-cut lettuce and spinach including chopped iceberg, shredded iceberg, chopped romaine, and pre-washed and cleaned whole-leaf spinach. All these items would be terrific in a salad bar setting or for stir-fry dishes. Bag sizes vary per item. For further information write to PO Box 4070, Salinas, CA 93912-4070 or call (800) 772-4542.

Grimmway Farms, PO Box 81507, Bakersfield, CA 93380 offers various fresh and frozen produce items pre-cut to meet your needs. For example, you can purchase frozen baby whole carrots, smooth sliced carrots, crinkle cut carrots, bias cut carrots, or chunk carrots. For package sizes and further information call (805) 854-6250.

Natural Selection Foods offers several varieties of bulk organic baby greens from Earthbound Farm including mixed baby greens, baby spinach, mixed baby greens with fresh herbs, baby lettuce mix, Asian salad mix, and baby red and green romaine. For further details write to Natural Selection Foods, 1721 San Juan Hwy., San Juan Bautista, CA 95045 or call (888) 624-1004. You can also visit their website: www.nsfoods.com.

Foxy Organics from The Nunes Company, Inc., PO Box 673, Salinas, CA 93902, offers cauliflower (25-30 pounds per carton); celery (55-65 pounds per carton); celery hearts (29-33 pounds per carton); green onions (48 bunches per carton); iceberg lettuce (various amounts); radishes (24 bunches); green leaf lettuce (24 heads per carton); broccoli (20-24 pounds per carton); red leaf lettuce (24 heads per carton); romaine lettuce (24 heads per carton); romaine hearts (12 bags or 3 hearts per carton); and butter lettuce (24 heads per carton). For more information call (831) 751-7500 or visit their web site at <www.foxy.com>.

SAUCE

Cuisine Solutions offers ready-to-use Tomato Sauce with Basil. Contact Cuisine Solutions, 85 S. Bragg Street, Suite 600, Alexandria, VA 22312; (888) 285-4679.

SEASONINGS

San-J International, Inc., 2880 Sprouse Dr., Richmond VA 23231; (800) 446-5500 or (804) 226-8333; offers a wide selection of sauces you can use on many different types of vegetarian dishes. You'll find Tamari, Reduced Sodium Tamari, Teriyaki, Hot and Spicy Szechuan Sauce, and Thai Peanut Sauce. All come in 5-ounce, 10-ounce, 64-ounce, and 5-gallon size containers. You can visit their website at www.san-j.com

SOUP MIXES, BASES, AND BROTHS

RC Fine Foods is a purveyor of soup mixes and bases, seasonings, salad dressings, and dessert mixes. Many of their items do contain meat and dairy, but they have added several vegan items to their base and soup line, as follows: Vegetable Bouillon Base (request the variety without MSG) and Golden Vegetable Base. They are available in 6/13 ounces, 12/13 ounces, and 30-pound pails. Thirteen ounces of mix yields 4-5 gallons of broth. These bases can be used as a starter for hearty vegetable or bean soups or for light soups (just add cooked pasta or rice to the prepared bases). The prepared bases can also be used as a cooking liquid for vegetables, pastas, or grains. The dry base can be used as a flavoring agent for casseroles and stews.

Vegetarian Vegetable Soup Mix (request the variety without MSG): available in 12/18-ounce cases (yields 2 gallons of soup). Use as is or add extra vegetables, potatoes or grains.

Low Sodium Herbal Seasoning Mix (available in 12/8 ounces with no MSG): a blend of herbs and spices with no salt that can be used to season soups, stews, and salad dressings. For further information contact RC Fine Foods PO Box 236 Belle Mead, NJ 08502; (800) 526-3953). You can also visit their website: www.rc.finefoods.com

Scenario International Company, 4092 Deer Vale Dr., Sherman Oaks, CA 91403 offers The Organic Gourmet Vegetable Soup N' Stock Concentrate as well as Wild Mushroom Soup N' Stock Concentrate. Use these stocks to enhance the flavor of rice, beans, casseroles, main dishes, and even salad dressings. They do not contain MSG or hydrogenated oils and the vegetables are organically grown. Five 2.2-pound size jars each making 200 cups of stock can be purchased. This same company also offers vegetable bouillon cubes. For further information please call (800) 400-7772 or (818) 986-3777 or visit their website at www. organic-gourmet.com

SOUPS

Campbells is offering a line of vegan canned soups, based with beans or vegetable stock. Call (800) 879-7687 for ordering information.

Norpac offers several vegan soups for food service including Zesty Lentil and Orzo, Garden Vegetable, and more. Call (800) 822-2898 for further information.

Ridgefield's offers several vegan soups for food service. Contact them at (800) 800-2269.

SOY SAUCE AND TAMARI, ORGANIC

Eden Foods, Inc., 701 Tecumseh Rd., Clinton, MI 49236 is now offering 20-ounce containers of organic soy sauce and organic tamari on both the east and west coasts of the United States. For further details call (517) 456-7424 or call (800) 248-0301.

TOMATO PRODUCTS, ORGANIC

Muir Glen, Inc., 1250 N. McDowell Blvd., Petaluma, CA 94934 offers organic tomato sauce, organic diced tomatoes, organic tomato paste, organic whole peeled tomatoes, and organic tomato purée in 102-ounce cans. For information call (707) 778-7801 or (800) 832-6345. Visit their website at www.muirglen.com

Millina's Finest, 550 Monterey Rd., Suite B, Morgan Hills, CA 95037 manufactures organic ground peeled tomatoes with purée, organic diced tomatoes, and organic tomato purée in #10 can sizes. Call (800) 775-5297 for more details. Also, visit their website at www.ofpi.com

Enrico's offers organic pasta sauces, salsa, ketchup, and BBQ sauce. Some are available in a #10 can size. The products are available through Ventre Packing Co., Inc., 6050 Court Street Road, Syracuse, NY 13206; or call (315) 463-2384.

Toto's Gourmet Products include salsa and vegetarian chili in gallon size jars. Write to them at Mama Vida, Inc., 6503 Deancroft Rd., Baltimore, MD 21209 or call (410) 484-4066.

VEGETABLE SIDE DISHES

Simplot is offering several convenience-style vegetable side dishes, which can be easily made into vegan entrées. Under the Roastworks name, the Flame-Roasted Redskins and Vegetables (red rose potatoes tossed with red and green pepper strips and yellow onions, seasoned with chili), Peppers and Onions (bell peppers and onions with a fajita-style seasoning), and the Flame-Roasted Sweet Corn and Peppers (cut corn and red, green and yellow peppers with a Southwestern seasoning) are precooked, needing only 10-15 minutes in the oven. They come 6-2.5 pounders packed to a case. Served on a bed of cooked beans or grains, these products make fast and colorful dishes. You can also top a veggie burger with the peppers or corn and create a "burger" dinner. For more information call (800) 572-SPUDS (Simplot in Boise, ID)

Cuisine Solutions offers ready-to-use side dishes for the chef. All products are made to fit upscale menus, as if a chef had been preparing them. Many hotel chains are supplementing their menus with these products. Among the vegan offerings are Sicilian Salad (mixed beans, artichokes, and sundried tomatoes in herbed vinaigrette) and Yellow and Red Papaya relish with Vegetable Medley. Side dishes come in eight 2-pound pouches. All products are immersed in boiling water (or placed in a steamer) for preparation and are very easy to prepare. Cuisine Solutions is an international company with headquarters in France, Norway, and the USA. Contact Cuisine Solutions, 85 S. Bragg Street, Suite 600, Alexandria, VA 22312; (888) 285-4679.

WRAPS

Specialty Brands Inc. distributes Pacific Tortilla Kitchen Brand wrap sandwiches including a vegan stir-fry wrap served in a tomato sesame tortilla. These wraps can be purchased in cases of 48. For more information call (800) 548-6363 or write to Specialty Brands Inc., PO Box 5647, Riverside, CA 92517.

Appendix C

RESOURCES

BOOKS

<u>Quantity Cooking Information</u> (not necessarily vegetarian information, but includes how to set up banquets, amounts to prepare, how to purchase in quantity, etc.):

- CATERING LIKE A PRO (Halvorsen) ISBN 0-471-00688-2, 1994, John Wiley & Sons, Inc.
- FOOD FOR FIFTY (Shugart and Molt) ISBN 0-02-4103410-1, 1993 MacMillan Pub.
- PROFESSIONAL BAKING (Wayne Gisslen) ISBN 0-471-595-9-8, 1994, John Wiley & Sons, Inc.
- PROFESSIONAL COOKING (Wayne Gisslen) ISBN 0-471-83848-9, 1998, John Wiley & Sons, Inc.
- PROFESSIONAL VEGETARIAN COOKING (Ken Bergeron) ISBN 0-471-29235-4, 1999, John Wiley & Sons, Inc.

<u>Vegan Nutrition</u>:

- BECOMING VEGETARIAN (Melina, Davis, and Harrison) ISBN 1-57067-013-7, 1995, Book Publishing Company
- SIMPLY VEGAN (Wasserman and Mangels) ISBN 0-931411-20-3, 1999, The Vegetarian Resource Group
- THE VEGETARIAN WAY (Messina and Messina) ISBN 0-517-88275-2, 1996, Three Rivers Press

PERIODICALS

- VEGGIE LIFE published by EGW Publishing Company
- VEGETARIAN JOURNAL published by The Vegetarian Resource Group
- VEGETARIAN JOURNAL'S FOODSERVICE UPDATE published by The Vegetarian Resource Group
- VEGETARIAN TIMES published by Primedia

ORGANIZATIONS AND WEBSITES

THE VEGETARIAN RESOURCE GROUP
PO Box 1463, Baltimore, MD 21203
(410) 366-VEGE
www.vrg.org

NATIONAL ASSOCIATION OF COLLEGE AND UNIVERSITY FOOD SERVICES
1405 South Harrison Road, Suite 305
Manly Miles Bldg., M.S.U., East Lansing, MI 48824-5242
(517) 332-2492
www.nacufs.org/nacufs

THE AMERICAN DIETETIC ASSOCIATION
216 W. Jackson Blvd.
Chicago, IL 60606-6995
(312) 899-0040
www.eatright.org

BACKGROUND INFORMATION ON SOME VEGAN INGREDIENTS

The following article first appeared in *Vegetarian Journal* and was researched and written by Caroline Pyevich.

WHY IS WINE SO FINED?
Although wine usually only contains grapes, yeast, and a small amount of sulfites which are added and created during fermentation, the processing of wine introduces small amounts of substances which may be of concern to vegetarians and vegans.

Every wine is different and no uniform formula exists for producing wine. Wine reflects where it was grown. The soil gives the wine its flavor, which is why wine produced in certain areas has a distinct taste. Winemakers may not choose to extensively process their wine in order to retain some of these natural qualities.

A clarifying or fining agent makes wine clear by removing proteins in the wine. The agents eventually settle out of the wine. Different proteins serve as clarifying agents depending upon both the type of wine and the desired flavor. Lab trials determine both the clarifying agent and quantities used. The fining agents have an opposite polarity to that of the wine. Therefore, the agents solidify with the protein remains in the wine and can be removed.

Some clarifiers are animal-based products, while others are earth-based. Common animal-based agents include egg whites, milk, casein, gelatin, and isinglass. Gelatin is an animal protein derived from the skin and connective tissue of pigs and cows. Isinglass is composed of the bladder of a sturgeon fish. Bentonite, a clay earth product, also serves as a popular fining agent.

Organic agents are more likely to be used in the clarification of premium wines. Premium wines typically cost more than $7 a bottle and are produced from grapes grown in desirable locations. According to Bouchaine Vineyard, twenty-five percent of the premium wine produced in the United States is clarified with an organic protein.

Egg whites from chicken eggs are exclusively used for red wine clarification and are removed before the wine is bottled. The egg whites have not been specially processed or separately distributed for the wine industry. They are regular, store-bought eggs or farm eggs. Two or three egg whites can clarify a 55-gallon barrel of wine.

Winemakers in France (Burgundy) commonly utilize egg whites in their production because they can use the whites of the eggs after the yolks have already been added to their foods. Egg whites generally clarify more expensive wines (above $15) or wines that are expected to age.

Large producers of wine in the United States do not usually use egg whites as a fining agent, and they may implement potassium caseinate as a substitute for eggs. Whole milk and casein are two other possible fining agents in some red wines.

Gelatin can clarify either white or red wine. Gelatin pulls suspended material out of wine, and less expensive wines may use this material. One-sixteenth of a pound of gelatin can clarify 1000 gallons of wine.

Gelatin serves as a finishing agent in some wine and beer. A finishing agent adds a "final touch" to the quality and clarity of the wine without making any radical change in its flavor. Gelatin may also be used in addition to another fining agent and is removed after the clarification process.

Although the clarifying agents for red wine are animal products, many pro-ducers of red wine do need to use any clarifying agent to remove tannins. By pressing the wine at an early stage of the winemaking process, the tannins can be removed without the additional proteins.

Isinglass, sturgeon's bladder, is used to fine selective white wine. Germany, who initially introduced this method, is one of the main countries that still uses this technique. Some American wineries use isinglass to clarify white wine or chardonay, but this substance is not commonly incorporated in wine production. Activated carbon or bentonite are alternative clarifiers of white wine.

The most popular substance used to remove the proteins of domestically produced white wines is bentonite. It is a silica clay, which picks up the organic proteins left by the grapes. If left in the wine, these proteins would denature and form long molecular strands. This process would result in wine that is either hazy wine or has loose sediments floating in it. Therefore, bentonite acts as an agent to improve the cosmetic appearance of the wine for the consumer.

Bentonite fines most inexpensive wines. Two to three pounds of bentonite clarifies 1000 gallons of wine.

Several other fining agents exist. Sparkaloid, a diatomaceous earth, clarifies white and red wine. Italian wine may be fined with either eggs, milk, or blood. Although blood of large mammals may serve as a clarifier in some Old Mediterranean countries, its use is forbidden in wine from either the United States or France.

Both the clarifying agents and the removed proteins coagulate on the bottom of the wine tank or barrel. They are then removed through either a settling process or a cellulose fiber filter. The ingredient list of a wine will not state the clarifier as an ingredient because it is taken out of the final product. Calling or writing to a particular wine company may be the best way to discover which fining agent they use.

Wine may also be filtered to remove impurities. A wine can be filtered and not clarified, or clarified and not filtered. A wine marked UNFILTERED has not passed through a filtering substance, such as a plastic micropore filter. UNFINED wines have not had a clarifying agent passed through them. Even though a wine label may state it is unfined, this may not always be the case. According to one California winery, some companies may mark a bottle of wine as unfined for a marketing technique because no one avidly scrutinizes the wine producers to verify these claims.

Kosher wines may be more likely to avoid the use of the animal-based clarifying agents, but not all do so. The Union of Orthodox Jewish Congregations (OU) stated that all of their Kosher certified American-made wines do not currently use either gelatin, isinglass, or egg whites. They cannot vouch for the status of the international Kosher wines.

The Orthodox Union also claimed that a wine could theoretically be certified as Kosher if it contained egg whites or if the gelatin were completely removed from the final product. They did not reveal any general rule for certifying wine as Kosher and claimed that each certification agency may use different criteria for certifying wine. Star-K, another certification organization, also showed no aversion to the use of egg whites.

Kof K claimed that Kosher wine is not clarified with either gelatin or isinglass in America. Egg whites, a kosher item, would be a permissible agent. Kof K mentioned that paper is sometimes used to clarify Kosher wine, as the paper adheres to the impurities. Kosher wine is a specialty item and is produced directly for the Kosher market.

The following article first appeared in *Vegetarian Journal* and was researched and written by Rachel Himmelheber.

VEGAN BAKING

A glance at the ingredient list of a loaf of bread from most commercial bakeries can be astounding: the list is long and the names are often unpronounceable. However, the thought of baking your own bread in quantity can sometimes be just as frightening. Homemade bread has the unfair reputation of being a time-consuming, tedious process, one that only a master baker could possibly successfully undertake. Fortunately, these assumptions are false, particularly if you want to make large batches of bread. With a few pieces of equipment, some beginning recipes, and several tips to get you started, you should be well on your way to making delicious homemade bread with a minimum of time and unnecessary ingredients.

First, I recommend finding some traditional, small batch bread recipes that you like and multiplying them, rather than searching for large batch recipe cookbooks. Most bread recipes make two loaves of bread; I suggest multiplying by six. Twelve loaves of bread is more manageable than it sounds if you are using a commercial mixer with a bread hook attachment. Second, if your facility does not own a commercial mixer or a bread hook attachment, I strongly suggest purchasing one. They are expensive, but they more than pay for themselves. Many have more uses than just mixing bread; some come with shredding attachments as well as other mixer attachments such as whisks and paddles. The paddle attachment can be used for any quick bread recipes, while the bread hook could mix and knead your bread entirely for you.

While the bread hook could do all of the kneading process for you, I don't recommend this approach. I believe the taste and quality of the bread suffers without any hand kneading. Mix all of the ingredients in your mixer and continue adding flour and allowing the machine to "knead" your bread until the dough just begins to stay together in one piece. I then, with the help of liberally floured hands, take my dough out of the mixer and hand knead it on a floured board or table. Kneading is really very simple. If you have never done it before, James Beard's *Beard on Bread* has a very detailed explanation with pictures that is invaluable. Depending upon your mixer and the time you have allowed your bread in the mixer, your hand kneading time may vary anywhere from three to ten minutes. Basically, your bread is ready for its first rising when the dough is smooth and elastic, not sticky or lumpy.

Bread recipes, particularly quick bread recipes, are often chock-full of butter, milk, and eggs. These additions substantially increase the bread's fat and cholesterol level. Butter, milk, and eggs also make your bread unappealing to vegan diners. Milk and butter are easily replaced with soy milk or rice milk and margarine, oil, or shortening. Eggs, however, are more difficult to replace. Eggs act as a binder, helping to keep your bread together, as well as a lightener, making your bread fluffier. In some quick breads, eggs can be replaced with a combination of baking powder, baking soda, oil, and bananas. Puréed tofu can also be substituted, as it is in the Dinner Roll recipe on page 237. If your diners are not vegans, lowfat yogurt is a good substitute for eggs in quick bread or muffin recipes. Simply replace each egg with one tablespoon of lowfat or nonfat yogurt. The yogurt results in a lighter muffin than the tofu does. (While I have not tried soy yogurt as an egg substitute, I think it could possibly be a viable option for vegans.)

If you are concerned with fat content, there are many lowfat soy milks on the market now. I have also successfully replaced the oil or margarine in some breads with water, as in the Cinnamon Raisin Bread on page 236, or with mashed bananas or applesauce (in quick breads). Light tofu also works just as regular fat tofu would. However, light or nonfat margarine are not good for baking. You may replace the margarine used to oil your bowl for the rising and your baking sheets with lowfat cooking spray.

It has been said that while cooking is an art, baking is a science. And, while it is true that there is less room for improvisation in baking, many bread recipes are extremely adaptable. If you find a good basic recipe, such as the French Bread recipe on the next page, you can add to that and come up with many variations.

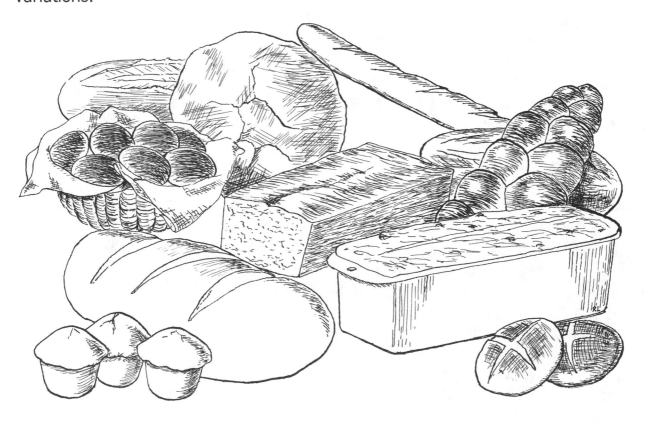

Basic French Bread
(Makes twelve medium-size loaves)

10 Tablespoons yeast
3-3/4 cups warm water (wrist temperature, about 100-115 degrees)
12 cups cool water (3 quarts)
6 Tablespoons salt
About 40 cups of unbleached white flour (approximately 10 pounds)

Proof the yeast in the warm water. (Sprinkle the yeast in the warm water and set it aside. Your yeast has "proofed" when the mixture foams, swells, and bubbles. This step ensures that your yeast has not spoiled.) Meanwhile, pour the salt into your mixing bowl and add the cool water. Add the yeast when it is ready. Then, slowly add the flour, mixing between additions. (I keep the mixer on the entire time. This step helps to reduce the amount of gas bubbles in your bread, as well as making for a smoother, less lumpy loaf overall.)

When the bread begins to form one cohesive mass that stops sticking to the sides of the bowl, turn it out onto a floured board. Knead in some more flour until the dough is smooth and elastic. (Do not be alarmed if your flour amount varies from the suggested 40 cups. You may need more or less depending on the quality of the flour and even the weather.) When your dough is ready, put it in oiled bowls, and turn it around a few times to make sure the loaves are coated with the oil. (This step prevents your bread from cracking and drying out.) Cover the bread with a towel. Leave the bowls in a warm, dry place until it has doubled in size, about 45 minutes to 1-1/2 hours.

When the dough has doubled, punch it down, knead it for a few minutes to rid it of the gas bubbles, and form into loaves (round loaves, braided loaves, baguettes, etc.). Place on oiled baking sheets and let rise again, 30 to 45 minutes. Slash your loaves diagonally a few times with a serrated knife and brush with cold water, oil, or melted margarine. Bake in a 335-degree commercial oven for 25 minutes or until golden brown. The loaves will sound hollow when tapped if they are done. If the bottoms are soft, remove from the baking sheet and allow them to cook for five more minutes directly on the oven rack.

Variations: All the variations of French Bread listed below make 12 medium-size loaves of bread. If you make braided loaves, it may make less.

Wheat Bread
Replace up to 30 cups of flour with whole wheat. I Like a 50/50 mix. The more whole wheat flour, the denser and heavier your bread will be. It will also rise less.

Cracked Wheat Bread

This bread calls for 20 cups of white flour (about 5 pounds), 15 cups of whole wheat (about 3-1/4 pounds), and 5 cups of cracked wheat or bulgur wheat. Add the cracked wheat to the water and the salt in the mixing bowl first. This bread is wonderfully crunchy and is perfect for sandwiches. It makes beautiful round loaves or braided loaves, particularly when sprinkled with additional cracked wheat. Resist the temptation to cut into it while still warm. It is particularly delicate.

Cinnamon Raisin Bread

This bread can be made with half wheat and half white flour, but I prefer this bread when made with all unbleached white. Add 3-1/2 cups brown sugar to the water and salt. If your brown sugar is hard and crumbly, try to dissolve all of it. Then, add an additional cup of water. This water replaces the recipe's oil. Add 5 cups of raisins and 2-1/2 Tablespoons of cinnamon to the mixing bowl. Mix as usual. This bread will not sound hollow; it is a soft bread. Therefore it is done when it is properly browned, about 25 minutes. Do not cut this bread until it is cool; it will be very moist and doughy in the middle while warm. This bread is wonderful served with a powdered sugar icing or glaze as a brunch or breakfast dish.

Rosemary-Onion Bread

Add a minimum amount of wheat flour to this bread; it is much better as a light, fluffy loaf. Replace the salt with 6 Tablespoons garlic salt. Add 4 Tablespoons dried rosemary, slightly crushed with your fingers. Add 1-1/2 finely chopped large onions to the mixture. (If you prefer, you may use the equivalent of granulated onions. Do not use onion powder.) I also like to add about 2 cups of sugar to this bread; it is optional, but I feel it really brings out the flavors.

Granola Bread

Reduce the water in your bowl to 8 cups. Use the 4 cups of water to soak 6 cups of oats for about 10 minutes. (This water should be hot, but it need not be boiling.) Add the oats to the water and salt. Add 4 cups brown sugar, 3 cups chopped walnuts, 3 cups raisins, 2-1/2 cups sunflower seeds, and 1-1/2 tea-spoons each cinnamon, nutmeg, and allspice. Add 1 teaspoon cloves. This bread is a dense bread by nature; add up to 30 cups wheat flour in place of the white. (This bread, like the Cinnamon Raisin, may not sound hollow when done.) Serve the bread with a warm beverage at breakfast.

Light Dinner Rolls (Makes about 200 medium-size rolls)

10 Tablespoons yeast
2-1/2 cups warm water
3-1/2 cups melted margarine
12 cups hot soy milk (3 quarts)
2-1/2 cups sugar
3 Tablespoons salt
2-1/4 cups blended soft tofu, mixed in a blender or food processor
20 cups unbleached white flour (about 5 pounds)
15 cups whole wheat pastry flour (about 3-1/4 pounds)

Proof yeast. Add ingredients to bowl in order given. Mix. Knead. Let rise. Punch down. Knead. Roll out into individual crescents or knots of desired size. Let rise again. Brush with additional margarine if desired. Bake at 335 degrees for 15 minutes or until golden brown.

Your local distributor will carry 50-pound bags of unbleached white and whole wheat flour. They probably will not carry anything more exotic. Try your local co-op, health food store, or one of these distributors.

Montana Flour and Grains, Inc.
P.O. Box 517
Fort Benton, MT 59442
406-622-5436, FAX 406-622-5439
www.kamut.com
Includes some organic flours, wheat berries, rye and rye flour, and whole wheat pastry flour

Natural Way Mills, Inc.
Route 2, Box 37
Middle River, MN 56737
218-222-3677, FAX 218-222-3408
Organic, will ship some 5 and 10 pound bags, millet, soy, brown rice, corn, barley, and more

Tips For Baking Bread

- Have separate measuring cups for wet and dry ingredients. Use four cup measuring cups, if possible. It is important to remember that the flour amounts are not exact, whether you follow the cups or the pound suggestions. Your bread is ready when it is smooth and elastic.

- Invest in some rubber scrapers to clean your cutting boards after each kneading. Little pieces of old bread can get into your next batch and ruin it.

- Use more flour than you think you need on your rolling pin, on your board, and on your hands. There is nothing more annoying than bread that sticks everywhere.

- Begin with your mixer on the lowest possible speed, but gradually increase the speed. This step will help to pick up any hard, crumbly pieces of bread stuck at the bottom of the dough.

- Bread is done with the kneading process when it springs back from your finger. It is finished rising when it does not spring back but starts to deflate.

- Try not to bake on rainy or humid days. If you must, be aware that this weather could negatively affect your bread.

- Spruce up a dull loaf of bread by sprinkling the top with sesame or poppy seeds before it is baked. Fresh or dried herbs or a maple syrup and oatmeal combination also looks nice on top of your loaf.

- You can also liven up a dull loaf with a flavored spread. Simply combine softened margarine with cinnamon and brown sugar, or dried herbs and garlic, or try olive oil, margarine, chopped bell peppers, black olives, chopped sundried tomatoes, garlic, basil, oregano, and parsley. Serve with your freshly baked bread. Your diners will eat your bread more quickly if it has a spread to go with it. Experiment with different kinds depending upon your leftovers; almost any combination works well. For spreads involving dried herbs, you may want to refrigerate them overnight to allow the herbs to soften and the flavors to blend.

- The quickest loaves to form resemble sausage rolls; simply roll out 1/12 of your dough into a rectangle. Tuck in two edges and roll up the other edge closest to you. Place seam side down on your baking sheet or loaf pan.

The following article first appeared in *Vegetarian Journal* and was researched and written by Caroline Pyevich.

HONEY PRODUCTION

While some vegetarians eat honey and many vegans avoid eating honey, not everyone understands the ramifications of using bees for honey production and agricultural pollination. Beekeeping involves more than simply removing honey from the hive. The recent decline in the native bee population has increased agricultural reliance on the managed honeybee.

What is Honey?

Honey is produced by honeybees, a vegetarian insect which evolved millions of years ago from an insect-eating wasp. Honeybees eat pollen to obtain protein, fat, and vitamins, and they make honey from the nectar of flowers for an energy source. Bees reduce the water content of the nectar both by fanning it with their wings and manipulating the liquid in their mouth. Bees create honey through the use of their digestive enzyme, invertase. This enzyme converts the sucrose of the gathered nectar into equal parts of the sugars glucose and fructose in the bee's honey stomach (1).

Food for Bees

Bees normally eat nectar, but they may be fed a 50:50 solution of sucrose and water, which is the same ratio as that in nectar. The solution is sometimes given to the bees in the early spring to stimulate the queen to lay more eggs and build up the size and strength of the colony. Bees will receive the sugar solution if the beekeeper removed too much honey during the year because each hive requires fifty to sixty pounds of honey in the fall to survive the entire winter.

Bees are not fed the sucrose solution during the collecting season when they produce enough honey to supply both the beekeepers and the hive demands. Bees will continuously gather nectar and produce honey regardless of the amount of honey which they have stored (2). However, bees sometimes collect more nectar when they are provided with more storage room. Bees naturally live in a tightly crowded hive, and beekeepers often allow more room in the hive so the bees will produce more honey (3). The honey bees make from the sucrose solution will not have the distinct taste of honey produced from nectar (4).

Beekeepers sometimes feed pollen substitutes to the bees in early spring when there is not enough natural pollen in the foraging area. Some ingredients of a homemade pollen substitute include powdered skim milk, dried brewers' yeast, and dried egg yolk. Some bees are never fed either sugar or pollen substitutes (1).

Treatment of the Hive

Beekeepers burn, smoke, and add chemicals to the hive. Beekeepers burn a hive when the bees are infected with American Foulbrood, a fatal and highly contagious bacterial disease in bees. No known treatment eliminates this bacteria which easily transfers from one hive to the next through either honey or equipment contamination (4). Burning the infected hive may prevent the spread of the disease.

Recently, the practice of fumigation has become available in a few states. This method eliminates the need to burn the hive, as the infected bees are poisoned with calcium cyanide. Beekeepers may also purposely kill bees when an overly aggressive colony could be harmful to the public. Introducing a gentle queen to the colony is a more typical way to deal with this situation (4).

Beekeepers use smoke puffs to reduce their chances of being stung when opening the colony. A puff of smoke is applied for about 30 seconds to mask an alarm pheromone, which the bees normally spread throughout the colony when they are disturbed.

Large scale beekeepers are more likely to use caustic chemicals to repel bees when removing honey from the hive. The chemicals are sprinkled on acid boards and do not directly contact the bees. These fumes drive the bees away from the honey. A convenient, non-chemical alternative to both smoke and chemicals is the bee escape, a one-way exit trap, in which bees are separated from the part of the man-made hives containing honey. The bee blower, similar to a modified leaf blower, is another popular method of quickly removing the bees (5).

Beekeepers obtain bees either from catching stray swarms, taking bees from a tree, buying an established colony, or purchasing packaged bees. Entire colonies or single queens may be bought. Packaged queen bees can be selectively bred for characteristics such as honey production, color, size, pollination ability, and gentleness. Genetic engineering has not been done on bees.

Pesticides

The improper application of pesticides and herbicides on crops can kill the bees that pollinate and gather nectar from these fields. According to federal regulations, certain chemicals cannot be applied to the areas bees pollinate or must be introduced after the bees have already collected nectar (6).

Pesticides, which are contact, stomach, or respiratory toxins can affect the nervous system of the bee so that it can no longer locate food sources. The bees which pollinate these chemically-treated crops will die. While honeybees are easily transported off treated fields, ground-nesting native bees must remain there. Therefore, pesticides are more likely to harm native bees than honeybees.

Chemicals cause more problems in areas where irrigation systems are commonly used, and bees that rely upon irrigation as a water source can die from consuming the water's chemicals. Researchers are currently investigating pesticide alternatives such as the use of biological control of insects and weeds.

Bee Pollination

In America's present agricultural situation, the honeybee plays a key role in pollinating over ninety crops. Pollination is the transfer of pollen from the anther, a male part of the flower, to the stigma, a female part. Pollination is necessary for plant reproduction. Bees carry pollen from one plant to another when they collect both nectar and pollen. While wind assists in the pollination of grasses and grains, insects are necessary agents for the pollination of a wide variety of fruits and vegetables (7).

In the United States, one-third of all food consumed by humans somehow requires the pollination performed by honeybees. Cantaloupes, blueberries, apples, cranberries, and squash are just some of the foods pollinated by the honeybee. Clover and alfalfa are used in animal feed and are also pollinated by the honeybee.

Bees assist in the pollination of about eighty percent of the agricultural crops that require insect pollination. Farmers often rent bee colonies to pollinate vast acres of crops, and migratory beekeepers move around the United States to sell their pollination services during times of high demand. Beekeepers gather in California each year to service the almond crop, which would not be as large without the honeybees (5).

The different types of honey vary according to the type of crop which the honeybee visits. Clover honey, one of the most popular types of honey, is made from the nectar of clovers, which are used in animal feed. Other types of honey, such as orange blossom honey, result from the pollination of citrus fruits.

Honey production and pollination may be related, but are not the same process. For example, while honeybees can pollinate pickling cucumbers, they do not produce a substantial amount of honey from this forage. Similarly, some beekeepers only manage bees for honey production and do not rent their hives to pollinate crops (8). Often a beekeeper and a grower both benefit from the bees' forage of a field.

The honeybee was introduced to North America from Europe for its honey and wax production, and this general pollinator can adequately service a wide variety of crops. Indigenous bees cannot pollinate some imported crops, such as varieties of apples and pears. These bees also do not produce the type of honey preferred by humans, and the cells of their hive are not made of wax. Therefore, humans commonly manage the honeybee rather than the native bee.

What about the Native Bees...

Recently, the need for honeybees has increased because of their pollination ability. Both the decrease in wild bee population and the intensive pollination needs of today's agriculture have resulted in a new demand for honeybees. Although previous pollination was left to chance, the large crop yield demands of modern agriculture require the service of the honeybees in order to secure a completely pollinated crop. Honeybees are useful because they can be moved and maintain a strong populations throughout the year (5).

Native species are better suited to pollinate many crops in America, but not all of the native species can promise the high pollination rate of the honeybee. For example, although native bees are physically adapted to pollinate cranberries better, honeybees will still pollinate this crop when no other source of nectar exists. Farmers then utilize honeybees to pollinate their many acres of cranberries (9).

Modern agriculture promotes planting large acres of one type of crop, and all of the flowers of this crop bloom simultaneously. Native bees are often specific pollinators of one type of crop, and not enough bees of a particular variety exist to sufficiently pollinate vast acres of one bloom (10). For example, a watermelon blossom can require up to eight visits by a bee before it is adequately pollinated. The native bees can no longer perform this task alone.

New attempts have been made to introduce native species in greenhouse agriculture and many backyard gardeners and organic growers rely on native species to pollinate their produce (8). Most large-scale farmers resort to using the honeybee for some of their crop pollination.

A combination of factors has contributed to the decrease in wild bee population. The vast destruction of the native bees' habitat for purposes of urbanization and large-scale agriculture have greatly reduced the number of wild bees. For example, blueberry fields grow naturally when a forest in a suitable location is cut down, but the native bees are destroyed by this interference. Honeybees must then be introduced in order to pollinate the blueberries which will grow in this cleared area, even though native bees are better adapted to pollinate this plant efficiently (5).

Other problems threatening the wild bees include pesticides and irrigation systems, which destroy the nests of the bees inhabiting treated fields. Bees also can be injured during the mechanized harvest of crops.

Parasites

A more recent problem for both native and managed bees is parasitic mites. Two types of mites, tracheal and varroa, affect the world's bee population. The mites are a natural parasite of the honeybee and the bees have little resistance to the deadly invaders. The mites entered the United States from foreign lands even though federal regulation has prohibited the transfer of honeybees into the United States since the 1923.

Beekeepers combat tracheal mites, which live in the breathing tubes of the bee, by placing a mixture of Crisco and sugar in the hive to disrupt the scent-tracking mechanism of the mites. Placing menthol (mint) crystals in perforated bags inside the hive can also reduce tracheal mites (4).

The varroa mite can kill an entire colony within one to two years after infection. This mite is treated with an approved chemical, a fluvalinate, which is not used while the bees are producing honey for human consumption. Fluvalinate has not been detected in honey because this chemical is fat soluble and honey contains no fat (5). The fact that only one approved chemical exists to treat varroa mites suggests that the mites may soon become resistant to it. If so, the bee population would be severely decimated.

Managed bees, unlike wild bees, are fed antibiotics as a preventive measure against secondary diseases precipitated by mite infestation. Therefore, wild bees have a high risk for these diseases. The antibiotics show no adverse side effects to the bees (4).

Conclusion
From this information, we see that if we are to continue with current agricultural practices, we will increasingly rely upon the honeybee to pollinate our crops and if people continue to eat honey, beekeepers will keep on selling honey. Although bees could be managed strictly for their pollinating ability without using their honey, this system could affect agricultural costs. How does the bee fit into this situation?

Managed bees may be more likely to avoid the pesticides, mites, and disruption of their homes that typically threaten native bees. However, one reason the managed bees have a better survival rate than the native bees is that humans have interfered with the natural habitat of the native bees through the use of pesticides, forest clear-cutting, accidental introduction of parasites, and monoagriculture.

Although honey production may have been the initial reason for the importation of honeybees to America, it is no longer the sole reason that these bees are important to humans. The use of managed bees may be the only way modern agriculture can sustain itself. The question remains as to whether we could practically reintroduce a more "natural" system of pollination into our modern society.

Bibliography

1) Odlum, Melanie. <u>Beekeeping in Maryland</u>. University of Maryland, 1984.
2) Szabo, T., Sporns, P., & Lefkovitch, L. "Effects of frequency of honey removal and empty comb space on honey quantity and quality." <u>BeeScience</u>. 2.4 (1992): 187-92.
3) Smith, Barton (Maryland State Apiary inspector) – Personal interview. June 1996.
4) Ernie Miner (a bee-supply dealer in Maryland who is also a part-time state inspector) – Personal interview. 11 June 1996.
5) Morris, David (President of the Maryland State Beekeepers Association) – Personal interview. 11 June 1996.
6) Levin, M.D., "Using honey bees to pollinate crops." USDA leaflet Number 549: 1986.
7) McGregor, S. E. "Pollination of crops." <u>USDA Agriculture Handbook 355</u>. 107-17
8) Hachiro Shimanuki (Research Leader for the USDA Bee Research Department) – Personal interview. 13 June 1996.
9) Batra, Suzanne (researcher at USDA Bee Research Labs) – Personal interview. 12 June 1996.
10) Batra, Suzanne. "Solitary Bees." <u>Scientific American</u>. 250.2 (1984): 120-7.

Selecting Sweeteners:

Some vegans refrain from using refined white cane sugar, as it may be filtered with materials containing bone. Vegans also refrain from using honey, as it is considered an animal product. Here is a short guide to some vegan sweeteners.

1. **Dehydrated Sugar Cane Juice (also called "Sucanat," an abbreviation for sugar cane, natural):** This is a light brown, granular sweetener that taste like a mild molasses. It can be substituted, ounce for ounce, for refined sugar and can be ground (manually by mortar and pestle, mechanically by a food processor) for a finer texture for baking and frostings. Beware that there is also a Sucanat product that contains honey and it is not vegan.

2. **Date Sugar:** made from ground, dried dates, and is dark brown and has a sugary texture. It can be substituted, ounce for ounce, for refined sugar and should be stored tightly sealed in a cool, dry place. It can be ground for a finer texture.

3. **Granular Fruit Sweetener:** made from grape juice concentrate blended with rice syrup. This is a dry mix that is about 80 percent as sweet as refined sugar. For 8 ounces of refined sugar, use 12 ounces of this sweetener.

4. **Rice Syrup:** a brown liquid that resembles butterscotch in flavor. It is made from mixing cooked brown rice with dried barley and enzymes. The enzymes convert rice starch to the sugar maltose. For each cup of refined sugar, use 1-1/3 cups of rice syrup (and reduce liquid in recipe by 1/4 cup).

5. **Barley Malt Syrup:** similar to rice syrup. Use in equivalent amounts.

6. **Fruit Juice Concentrates:** order extra when ordering your frozen juices. Use 2/3 cup of concentrate for 1 cup refined sugar (and reduce liquid by 1/3 cup). If using for baking, add 1/4 teaspoon baking soda for every cup concentrate used (to neutralize acidity).

7. **Maple Syrup:** this natural syrup is two-thirds as sweet as refined sugar. Maple sugar is also available. Look for pure maple syrup or sugar. Artificially flavored syrups may contain refined sugar.

8. **Molasses:** two-thirds as sweet as refined sugar. Use in dishes, which can support its strong (and wonderful) flavor, such as baked beans, oatmeal, and other grain cookies and breads, gingerbread, and cornbread.

GARNISHES

The old adage, "You eat first with your eyes," is absolutely true. If it doesn't look good, no one is going to try it.

Be sure that your basic plate presentation is solid (using the right sized plates, getting the food in the plate, placing different items in an attractive way on the plate, etc.). Then move onto garnishing.

Garnishing can serve several purposes. It can draw the customer's eye to the area you would like to highlight; it adds color (tofu tastes good, but it sure isn't pretty); and it can add a dash of flavor or texture, serving as an accent. Garnishing tells your customers that you care.

When planning your garnishes consider cost (the garnish should not cost more than the food item; an example would be using a small pineapple wedge rather than a whole pineapple slice), labor (radish roses for 500 is ambitious, but too time-consuming), color, texture, and time. Think about adding a cool garnish to a hot dish, such as sliced cucumbers and raw broccoli sprouts to accent a hot Asian noodle dish. We do this all the time with that traditional American dish, chili – always served with chopped onions, and for fancy chili occasions with chopped tomatoes, chopped bell peppers, and fresh cilantro. Here are some garnishing suggestions:

CENTERPIECES
Pineapple trees: Core a whole pineapple, insert a length of metal or PVC pipe and then six or seven more pineapple (with the tops cut off). Top with banana leaves or long ferns; add skewers of fruit (kiwi, berries, melon wedges, grapes, etc.) to the pineapple.

Bouquets: can be carved out of fruit and veggies (if you have the time and the skill) or create an herb bouquet from fresh lavender, basil, thyme, oregano, and flowering chives.

Fruit Creations: Hedgehogs from mangoes (score with "X" and turn inside out), peacock watermelons (watermelon is base, use skewers of sliced kiwi for tail), and apple swans

Edible Baskets: orange, papaya, tomato, pepper, pineapple, peeled melons, etc.

PLATE GARNISHES

Veggies: peppers, radishes, cherry tomatoes, cucumber spears and slices, zucchini and yellow squash spears and slices

Fruit: orange slices, berries, melon balls, kiwi slices or wedges, pear or apple slices or wedges (dipped in orange juice to avoid browning), dried fruit combos, pineapple slices or wedges, sliced fresh peaches or apricots (in season), grape clusters

Fresh herbs: basil, cilantro, sage (check out all the varieties, such as purple and lemon), oregano, rosemary, parsley (lots of varieties), cilantro, mint, spearmint, peppermint, flowering chives and garlic (and their flowers)

Crunchy Stuff: nuts (toasted, roasted, or steamed), seeds (raw or toasted), wheat germ, granola, croutons (experiment with different seasonings), crumbled cold cereal. Baked or fried chips (potato, tortillas in all different colors, or veggie; we thinly slice apples, carrots, beets, salsify, and parsnips and bake at 400 degrees until crisp to make our own chips)

Veggies as Underliners: leaves of kale, romaine, head lettuce (also known as iceburg), butter lettuce, endive, bok choy, spinach; shredded red or green cabbage, lettuces; thinly sliced tomatoes, cucumbers, carrots

Brochettes: make mini fruit or veggie brochettes on 4-inch skewers. Serve cold or grilled (yes, you can grill the fruit, drizzled with a little maple syrup)

Examples Brochettes:

FRUIT	VEGGIE
Assorted melon wedges	Cherry tomato, bell pepper wedges, onion wedges
Grapes, strawberries, pine-apple wedges	Mushroom caps, zucchini wedges, red pepper wedges
Pear, apple, and grape (Dipped in orange juice to avoid browning)	Radish, green onion, carrot wedges

OTHER FUN STUFF

For soups: popcorn, seasoned croutons, shredded raw carrots and zucchini, chopped onions, tomatoes, chopped multi-colored bell peppers, diced pimientos, chopped fresh herbs, bread sticks

For side dishes and entrées: chopped, sautéed celery and onions, veggie "bacon" bits, chopped nuts, chopped fresh herbs, parsley, mint, and cilantro leaves, sliced pimientos, tomato wedges, chow mein noodles, lemon slices, shredded green and red cabbage, shredded carrots

For hot cereals, puddings, custard, etc.: chopped nuts (such as almonds, hazel nuts, walnuts, peanuts, pecans, etc.), toasted seeds (sesame, sunflower), shredded coconut, chopped dried fruit (raisins, dates, figs, peaches, apricots, persimmons, papaya, mango, blueberries, etc.), carob, chocolate or peanut butter chips, ground spices (cinnamon, nutmeg, ginger, cloves, etc.), cocoa powder, cookie or cake crumbs

CREATING THE PLATE

Remember the "KISS" method: keep it simple, student (we've heard other versions of this, but this is a family book!). You may only need an orange slice or several leaves of basil to complement your plate. Don't use so much garnish that the customer becomes confused when looking at the plate. Here are some other guidelines collected over the years:

- Use the correct size plate or dish – food falling over the sides of a too-small plate doesn't look as if the customer is getting more for his money, it just looks sloppy (and is difficult to eat from); a too-large plate looks as if the customer isn't getting much food.
- Think colors – if you can (depending on your china situation), avoid serving mashed potatoes on white plates; it's boring. If you have only white plates, then choose a colorful garnish.
- Think height – use an underlining plate with a soup bowl or place a salad plate on top of a dinner plate for more height (looks more elegant and moves the eye around).
- Use underliners, such as paper doilies, linen or paper napkins (under the plate), or sliced or shredded fruit or cooked grains (as in stewed tomatoes served on an underliner of couscous). This adds color and height.
- Parsley and lemon wedges are not the only garnishes in the world; vary garnishes from dish to dish and meal to meal.

- If it's on the plate, be sure it's edible (except for doilies and skewers); chances are, if you serve it, someone will eat it. So keep the lilies and the nightshade (both very poisonous flowers) off the plate.
- Garnishes can go on top, on the side or even under food (think of shredded purple cabbage as a colorful underliner); experiment with placement.

BOOKS ON GARNISHING
- BEAUTIFUL FOOD (Fobel) ISBN 0-442-22730-2, 1983, VNR Publishers
- EDIBLE ART (Larousse) ISBN 0-442-25832-1, 1987, VNR Publishers
- ART OF GARDE MANGER (Sonnenschmidt and Nicolas) ISBN 0-8436-2223-7, 1994, VNR Publishers

RECIPES
Following are some recipe ideas that can bring more color to the table.

WATERMELON SALSA

Yield: 25 one-ounce servings

Use this as a condiment or as a salad dressing or even as a cold sauce with hot rice or grains.

INGREDIENTS	MEASURE	METHOD
Watermelon, seeded and diced	2-1/2 pounds	In a large bowl, gently mix watermelon, chilies, onion, and ginger. Refrigerate for 20 minutes. Add cilantro and pepper and toss lightly.
Fresh chilies, chopped	5 ounces	
Red onion, diced	4 ounces	
Ginger, fresh and grated	2 ounces	
Fresh cilantro, minced	3 ounces	
Black pepper, ground	1/2 ounce	

Total Calories per Serving: 21   Total Fat as % of Daily Value: <1%   Protein: 1 gm   Fat: <1 gm
Carbohydrates: 5 gm   Calcium: 9 mg   Iron: <1 mg   Sodium: 3 mg   Dietary Fiber: <1 gm

MANGO SALSA

Yield: 25 one-and-half-ounce servings

This aromatic salsa complements mildly seasoned entrées and side dishes (and looks great on the table).

INGREDIENTS	MEASURE	METHOD
Ripe mangoes, peeled and chopped	3 pounds	Combine all ingredients in a large bowl. Chill for at least 1 hour before serving.
Sweet onions, chopped	1 pound	
Fresh chilies, chopped	3 ounces	
Red pepper flakes	1/2 ounce	
Fresh cilantro, chopped	2 ounces	
Fresh lime juice	2 ounces	
Vinegar	1 ounce	

Total Calories per Serving: 45   Total Fat as % of Daily Value: <1%   Protein: 1 gm   Fat: <1 gm
Carbohydrates: 12 gm   Calcium: 12 mg   Iron: <1 mg   Sodium: 2 mg   Dietary Fiber: 2 gm

AVOCADO SALSA

Yield: 25 one-and-half-ounce servings

This salsa is cool to the eye and to the taste bud.

INGREDIENTS	MEASURE	METHOD
Ripe avocados, peeled and mashed	2-1/2 pounds	Mix avocados, onions, chilies, tomatoes, lime juice, and red pepper flakes until well combined.
Onions, chopped	1/2 pound	
Fresh chilies, chopped	3 ounces	
Tomatoes, chopped	5 ounces	
Lime juice	4 ounces	
Red pepper flakes	1 ounce	
Cucumbers, peeled and diced	1/2 pound	Add cucumbers and cilantro and mix until cucumbers are well coated.
Fresh cilantro	2 ounces	Chill until ready for service.

Total Calories per Serving: 82   Total Fat as % of Daily Value: 11%   Protein: 1 gm   Fat: 7 gm
Carbohydrates: 5 gm   Calcium: 12 mg   Iron: 1 mg   Sodium: 7 mg   Dietary Fiber: 1 gm

MAPLEBERRY VINAIGRETTE

Yield: 25 one-ounce servings

This salad dressing will add color and new flavor to cool greens and fruits salads.

INGREDIENTS	MEASURE	METHOD
Cranberry Juice	18 ounces	In a large bowl, whisk all ingredients
Vegetable oil	4 ounces	together until combined. Refrigerate
Maple syrup	3 ounces	until ready to serve.

Total Calories per Serving: 63   Total Fat as % of Daily Value: 6%   Protein: 0 gm   Fat: 4 gm
Carbohydrates: 6 gm   Calcium: 5 mg   Iron: <1 mg   Sodium: 1 mg   Dietary Fiber: 0 gm

FRESH BASIL PESTO

Yield: 25 one-ounce servings

Got the white-pasta blahs? Toss pasta, rice, and grains with this colorful sauce or use it as a topping for bread or as a dip for bread sticks.

INGREDIENTS	MEASURE	METHOD
Fresh basil, washed and dried*	3 pounds	Place all ingredients in a food processor (by batches) and process until the mixture is coarsely puréed. Store, covered in the refrigerator until ready to serve.
Pine nuts	12 ounces	
Fresh garlic, minced	3 ounces	
Olive oil	10 ounces	
Black pepper, coarsely ground	1 ounce	

Note: If fresh basil is not available, spinach leaves may be used instead.

Total Calories per Serving: 193   Total Fat as % of Daily Value: 28%   Protein: 5 gm   Fat: 18 gm
Carbohydrates: 6 gm   Calcium: 97 mg   Iron: 2 mg   Sodium: 2 mg   Dietary Fiber: 1 gm

Appendix E

FOOD SAFETY POINTERS

Handling food safely is of the largest importance. Food can be the perfect medium for spreading disease if the proper techniques are not used at every step of the operation. This means:

- purchasing food from reputable purveyors
- receiving the food properly (did it come in thawed or frozen)
- knowing what the expiration date is
- making sure the delivery truck was properly refrigerated
- storing food at correct temperatures
- sealing food away from chemical and insect contamination
- preparing food with sanitized hands and equipment
- serving items in a safe manner
- storing and utilizing leftovers according to the rules of safe food handling

In addition, see Chapter 2 for food safety resources.

TEMPERATURES

Remember the slogan, "Keep hot foods hot and cold foods cold." This translates to 140 degrees or above for holding hot food and 40 degrees or below for holding cold food. All prepared leftovers (such as soups, stews, and sauces) must be reheated to at least 165 degrees for re-service (and remember food only has two chances for service: the original preparation time and one reheat. After this, food must be discarded).

To reiterate, all perishable foods must be kept above 140 or below 40. The range between 41-139 degrees is called the "temperature danger zone," and is the range in which bacteria grow the most rapidly. If you discover that any food has been stored in the danger zone for 2 hours (some authorities will allow 4 hours, but we like to be very strict in this area), discard it. Better to lose some money than to lose a customer (possibly permanently).

STORAGE LIFE OF SELECTED FOODS

This will give you an idea of how long some foods will be safe to consume (if held under the correct conditions):

Food Item	Storage Temperature (Fahrenheit)	Maximum Period	Remarks
REFRIGERATED			
Fresh tofu (Not aseptically packaged)	38-40	7 days	Store covered, change water every day
"Fake meat" Casserole (Cooked with seitan, tempeh, etc.)	32-36	2 days	Store covered, reheat to 165
Prepared egg replacer (powder mixed with water)	40	2 days	
Leftover gravy, sauce	32- 36	1-2 days	Very perishable
Stuffing	32-36	1-2 days	Very perishable
Applesauce	38-36	3 days	
Soy or rice milk, opened	38-40	7 days after opening	
Fresh apples	40	2 weeks	
Citrus fruit	40	1 month	
Grapes	40	1 week	
Potatoes	40	2 months	
Tomatoes	40	5 days	

<u>DRY STORAGE</u> (be sure your food storage area is clean, dry, and cool with adequate light and ventilation. All food is to be stored 6 inches from the floor and 3 inches from the ceiling and needs to be in airtight containers, properly labeled)

Coffee and tea	7- 12 months
Carbonated soda	indefinitely
Canned soup, vegetables, fruit	1 year
Salad oil	6-9 months
Flour	9-12 months
Baking powder and soda	8-12 months
Dry yeast	14 months
Syrup	1 year
Grains	8 months
Cold cereal	6 months
Pasta	3 months
Parcooked rice	8-12 months
Dried beans	1-2 years
Nuts	1 year
Jelly, fruit preserves	6 months
Peanut butter	6 months

<u>FROZEN</u> (temperatures can range from −10 to 0 degrees)

Fruit (such as strawberries)	8-10 months
Fruit juice	8-10 months
Vegetables	6-8 months
Potatoes (such as French fries)	2-4 months
Soy ice cream	3 months
Pie shells	1-2 months
Baked cakes	2-4 months
Yeast dough (unbaked)	1-2 months
Tofu, seitan, tempeh	1-3 months

STOCK ROTATION

FIFO (first in, first out) is a tradition worth enforcing in all your storage areas (pantry, refrigerators, freezers, chemical lockers, etc.). Don't have a FISH (first in, still here) establishment. Set up a rotation system that is easy with which to adhere. Some kitchens simply use markers and place dates on all cans and containers (to combine this with inventory systems, you can add a price with the date) and others use a colored dot system.

RESOURCES FROM THE VEGETARIAN RESOURCE GROUP

If you are interested in purchasing any of the following VRG titles, please send a check or money order made out to The Vegetarian Resource Group (Maryland residents must add 5% sales tax) and mail it along with your order to The Vegetarian Resource Group, P.O. Box 1463, Baltimore, MD 21203. Make sure you include your shipping address. You can fax your order to (410) 366-8804 or call (410) 366-8343 9 am to 6 pm EST to order with a Visa or MasterCard credit card. Price given includes postage in the United States. Outside the USA please pay in US funds by credit card or money order and add $3.00 per book for postage. You can also order these books online at www.vrg.org

SIMPLY VEGAN
Quick Vegetarian Meals, 3rd Edition
By Debra Wasserman & Reed Mangels, Ph.D., R.D.

Simply Vegan is an easy-to-use vegetarian guide that contains over 160 kitchen-tested vegan recipes (no meat, fish, fowl, dairy, or eggs). Each recipe is accompanied by a nutritional analysis.

Reed Mangels, Ph.D., R.D., has included an extensive vegan nutrition section on topics such as Protein, Fat, Calcium, Iron, Vitamin B12, Pregnancy and the Vegan Diet, Feeding Vegan Children, and Calories, Weight Gain, and Weight Loss. A Nutrition Glossary is provided, along with sample menus, meal plans, and a list of the top recipes for Iron, Calcium, and Vitamin C.

Also featured are food definitions and origins, and a comprehensive list of mail-order companies that specialize in selling vegan food, natural clothing, cruelty-free cosmetics, and ecologically-based household products. TRADE PAPERBACK $13

VEGAN HANDBOOK

Edited by Debra Wasserman & Reed Mangels, Ph.D., R.D.

Over 200 vegan recipes including the basics, international cuisine, and gourmet dishes can be found in this book. Also includes sports nutrition, a seniors' guide to good nutrition, dietary exchange lists for meal planning, online resources, feeding vegan kids, vegetarian history, and much more. The book is 256 pages. TRADE PAPERBACK, $20

MEATLESS MEALS FOR WORKING PEOPLE

Quick and Easy Vegetarian Recipes, 2nd Edition
By Debra Wasserman & Charles Stahler

Vegetarian cooking can be simple or complicated. The Vegetarian Resource Group recommends using whole grains and fresh vegetables whenever possible. For the busy working person, this isn't always possible. Meatless Meals For Working People contains over 100 delicious fast and easy recipes, plus ideas which teach you how to be a vegetarian within your hectic schedule using common convenient vegetarian foods. This 192-page handy guide also contains a spice chart, party ideas, information on quick service restaurant chains, and much more. TRADE PAPERBACK, $12

THE LOWFAT JEWISH VEGETARIAN COOKBOOK

Healthy Traditions from Around The World
By Debra Wasserman

The Lowfat Jewish Vegetarian Cookbook contains over 150 lowfat, vegan international recipes. Savor potato knishes, Polish plum and rhubarb soup, Indian curry and rice, Greek pastries, and spinach pies. Feast on Romanian apricot dumplings, North African barley pudding, pumpernickel and Russian flat bread, sweet fruit kugel, Czechoslovakian noodles with poppy seeds, and Russian blini. Celebrate with eggless challah, hamentashen for Purim, Chanukah latkes, mock "chopped liver," Russian charoset, eggless matzo balls, and Syrian wheat pudding.

    Breakfast, lunch, and dinner menus are provided, as well as 33 unique Passover dishes and Seder ideas, and Rosh Hashanah Dinner suggestions. Each recipe is accompanied by a nutritional analysis. TRADE PAPERBACK $15

NO CHOLESTEROL PASSOVER RECIPES
100 Vegan Recipes
By Debra Wasserman & Charles Stahler

For many, low-calorie Passover recipes are quite a challenge. Here is a wonderful collection of Passover dishes that are non-dairy, no-cholesterol, eggless, and vegetarian. It includes recipes for eggless blintzes, dairyless carrot cream soup, festive macaroons, apple latkes, sweet and sour cabbage, knishes, broccoli with almond sauce, mock "chopped liver," no oil lemon dressing, eggless matzo meal pancakes, and much more. TRADE PAPERBACK $9

VEGETARIAN QUANTITY RECIPES
From The Vegetarian Resource Group

Here is a helpful kit for people who must cook for large groups and institutional settings. It contains 28 vegan recipes including main dishes, burgers, sandwich spreads, side dishes, soups, salads, desserts, and breakfast. Each recipe provides a serving for 25 and 50 people, and a nutritional analysis. The kit also contains a listing of over 140 companies offering vegetarian food items in institutional sizes and "Tips for Introducing Vegetarian Food into Institutions." PACKET $15

VEGETARIAN JOURNAL'S
FOODSERVICE UPDATE NEWSLETTER
Edited by The Vegetarian Resource Group staff

This quarterly newsletter is for food service personnel and others working for healthier food in schools, restaurants, hospitals, and other institutions. Vegetarian Journal's Foodservice Update offers advice, shares quantity recipes, and spotlights leaders in the industry who are providing the healthy options being looked for by consumers. NEWSLETTER $30 includes both Vegetarian Journal and Vegetarian Journal's Foodservice Update. Inquire about foreign rates.

VEGETARIAN JOURNAL'S GUIDE TO NATURAL FOODS RESTAURANTS IN THE U.S. & CANADA

For the health-conscious traveler, this is the perfect traveling companion to insure a great meal or the ideal lodgings when away from home or if you are looking for a nearby vegetarian place. There has been a delightful proliferation of restaurants designed to meet the growing demand for healthier meals. To help locate these places, there is now a single source for information on over 2,000 restaurants, vacation resorts, and more.

The Vegetarian Journal's Guide to Natural Foods Restaurants (Avery Publishing Group, Inc.) is a helpful guide listing eateries state by state and province by province. Each entry not only describes the house specialties, varieties of cuisine, and special dietary menus, but also includes information on ambiance, attire, and reservations. It even tells you whether or not you can pay by credit card. And there's more. Included in this guide are listings of vegetarian inns, spas, camps, tours, travel agencies, and vacation spots. TRADE PAPERBACK $16

LEPRECHAUN CAKE AND OTHER TALES
A Vegetarian Story-Cookbook
By Vonnie Winslow Crist and Debra Wasserman

This vegan story-cookbook is for children ages 8 through 11. The book includes a glossary of cooking terms, clean-up and preparation instructions, and safety tips. Children will love preparing and eating the delicious recipes. A leprechaun in the kitchen, a baby dragon down the block, friendly forest deer from South America, and the Snow Queen's Unicorn teach children and adults who love them, about friendship, caring, and healthy cooking. TRADE PAPERBACK $11

FOOD INGREDIENT GUIDE
The Guide to Food Ingredients is a 28-page reference to over 200 mysterious ingredients found on food labels. What makes this food ingredients dictionary unique is that it lists the commercial source for each ingredient. You can quickly determine whether various ingredients are vegetarian, vegan, or neither. For example, did you know that carmine is a food coloring derived from beetles? Also, carrageenan is a seaweed product, which is a common jelling agent. HANDOUT $4

To order additional copies of

VEGAN IN VOLUME –
VEGAN QUANTITY RECIPES FOR EVERY OCCASION
send $20 (postage included) per book to
The Vegetarian Resource Group, PO Box 1463, Baltimore, MD 21203.
(Outside the USA, pay in US funds only
and add $3 per book for additional postage.)

WHAT IS THE VEGETARIAN RESOURCE GROUP?

Our health professionals, activists, and educators work with businesses and individuals to bring about healthy changes in your school, workplace, and community. Registered dietitians and physicians aid in the development of practical nutrition related publications and answer member or media questions about the vegetarian lifestyle.

Vegetarian Journal is one of the benefits members enjoy. Readers receive practical tips for vegetarian meal planning, articles on vegetarian nutrition, recipes, natural food product reviews, and an opportunity to share ideas with others. All nutrition articles are reviewed by a registered dietitian or medical doctor.

The Vegetarian Resource Group also publishes books and special interest newsletters such as Vegetarian Journal's Foodservice Update and Tips for Vegetarian Activists.

To Join **The Vegetarian Resource Group**
and Receive the Bimonthly **Vegetarian Journal** for One Year
Send $20.00 to The Vegetarian Resource Group
P.O. Box 1463, Baltimore, MD 21203.
(Mexico/Canada send $30 and other foreign countries
send $42 in US funds only.)
Orders can be charged over the phone by calling (410) 366-8343
or faxed by calling (410) 366-8804. Our e-mail address is vrg@vrg.org
Visit our web site at: www.vrg.org

Index by Subject

Index to Recipes

Index by Major Ingredients